Educational Linguistics in Practice

BILINGUAL EDUCATION & BILINGUALISM
Series Editors: **Colin Baker** (*Bangor University, Wales, UK*) and **Nancy H. Hornberger** (*University of Pennsylvania, USA*)

Bilingual Education and Bilingualism is an international, multidisciplinary series publishing research on the philosophy, politics, policy, provision and practice of language planning, global English, Indigenous and minority language education, multilingualism, multiculturalism, biliteracy, bilingualism and bilingual education. The series aims to mirror current debates and discussions.

Full details of all the books in this series and of all our other publications can be found on http://www.multilingual-matters.com, or by writing to Multilingual Matters, St Nicholas House, 31–34 High Street, Bristol BS1 2AW, UK.

BILINGUAL EDUCATION & BILINGUALISM
Series Editors: **Colin Baker** (*Bangor University, Wales, UK*) and
Nancy H. Hornberger (*University of Pennsylvania, USA*)

Educational Linguistics in Practice

Applying the Local Globally and the Global Locally

Edited by

Francis M. Hult and Kendall A. King

MULTILINGUAL MATTERS
Bristol • Buffalo • Toronto

Library of Congress Cataloging in Publication Data
Educational Linguistics in Practice : Applying the Local Globally and the Global
Locally/Edited by
Francis M. Hult and Kendall A. King.
Bilingual Education & Bilingualism
Includes bibliographical references and index.
1. Language and education. 2. Education, Bilingual. I. Hult, Francis M.
II. King, Kendall A.
P40.8.E38 2011
404'.2071—dc22 2011000604

British Library Cataloguing in Publication Data
A catalogue entry for this book is available from the British Library.

ISBN-13: 978-1-84769-353-2 (hbk)
ISBN-13: 978-1-84769-352-5 (pbk)

Multilingual Matters
UK: St Nicholas House, 31–34 High Street, Bristol BS1 2AW, UK.
USA: UTP, 2250 Military Road, Tonawanda, NY 14150, USA.
Canada: UTP, 5201 Dufferin Street, North York, Ontario M3H 5T8, Canada.

The policy of Multilingual Matters/Channel View Publications is to use papers that
are natural, renewable and recyclable products, made from wood grown in
sustainable forests. In the manufacturing process of our books, and to further support
our policy, preference is given to printers that have FSC and PEFC Chain of Custody
certification. The FSC and/or PEFC logos will appear on those books where full
certification has been granted to the printer concerned.

Typeset by Integra Software Services Pvt. Ltd, Pondicherry, India.

For Nancy H. Hornberger
on the occasion of her sixtieth birthday

Contents

**Section III: Policy and Planning for Linguistic Diversity in
Education**

About the Authors

Colin Baker is Pro Vice Chancellor at Bangor University, Wales, UK. He is the author of 15 books and over 60 articles on bilingualism and bilingual education, with specific interests in language planning and bilingual education. His book *Foundations of Bilingual Education and Bilingualism* (Multilingual Matters, 1993, 1996, 2001, 2006) has sold over 100,000 copies and has been translated into six languages. His *Encyclopedia of Bilingualism and Bilingual Education* (Multilingual Matters, with S.P. Jones) won the British Association for Applied Linguistics Book Prize Award for 1999. His *Parents and Teachers Guide to Bilingualism* was first published in 1995, with further editions in 2000 and 2007. He edits two Multilingual Matters book series and is Editor of the *International Journal of Bilingualism and Bilingual Education*. In addition to his academic activities, Colin Baker has held three UK government appointments.

Melisa Cahnmann-Taylor, Associate Professor of Language and Literacy Education at the University of Georgia, is the co-author of *Teachers Act Up! Creating Multicultural Communities Through Theatre* (Teachers College Press, 2010) and *Arts-Based Research in Education: Foundations for Practice* (Routledge, 2008). She studies multicultural education and multilingual classrooms as sites of social conflict, where possibilities exist for social change, justice and democracy. Her research methodologies embrace qualitative, feminist, poetic, narrative and arts-based approaches. She is most interested in theoretical and empirical work that excites teachers about the depth and possibility to improve the education of all children, especially children for whom standard English is not a first language. Cahnmann-Taylor judges an annual poetry contest for the Society for Humanistic Anthropology and serves as associate editor of *Critical Inquiry in Language Studies*.

Serafín Coronel-Molina is an assistant professor in the Department of Literacy, Culture, and Language Education at the School of Education, and an adjunct faculty member in the Department of Anthropology, the American Studies Program, and the Latino Studies Program at Indiana University. He is an educational linguist and sociolinguist. His research on Andean sociolinguistics, politics of language and language contact has been published in a number of book chapters and journals, such as the *International Journal of the Sociology of Language,* the *International Journal of Bilingual Education and Bilingualism, Amerindia,* the *School for International Training Ocassional Papers* and the *Latin American and Caribbean Ethnic Studies.* He has also co-edited with Linda Grabner a book titled *Lenguas e Identidades en Los Andes: Perspectivas Ideológicas y Culturales* (Abya-Yala, 2005). He is currently working on a book manuscript titled Language Policy and Planning, and Language Ideologies in Peru: The Case of Cuzco's High Academy of the Quechua Language.

Angela Creese is Professor of Educational Linguistics at the School of Education, University of Birmingham. Her research interests are in multilingualism, linguistic ethnography, education of linguistic minority students, discursive negotiation of identities in multilingual contexts and teacher collaboration in multilingual schools. She is author of a number of books and articles on multilingualism and linguistically diverse classrooms. Her books include *Multilingualism: A Critical Perspective* (2010); *English as an Additional Language: Approaches to Teaching Linguistic Minority Students* (2010); *Volume 9: Ecology of Language, Encyclopedia of Language and Education* (2009); *Teacher Collaboration and Talk in Multilingual Classrooms;* (2005) and *Multilingual Classroom Ecologies* (2003). She is an associate editor of the journal *Anthropology & Education Quarterly.*

Daryl Gordon is an Assistant Professor at Adelphi University's TESOL Program, where she teaches courses in ESL methodology, second language acquisition, sociolinguistics and action research methods. Her research interests include gendered second language socialization, transnational literacy, the discourse of citizenship within naturalization education, immigrant access to health care and action research in teacher education. Her articles have appeared in *Education and Anthropology Quarterly, TESOL Quarterly* and the *Journal of Southeast Asian American Education & Advancement.* She has presented research findings at national and international conferences including the American Association of Applied Linguistics (AAAL), the American Education Research Association (AERA), the American Anthropological Association (AAA) and the TESOL Convention. She has taught and designed curricula for English language learners and conducted professional development for ESL teachers in the US, Mexico and the Lao People's Democratic Republic.

Mike Grover is the co-founder of Multilingual Matters. Well established within the field, Multilingual Matters is an international independent publishing house focusing on bilingualism, second/foreign language learning, sociolinguistics, translation and interpreting.

Francis M. Hult is Assistant Professor of Applied Linguistics in the Department of Bicultural-Bilingual Studies at the University of Texas at San Antonio. His research examines the globalization of English as it relates to language planning and multilingualism, with a particular focus on Sweden. He is the founder and manager of the Educational Linguistics List. His work appears in journals such as the *International Journal of the Sociology of Language, Language Problems and Language Planning*, and *Language Policy*. He is the co-editor (with Bernard Spolsky) of the *Handbook of Educational Linguistics* (Blackwell, 2008) and the editor of *Directions and Prospects for Educational Linguistics* (Springer, 2010).

David Cassels Johnson is Assistant Professor of Education at Washington State University. He investigates the interaction between language policy and educational equity from a sociolinguistic perspective. Recent publications appear in *Applied Linguistics, Language Policy* and the *International Journal of Bilingual Education and Bilingualism*.

Kendall A. King is Associate Professor of Second Languages and Cultures at the University of Minnesota, where she teaches about and conducts research on language policy, sociolinguistics and bilingualism. Recent projects have examined transmigration, parenting practices and Spanish-Quichua-English language learning and use in Washington D.C., Minneapolis and Saraguro, Ecuador, and the relationship across (im)migration status, second language learning and school engagement for Latino youth. Her recent work appears in the *Modern Language Journal, Discourse Studies, Applied Linguistics* and the *International Journal of Bilingual Education and Bilingualism*. She is an editor of the journal *Language Policy*.

Marilyn Martin-Jones is Emeritus Professor at the University of Birmingham and the former founder-Director of the MOSAIC Centre for Research on Multilingualism. Over the last 30 years, she has been involved in research in bilingual and multilingual contexts in England and in Wales.

She has a particular interest in the ways in which language and literacy practices contribute to the construction of identities, in local life worlds and institutional contexts and the ways in which such practices are bound up with local and global relations of power. These themes are reflected in her publications: e.g. *Multilingual Literacy Practices: Reading and Writing Different Worlds* (with Kathryn Jones, John Benjamins, 2000); *Voices of Authority: Education and Linguistic Difference* (with Monica Heller, Ablex, 2001) and *Multilingualism: Global and Local* (Routledge, forthcoming).

Teresa L. McCarty is the Alice Wiley Snell Professor of Education Policy Studies and Applied Linguistics, and co-director of the Center for Indian Education at Arizona State University, USA. Her research focuses on Indigenous language planning and policy, critical literacy and ethnographic studies of minoritized schooling. She has been a Kellogg National Fellow and is a current fellow of the American Educational Research Association and the Society for Applied Anthropology. She served as the editor of *Anthropology and Education Quarterly*, and is the co-editor of the *Journal of Indian Education* and associate editor of *American Educational Research Journal* and *Language Policy*. Her recent books include *Ethnography and Language Policy* (Routledge, 2011); *Language, Literacy, and Power in Schooling* (Erlbaum, 2005); *A Place To Be Navajo – Rough Rock and the Struggle for Self-Determination in Indigenous Schooling* (Erlbaum, 2002); and *'To Remain an Indian': Lessons in Democracy from a Century of Native American Education* (with K. T. Lomawaima, Teachers College Press, 2006). She is presently working on a book project with Nancy Hornberger entitled Globalization from the Bottom Up: Indigenous Language Planning and Policy in Globalizing Spaces and Places.

Richard Ruiz received degrees in French Literature at Harvard College and in Anthropology and Philosophy of Education at Stanford University. He was faculty member in Educational Policy Studies at the University of Wisconsin-Madison before joining the College of Education at the University of Arizona, where he is currently a professor in Language, Reading and Culture. He works in language planning and education in many contexts in the US and internationally. In 2009, he was appointed Director of the Summer Language Planning Institute in Aruba for the purpose of facilitating the study and implementation of models for introducing Papiamento into Aruban schools.

Ellen Skilton-Sylvester is Professor of Education and the Director of Global Connections at Arcadia University. She completed her doctoral work in educational linguistics at the University of Pennsylvania and received the Outstanding Dissertation Award from the Council on Anthropology and Education of the American Anthropological Association. She is an educational anthropologist interested in language policy, literacy and identity. Her scholarly work has focused on biliteracy, immigrant education in the United States, and global citizenship/citizenship education. Recent publications have included articles in the *Interamerican Journal of Education for Democracy* and *Perspectives on Urban Education* as well as chapters in edited volumes: *Global Philadelphia: Immigrant Communities Old and New, Handbook of Practice and Research in Study Abroad: Higher Education and the Quest for Global Citizenship,* and *Adult Biliteracy in the United States: Sociocultural and Programmatic Responses.* She is currently serving as an associate editor for *Anthropology and Education Quarterly.*

Brian Street is Professor of Language in Education at King's College London and visiting professor of education in the Graduate School of Education, University of Pennsylvania. Street undertook anthropological fieldwork on literacy in Iran during the 1970s and taught social and cultural anthropology for over 20 years at the University of Sussex before taking up the chair of language in education at King's College. Street has a long-standing commitment to linking ethnographic-style research on the cultural dimension of language and literacy with contemporary practice in education and in development. He has written and lectured extensively on literacy practices from both a theoretical and an applied perspective. In 2008, Street received the Distinguished Scholar Lifetime Achievement Award from the (US) National Reading Conference.

Viniti Vaish is Assistant Professor at Nanyang Technological University's National Institute of Education. She is affiliated with the English Language and Literature Department and the Centre for Research in Pedagogy and Practice. Viniti conducts research in India and Singapore. She is currently Principal Investigator for a project on the Learning Support Program in Singapore, which is an early intervention program on reading. She teaches courses on bilingualism, qualitative research methods and language and literacy.

Manka Varghese is an Associate Professor at the University of Washington's College of Education. Her research and teaching focus on the preparation of teachers of linguistic minority students as well as the social, academic and cultural experiences of linguistic minority students in K-12 schools. Her work has appeared in journals such as *TESOL Quarterly; Journal of Language, Identity and Education; Linguistics and Education; Language and Education; Equity and Excellence in Education;* and *Journal of Latinos and Education.* She also has authored several book chapters and co-edited a volume entitled *Bilingualism and Language Pedagogy.*

Shuhan Wang is Deputy Director of the National Foreign Language Center (NFLC), University of Maryland. From 2006 to 2009 Shuhan served as the Executive Director for Chinese Language Initiatives at the Asia Society, and from 1998 to 2006 she was Education Associate for World Languages and International Education for the Delaware Department of Education. Currently, the NFLC administers the STARTALK Project, a multiyear federally funded initiative that promotes the study and teaching of critical languages such as Arabic, Chinese, Hindi, Persian, Russian, Swahili, Turkish and Urdu in the United States. As Co-Principal Investigator, Shuhan and the STARTALK team are leading the effort to enhance foreign language capacity. Her research interests include world language and heritage language education, curriculum and material design, teacher education and development, and language planning and policy. Shuhan received her PhD in Educational Linguistics from the Graduate School of Education, University of Pennsylvania.

Foreword

MIKE GROVER AND COLIN BAKER

I first met Nancy Hornberger in the mid-eighties at a Sociolinguistics Symposium in Cardiff. At that time Multilingual Matters was a relatively new publisher on the scene but was already establishing a reputation as being a friend for researchers in bilingualism, minority language studies and related subjects. We had a very small list of existing titles, but it was sufficient to attract Nancy to our stand and thus began a long and happy relationship that grew over time into the close contacts that currently exist between the publisher, its editors and authors.

Right from that first meeting we both realised that we shared a mutual interest in languages in a minority situation. For Nancy it was the Native languages of South America; for me, and my family, it was the situation of trying to maintain a second language that was far from common in the surrounding area.

Over the years we were to meet at more and more conferences, and during this time Nancy's academic reputation grew by leaps and bounds. When the book series *Bilingual Education and Bilingualism,* initiated by Multilingual Matters in 1994 with Colin Baker as its editor, needed an additional editor to take up some of the work load and broaden its scope in North America, Nancy was the obvious choice. She took up the reins in 1996 and has worked tirelessly with Colin to promote the series ever since.

Now roughly a quarter of a century after that first meeting, in no small part due to Nancy's encouragement, Marjukka and I can claim some sort of success in producing three separate multilingual entities. Our sons, Tommi and Sami, are not only bilingual but get much fun and satisfaction from learning yet more languages. It is on the professional front, however, where Nancy has helped us the most. Multilingual Matters, our third baby, now grown up and under Tommi's leadership, continues to be a major outlet for both theoretical and practical books on all aspects of bilingual education, multilingualism, multiculturalism (or whatever the latest fashionable and acceptable word is) and not least minority languages.

Thank you Nancy for those 25 years of friendship and encouragement.

Mike Grover

The long-standing partnership between Nancy and myself with Multilingual Matters begins with the commencement of a new book series, *Bilingual Education and Bilingualism*, that was initiated by Mike Grover in January 1994. Up to then, the major book series of Multilingual Matters was that commenced by Derek Sharp in 1982 simply entitled 'Multilingual Matters' (now edited by John Edwards). The 1980s and 1990s saw the rise of considerable academic and political interest in both bilingualism and bilingual education, increasing sales of books in this area, with such topics becoming higher on international conference agendas.

Multilingual Matters determined that a new book series was needed and would be named 'Bilingual Education and Bilingualism'. It would particularly, but not exclusively, concentrate on the many different forms of bilingual education, using a multidisciplinary perspective, to include politics and pedagogy, sociocultural and transnational issues, inclusive of boundary-breaking research as well as the philosophy, principles, policy, provision and practice of bilingual education. Following a delicious meal at Il Giardino (a small Italian restaurant on the seafront in Clevedon), I was asked to become the series editor.

Neither the publisher nor the editor anticipated the ever-increasing number of manuscripts submitted to the series, the very positive reception among academia of the initial tranche of books, nor the ever-expanding interest in bilingual education from academics, teachers, researchers, students, instructors and politicians. This interest was truly international, including the United States showing a strong and varied fascination with bilingual education. The publishers and myself therefore agreed that a co-editor was needed.

The search began. The person ideally needed to complement my profile: knowledgeable about the Americas rather than Europe; strong on qualitative research approaches rather than quantitative; interests in the anthropological, sociological and cultural dimensions rather than the psychological and political. Other attributes were mentioned: high standing in academia, immaculate efficiency and dedication to the series, and someone who could deal with both aspiring and well-established authors with tact and diplomacy, encouragement as well as focused advice. The search did not take long.

Soundings were taken among leading scholars whose advice was expert, impartial, reasoned and sensible. Various names were considered, but the one person who fitted the criteria best of all was Nancy Hornberger. Here was a person whose research and understandings were global rather than local, being expert in qualitative approaches to research, with an immense width of publications that included biliteracy and bilingualism, language planning and language revitalisation, with theoretical as well as grounded contributions. Nancy was asked and thankfully accepted.

From the early days of excellent cooperation as co-editor, it became apparent that Nancy was someone with an amazing international network, who not only was the central node with dozens of connections, but also someone who was immensely highly regarded as a person for her generosity of spirit, inspiration of the young, with an inherently positive and optimistic outlook, and whose standards and integrity were the highest and unquestionable.

The outstanding choice of Nancy as co-editor will be apparent to all those who have spoken to her, read her or received one of her supportive and gracious emails. Here is a highest rank international scholar with the serenity of a saint. Indeed, when I first asked Ofelia García what Nancy was like as a person, that was her keyword: serene. It stuck in my memory, and is so true.

Nancy has always been loyal, promoting the series, encouraging new scholars and advising well established scholars without fear or favour. She has worked tirelessly in giving advice, responding to unending requests for feedback on proposals, specimen chapters and whole manuscripts, working cooperatively with the publishing team and always maintaining excellent relationships.

To describe Nancy as an outstanding scholar, and one of the very best editors of books, encyclopaedia and book series in the world, is rather like characterising a superb wine only by its outward colour and bouquet. Anyone who has met Nancy, witnessed her charming, sensitive and sympathetic style of communication, who has listened to her consummate wisdom and deep sensibility, will know that here is a person who is gentle and gracious, charitable and caring, sagacious and serene.

Nancy, you have my unending gratitude for such a productive and rewarding partnership and loyal friendship. In the language of your Welsh ancestors: *diolch yn fawr iawn*.

Colin Baker

Introduction: Global and Local Connections in Educational Linguistics

FRANCIS M. HULT AND KENDALL A. KING

Since its inception, the transdisciplinary field of educational linguistics has been a nexus for multiple theories, methods and topic areas related to language (in) education (Hornberger, 2001; Hult, 2010; Spolsky & Hult, 2008). This intellectual diversity is framed by two constants, both of which are central to the field: a problem-centered approach and a global outlook. The field is problem-centered as it was formed – and continues to be shaped by – pressing real-world questions, many of which concern how best to provide equitable access to language and education for all students, and for linguistic and cultural minority students in particular. The field is global in the sense that it takes an international, often comparative approach to these problems, but also one that is locally grounded and culturally informed. For more than 25 years, Nancy H. Hornberger has been a leader in educational linguistics, setting the pace and embodying these constants in all of her work while inspiring others to do the same. This book is dedicated to her – and to her scholarship – in honor of her 60th birthday.

Nancy Hornberger joined the Graduate School of Education at the University of Pennsylvania (PennGSE) in 1985 as an assistant professor in what was then one of only two graduate programs in educational linguistics in the US.[1] Her scholarship, mentoring, teaching and consulting since then have been characterized by 'working the local globally and the global locally,' as she herself put it in a 2006 pro-seminar at Penn. This perspective is the inspiration for this book honoring Nancy Hornberger's contributions to educational linguistics.[2]

Beginning with her linguistic and educational work in Peru, where she studied relationships between Indigenous language education practices and bilingual education policy, Hornberger set the tone for educational linguistics research that is global in its perspective yet locally grounded in both educational practice and the close analysis of language use. This constant is evident in her consulting and research, which has taken her around the world to Bolivia, Brazil, El Salvador, Hong Kong, Mexico, New Zealand, Paraguay, Singapore and South Africa, among other locales, but also around the corner to schools and communities in the city of Philadelphia. For example, she has brought new insights to teacher training at institutions such as the Department of Linguistics at the University of Natal in South Africa; the Instituto de Estudos de Linguagem at the Universidad Estadual de Campinas in Brazil; the Andean Linguistics Program at the Colegio Andino in Peru; the Universidad Mayor de San Simón in Bolivia; and the National Institute of Education in Singapore as well as the School District of Philadelphia, for which she has served as an advisor to the superintendent, a professional development facilitator and a member of committees and task forces related to language minority students. Always wary of the expert's mantle, Hornberger rarely seeks to offer her own solutions to local issues, but rather strives to help educators develop the 'means to solve their own problems,' as she explained in her 2006 pro-seminar.

Hornberger has inspired a long line of scholars to follow her example, not least her many doctoral students. In her 25 years at Penn, she has supervised over 45 dissertations and served as a committee member on numerous others. Her students continue the tradition of problem-oriented language research with a global perspective, working in countries such as Botswana, Britain, Ecuador, Eritrea, Israel, Japan, Malaysia, Namibia, Pakistan, Peru, Sweden and Turkey as well as with many linguistic minority communities in the US. This book illustrates the impact that Hornberger's work has had on the field of educational linguistics as the authors – all of whom are her former students or close colleagues – strive to work 'the local globally and the global locally' in their research 'on (the role of) language (in) learning and teaching' (Hornberger, 2001: 19).

Central Themes

We have organized this book around three central themes of Hornberger's work: (1) bilingual education and bilingualism, (2) the continua of biliteracy, and (3) policy and planning for linguistic diversity in education. Each theme is first overviewed by a senior scholar in the field, and then aspects of that theme are developed with new data, theory and analysis by a series of original papers.

The first theme of the book reflects Hornberger's emphasis within educational linguistics on additive language learning, in the classroom and beyond. From the outset of her academic career, Hornberger has been a tireless advocate for policy and practice that promotes bi-/multilingualism as a resource for teaching and learning. The contributors in this first section each take up this theme in their own work. The second theme points to the many varied ways in which bi-/multiliteracies takes shape. In her influential continua of biliteracy model, Hornberger provides a heuristic that delineates and clarifies the multiple social, individual and ecological dimensions that influence language and literacy learning and use in multilingual settings (Hornberger, 1989; Hornberger & Skilton-Sylvester, 2000). Each of the contributors to this section illustrates that researching multilingual education requires careful attention to factors such as medium, context and mode of representation. The third and final theme focuses on the role that language policy and planning (LPP) plays in fostering (or constraining) linguistic diversity in education. Much like her work on the continua of biliteracy, Hornberger has brought to the field of LPP a much stronger understanding of how and why policy and planning should be analyzed within a multi-layered ecological system (Hornberger, 1994, 2002a). In this spirit, each of the contributors to this third section offers an account of aspects that influence LPP with respect to multilingual education in a particular context.

These lines of work are clearly *not* independent strands, but rather, both in practice and in Hornberger's scholarship, are intertwined. This book is rich in metaphorical references – to cooking (Ruiz), to onion peeling (Johnson), to dancing (Cahnmann-Taylor): the metaphor most apt for thinking about how these strands fit together is a braid. A woven braid is much stronger than unwound strands. At the same time, a braid renders some strands invisible at points; the supporting strand might be tucked in and twisted beneath the visible one on top. Hornberger's dissertation research and subsequent book (Hornberger, 1985, 1988) provides a perfect example of how these strands are woven together (see Martin-Jones, this book). This research was deeply rooted in years of life in the Andes with her husband, Esteban, and two children, Ch'uya and Cusi, and work as teacher, linguist and community member in rural Peru. One strand of that work examined national language planning efforts in Peru, and in particular the development and implementation of those officializing the Indigenous language of Quechua (Coronel-Molina, this book). Another strand of that same study analyzed bilingual education programs made possible through those national-level policy shifts and how these educational practices impacted student language learning as well as bilingual and biliterate development. Still a third strand of that work examined the relationship between school practices on the one hand and bilingual language use and language attitudes in community contexts on the other. As her early flagship study demonstrates – and indeed as is evident in so much of Hornberger's work – while detailed analysis of each of these threads is crucial and productive, any particular thread can only fully be understood when contextualized and viewed in the context of the other strands. Thus, although we have organized the contributions into three strands, the book as a whole reflects the holistic and dynamic perspective on language (in) education that is the hallmark of educational linguistics as a field and Hornberger's approach to it in particular.

Contributions and Contributors

The braid metaphor extends not just to the themes of Hornberger's work and to this book, but also to its contributors. Hornberger's professional life is tightly and meaningfully interwoven with that of her colleagues, students and mentors. The strength of that braid and the richness of those connections, both scholarly and personal, are abundantly evident here. The three thematic overviews are each written by a senior colleague with a close professional relationship to Nancy and, by extension, with the University of Pennsylvania's program in Educational Linguistics. Marilyn Martin-Jones, Brian Street and Teresa McCarty have been plenary speakers at the Ethnography in Education Research Forum, hosted annually at PennGSE by the Center for Urban Ethnography under Hornberger's direction (see Hornberger, 2002b). Martin-Jones and Street have also served as visiting professors in educational linguistics at Penn. Hornberger, in turn, has visited all three of their institutions and research contexts, and collaborated in myriad ways with their projects and students. More important than these institutional contacts are the deep connections that span their individual and collective scholarship, as detailed in the three thematic overviews.

Another strand in the braid is formed by Multilingual Matters. Colleagues Colin Baker and Mike Grover describe their long-standing relationship with Hornberger in the foreword to the book. We take this opportunity to thank them, as well as Tommi Grover and the entire MLM team, for their support of this project at every stage. Hornberger has had a long relationship with Multilingual Matters throughout her career, particularly as the co-editor of the *Bilingual Education and Bilingualism* series with Colin Baker, so we are delighted to work with them on this book.

Hornberger's mentor and dissertation advisor Richard Ruiz, the person who worked most closely with her at the start of her academic career, closes the book. As a doctoral student at the University of Wisconsin-Madison, Hornberger joined a small cadre of other students working with Ruiz in his Language Education Planning (LEP) research group, which would significantly influence her early work. Ruiz's supportive, humble and open stance as a mentor served as a model for how she would later mentor her own PhD students – including us. On a personal note, we have both benefitted tremendously in our own academic careers from Nancy Hornberger's careful guidance, and we continue to be inspired by her dedication as we mentor our own students and develop our own lines of research. Working together on this book in tribute to Hornberger has very much been, for both of us, a productive and enriching experience, and another turn in the braid.

Considering the many scholars whose work has been influenced by that of Hornberger in meaningful ways, we had to make difficult choices about the scope of this book. The main chapters were commissioned from students whose doctoral work Hornberger supervised at the University of Pennsylvania. Naturally, it would have been impossible to include all 45 students (and counting) so the range of chapters represents a sample of the varied conceptual, methodological and thematic strands that Hornberger has influenced within the field of educational linguistics. We also strove to represent the diversity in geographic and linguistic contexts that characterizes Hornberger's work. We asked the nine chapter contributors to present recent, original research, and to reflect on how their work has been influenced by but also extends or develops in some way one of Hornberger's theories or models. We thank all of our authors for their timely and insightful contributions.

Overview of the Book

In her thematic overview for Section I, *Marilyn Martin-Jones* traces the connections between Hornberger's scholarship, in particular her research on bilingual classrooms and communities, with investigations conducted across the globe. Martin-Jones, through her critical review of influences across these bodies of work, illustrates the ways in which local research has had global significance in shaping our understanding of bilingual processes and language policy, including both theoretical and methodological approaches.

The three chapters in this section resonate with Hornberger's close and systematic analysis of bilingualism in practice, both in and out of classrooms, as highlighted in the overview by Martin-Jones. *Manka Varghese's* contribution examines the tensions within the field of language teacher education. Drawing from a rich set of examples, Varghese builds and extends on Hornberger's writings that illustrate how educators can enact positive changes in restrictive language policy environments and, further, how these local practices can be productively examined and described as examples of possibility and potentials. *Viniti Vaish* expands on Hornberger's (2003) definition of biliteracy to analyze language use, and Hindi, Urdu and English code switching in Indian films. Her analysis reveals that the matrix language of these films is Hindustani, with the use of English and Urdu most often limited to borrowing for specific purposes. For instance, while Urdu references India's historical and imagined connections with Islamicate, it also problematizes simplistic renderings of terrorist characters. English, in turn, is used less as a language of colonial imposition and more often to reference not only middle-class non-resident Indians who are out of touch with Indian values, but also the practices and preferences of upper class Indians. *Angela Creese*, in her chapter, advances analytical vignettes as a methodology for investigating multilingual education. Drawing upon Hornberger's ethnographic work, Creese analyzes the role that fieldnotes and vignettes play in representing socially situated language use as well as the researcher's relationship to particular speech events and participants. She then goes on to explain how Hornberger's ethnographic approach resonates with the benefits and challenges her own team of nine researchers encountered during a major project exploring the multilingual repertoires of youth in four different communities. Vignettes, she concludes, provide rich ethnographic evidence that facilitates nuanced analysis of the multiple sociopolitical factors that intersect in everyday encounters.

In his thematic overview of Section II, *Brian Street* traces major developments in the study of literacy and the theoretical and methodological approaches that have coalesced, particularly in New Literacy Studies (NLS), in order to facilitate research that attempts to account for social and political issues. He then suggests ways in which Hornberger's highly influential continua of biliteracy model might potentially dovetail with the work undertaken in NLS, outlining key questions and challenges for future research that seeks to marry literacy with social justice.

The three chapters in this section all draw direct inspiration from the continua of biliteracy. *Ellen Skilton-Sylvester* re-revisits the continua of biliteracy, reflecting first on how the model interacted with her own development as a scholar. She then extends the continua to new contexts by considering how the continua of content helps us to analyze and understand recent restrictive language and education policy developments in the state of Arizona. *Daryl Gordon* uses both the continua of context and the continua of content to investigate literacy practices among Laotian women who have come to the US as refugees. She explores how one woman negotiates tensions between professional abilities and socially situated expectations about literacy, demonstrating that holistic research of workforce literacy requires looking beyond just functional abilities in reading and writing. In the final chapter for this section, *Melisa Cahnmann-Taylor* suggests the addition of a new set of continua to the model: empiricism of biliteracy. This new dimension, she argues, explicitly lifts forward epistemological issues that have long been encompassed in educational ethnography, particularly the empirical value of ambiguity, subjectivity and creativity in researching and representing biliteracy.

In her thematic overview for Section III, *Teresa L. McCarty* provides a critical review of the field of language policy and planning, and Ricento and Hornberger's (1996) 'onion metaphor' in particular. McCarty traces its genesis and development as an area of practice, and then focuses on present 'disciplinary reorientations' (Canagarajah, 2005: xvi) that investigate grounded manifestations of policy processes in practice. She focuses on two critical LPP questions, both closely linked to Hornberger's body of scholarship: (1) Can schools be agents for language and cultural maintenance and revitalization? and (2) Where is the practitioner in LPP practice? – highlighting the ways in which Hornberger's work 'points us toward the indefatigable promise of human agency in cracking open spaces of hope and possibility.' This sentiment is further explored in the chapters that make up this final section.

Building on Hornberger's work in the area of bilingual educational policy, *David Cassels Johnson* advances her concept of 'implementational and ideological space' (e.g. Hornberger, 2005). He draws on his ethnographic research on bilingual education in the School District of Philadelphia to distill five major principles for how educators engage with language policy. He illustrates that even within an ostensibly restrictive policy climate, teachers and administrators can find creative ways to foster multilingualism. Next, *Serafín Coronel-Molina* provides a historical overview and update on Peruvian politics and language planning. His chapter points to the long-standing gaps between public policy and popular languages attitudes, and to the deeply entrenched language ideologies and societal inequalities which threaten to undermine Indigenous language survival. *Shuhan Wang*, in turn, considers the history and development of Chinese-language teaching in the US, tracing both the development of Chinese heritage language schools and the growth of Chinese as a foreign-language instruction. Wang draws on Hornberger's ecology of language scholarship to point to the tensions inherent within these shifts, and concludes with policy-oriented recommendations for Chinese foreign language instruction and, by extension, other less commonly taught languages in the US.

The book concludes with *Richard Ruiz*'s reflections on the book's contents, which he describes as a 'cookbook' by Hornberger's students and colleagues. Ruiz considers Hornberger's earliest influences, the characteristics of her scholarship and approach to research which were evident from the outset of her career, and her lasting impact on her students and the field. Ruiz argues that Hornberger's body of work is as important as ever given the recent challenges to educational policy supporting linguistic diversity – both in Ruiz's home state of Arizona and around the world.

Since she first took the stage as a junior scholar, Hornberger has been a strong voice in the field, as a soloist and as a member of the choir. It is our hope that this book will serve both as a tribute to Hornberger's legacy and as a point of departure for the lyrics yet to be written about the topical, theoretical and methodological issues that continue to resonate in educational linguistics across the globe. Long may the songs of equity, access and multilingual education be heard!

Notes

1. The other was at the University of New Mexico (Hornberger, 2001: 1–2).
2. http://www.gse.upenn.edu/~hornberg/.

References

Canagarajah, S. (2005) Introduction. In A.S. Canagarajah (ed.) *Reclaiming the Local in Language Policy and Practice* (pp. xiii–xxx). Mahwah, NJ: Lawrence Erlbaum.

Hornberger, N.H. (1985) *Bilingual Education and Quechua Language Maintenance in Highland Puno, Peru*. PhD dissertation, University of Wisconsin-Madison.

Hornberger, N.H. (1988) *Bilingual Education and Language Maintenance: A Southern Peruvian Quechua Case*. Providence, RI: Foris Publications.

Hornberger, N.H. (1989) Continua of biliteracy. *Review of Educational Research* 59 (3), 271–296.

Hornberger, N.H. (1994) Literacy and language planning. *Language and Education* 8 (1, 2), 75–86.

Hornberger, N.H. (2001) Educational linguistics as a field: A view from Penn's program on the occasion of its 25th anniversary. *Working Papers in Educational Linguistics* 17 (1, 2), 1–26.

Hornberger, N.H. (2002a) Multilingual language policies and the continua of biliteracy: An ecological approach. *Language Policy* 1 (1), 27–51.

Hornberger, N.H. (2002b) Introduction to Special Issue. *Penn GSE Perspectives on Urban Education* 1 (2), http:www.urbanedjournal.org. Accessed 22 October 2010.

Hornberger, N.H. (ed.) (2003) *Continua of Biliteracy: An Ecological Framework for Educational Policy, Research and Practice in Multilingual Settings*. Clevedon: Multilingual Matters.

Hornberger, N.H. (2005) Opening and filling up implementational and ideological spaces in heritage language education. *The Modern Language Journal* 89, 605–609.

Hornberger, N.H. (2006, 26 January). Sabbatical sojourns: Working the local globally and the global locally. University of Pennsylvania, Philadelphia, PA.

Hornberger, N. H. and Skilton-Sylvester, E. (2000) Revisiting the continua of biliteracy: international and critical perspectives. *Language and Education* 14 (2), 96–122.

Hult, F.M. (ed.) (2010) *Directions and Prospects for Educational Linguistics*. Dordrecht: Springer.

Ricento, T. and Hornberger, N.H. (1996) Unpeeling the onion: Language planning and policy and the ELT professional. *TESOL Quarterly* 30 (3), 401–427.

Spolsky, B. and Hult, F.M. (eds) (2008) *The Handbook of Educational Linguistics*. Malden, MA: Blackwell.

Section I

Bilingual Education and Bilingualism

Thematic Overview I

Language Policies, Multilingual Classrooms: Resonances across Continents

MARILYN MARTIN-JONES

I still have vivid memories of the time, in the late 1980s, when I first read Nancy Hornberger's landmark ethnography of language practices and language ideologies in two rural school and community contexts in Puno, Southern Peru (Hornberger, 1988). At the time, the landscape of language policy research was dominated by studies of language planning processes and policy discourses at national level, studies which focused largely on policy documents, archival sources and interviews with policy-makers in different historical contexts. So, it was really heartening to come across Nancy Hornberger's work. Here was a researcher who, like me, was committed to approaching the study of language policy and bilingual education from the vantage point of the classroom, of teachers and learners and of local communities and who was convinced, as I was, that ethnography was best suited to this purpose, because of its emphasis on interpretive processes and on the situated nature of such processes.

In her early study in Peru, Hornberger provided us with rich and detailed insights into the daily interactional and organisational routines of life in the schools in the two rural communities where she carried out her research: one school where a Quechua/Spanish bilingual education project was being implemented and one where Spanish remained the dominant language of classroom life. Her meticulous account of the language and literacy practices, in Quechua and Spanish, that she had observed in these two local schools was contextualised in two main ways: firstly, with reference to the recent history of educational reform in Peru, to the introduction of a national bilingual education policy and to the complex processes involved in the implementation of the Experimental

Bilingual Education Project in Puno; and, secondly, with reference to the values associated with Quechua and with Spanish in the two local communities and the ways in which these values had been shaped by the history of conquest and the subsequent oppression and marginalisation of Quechua speakers in the Andean region of Peru.

It was precisely this kind of multi-layered analysis – one which combined the close study of the ebb and flow of multilingual communication in classroom and community settings with ethnographic and historical perspectives – that a small group of us at Lancaster University, in the north of England, were endeavouring to develop in the late 1980s and early 1990s. We called ourselves the Bilingualism Research Group. Several of the doctoral researchers in the group were engaged in ground-breaking research in schools in the global south. They all went on to publish their research and to contribute – with Hornberger, and with other scholars such as Canagarajah (1993) and Chick (1996) – to the creation of a distinct new strand of research related to education and language policy research in the global south, which documented the local ways in which teachers and learners made and remade centrally imposed policies in the recurring cycles of life in classrooms.

Jo Arthur Shoba was doing innovative research in primary classrooms in two schools in north eastern Botswana, where English was the 'officially approved classroom language' but where teachers made ample use of Setswana as a 'backstage language' (Arthur, 1996). Peter Martin was engaged in classroom-based research in primary schools in urban and rural settings in Brunei Darussalam, where a national bilingual education programme, in English and Bahasa Melayu, had been introduced. Martin was documenting, in illuminating detail, the ways in which teachers and students in these different settings were managing the challenges of the bilingual education programme (Martin, 1996). Lin Ndayipfukamiye was researching bilingual classroom discourse in grade five primary classrooms in Burundi, where students made the transition from Kirundi-medium education to a centrally imposed French-medium education. He provided a revealing account of the ways in which codeswitching between Kirundi and French served as a communicative resource for both teachers and students as students made this transition and as they coped with the constraints of the French-only language policy (Ndayipfukamiye, 1996).

Hornberger's research in Peru was an important point of reference for these researchers. There were powerful resonances between the language and literacy practices that she had documented in her study in Peru (Hornberger, 1988) and the practices in the classrooms they were observing and recording. The remarks that she made in the preface to her 1988 book still ring very true today, over two decades later:

> While the [Puno] schools and communities described are unique, those who read the descriptions will find many similarities between these schools and communities and communities and hundreds of other schools and communities in highland Peru, thousands in the highland Andes, and indeed millions in rural areas of the developing world. (Hornberger, 1988: xvi)

I have mentioned the work of some of the members of the Bilingualism Research Group at Lancaster at some length here because these are the studies that I am most familiar with and I was fortunate enough to engage in extended dialogue with the individuals concerned as their research unfolded. There were, of course, many other researchers working in other multilingual settings who were reading Hornberger's work in the late 1980s. Her study in Peru was widely cited and attracted a good deal of interest in post-colonial contexts. For example, when Jo Arthur Shoba returned from an early exploratory field trip to Botswana, I happened to have a copy of Nancy's book in my office and I showed it to Jo, encouraging her to read it. She smiled knowingly and told me that she had seen it on the desk of a colleague at the University of Botswana and had already made plans to get hold of a copy!

Ethnography of Language Education Policy: A Long-standing Research Tradition

Two decades on from Nancy Hornberger's seminal work in Peru, ethnography has come to occupy the centre ground in research on language education policy in multilingual settings. She has been at the forefront of a movement that has brought together two fields of research, with distinct histories, different orienting theories and empirical foci: on the one hand, research on language policy and planning and, on the other hand, research on multilingualism in school and classroom settings, which incorporated 'sociolinguistically-informed approaches to ethnographic research' (Hornberger, 1995: 245). I offer here a brief overview of the distinct histories of these two fields of research.

Research on language policy

The late 1980s and early 1990s saw a shift away from models of language policy research, that were formulated in an early sociolinguistics, grounded in structural functional thinking. New proposals were made for the development of approaches which could take account of the ways in which language policies contributed to the reproduction of asymmetrical relations of power in different political and historical contexts (e.g. Pennycook, 1989; Tollefson, 1991). These new proposals within the field of sociolinguistics reflected the wider influence across the social sciences of post-structuralist thought, particularly that which gave primacy to the role of discourse and culture in the reproduction of social inequality.

The new strand of work on language policy also reflected the influence of critical theory, with scholars being committed to engagement with questions of inequality and linguistic rights and wrongs (Pennycook, 2001; Tollefson, 2002). With this extensive new theory-building came a widening of the nature and scope of the field. Language policy research was now developed in the countries of the global north and west and there was greater concern with historical and ideological processes. However, the empirical focus was still on macro-level processes at the level of national and local governments and particular institutions.

Research on multilingualism in schools and classrooms

From the outset, research on multilingualism was guided by quite different epistemologies and orienting theories, although it was a field of study that was closely related to language policy. Within this field, there had been an early shift (in the late 1970s and early 1980s) towards interpretive and ethnographic research and to the close study of interactional processes. This intellectual shift was, of course, due to the incorporation of theoretical and methodological perspectives from the ethnography of communication (Hymes, 1974), ethnomethodology and conversation analysis (Garfinkel, 1972; Sacks *et al.*, 1974), interactional sociolinguistics (Gumperz, 1982) and micro-ethnography (Erickson & Shultz, 1982). The work of Gumperz (1982) was particularly influential in research on multilingualism, especially in the micro-analytic study of discourse practices and face-to-face interaction in local community contexts. This work was later taken forward by Auer (1984) in his proposals for the study of bilingual conversation.

By the late 1980s, these ethnographic and discourse analytic perspectives were being incorporated into research on bilingual classroom interaction. The largest early contribution to this new strand of research came from studies in post-colonial contexts, such as those described in the opening section of this chapter (including, of course, Hornberger's 1988 study in Peru). The 1990s then saw a diversification of research sites. Some studies were carried out with teachers and learners from linguistic minority groups (Heller, 1999; Jaffe, 1999). Angel Lin also did ground-breaking work in the changing political and sociolinguistic context of Hong Kong (Lin, 1996). Research was also undertaken in urban settings where some form of bilingual education provision was being made, in Europe or in North America, for learners of migrant or refugee origin (e.g. Creese, 2005; Freeman, 1998; Martin-Jones & Saxena, 1996; Rubinstein-Avila, 2002). In addition, research on bilingual talk was conducted in immersion programmes (e.g. Mejía, 1998), lifting the veil on communicative practices in an educational setting where there had long been a dominant discourse about sole use of the 'target language'.

In a key paper (Hornberger, 1995), Nancy traced the intersecting influences of different kinds of interpretive work (ethnography of communication, interactional sociolinguistics and sociolinguistic micro-ethnography) on research in multilingual classrooms. She called these different kinds of interpretive work: 'sociolinguistically-informed approaches' (1995: 245). The key concepts are superbly illustrated in this paper and I still recommend it as a foundational reference for doctoral researchers embarking on research in multilingual classrooms. Other reviews of research on bilingual classroom interaction have followed (e.g. Lin, 2008; Martin-Jones, 2000, 2007). Together with Hornberger (1995), they build a detailed picture of the thinking about theory and method guiding research in this area in the late 1980s and 1990s.

Some of the research in multilingual classrooms conducted in the mid-1990s drew on both interpretive *and* critical paradigms. I am using the term 'critical', here, in the sense of aiming to reveal links between the interactional routines of classrooms and the wider social and ideological order or, as Pennycook (2001) put it: 'mapping micro and macro relations' (2001: 5). Some examples of this critical, interpretive work are included in Heller and Martin-Jones (2001). The work of Heller (1999) pioneered this approach, drawing on post-structuralist theory, and particularly the work of Bourdieu (1991), in theorising the ways in which multilingual practices in schools and classrooms contribute to the reproduction or contestation of linguistic ideologies, language hierarchies and language policies.

These rich seams of critical and interpretive research in multilingual classrooms are still being developed in new contexts, providing yet deeper insights into processes of language policy-making at local levels and into the consequences of monolingual and bilingual policies for teachers and learners in different political and historical contexts. Studies conducted within the last few years include the following outstanding examples: research centering on the introduction of local bilingual education programmes in Mozambique (Chimbutane, 2009); research on the implementation of Lao-medium education in primary schools in the north-western region of Laos where minority languages are spoken (Cincotta-Segi, 2009); research in the US related to the implementation of Title III of the No Child Left Behind Act in the city of Philadelphia (Johnson, 2007); research in France on monolingual educational programmes for newly arrived migrant children (Bonacina, 2011); and research in complementary schools in the UK (Blackledge & Creese, 2010).

Language policy ethnography

Because, historically, there has been so little interaction between scholars working in the two fields of multilingualism and language policy, critical and interpretive studies of multilingual classroom interaction, of the type that I have just reviewed above, have not been thought of as contributing to the understanding of language policy development and implementation. However, as Hornberger and Johnson (2007) have noted, 'many ethnographies or qualitative studies illuminate the complexity of language planning and policy processes and the ways in which they create or restrict ideological and implementational space for multilingual pedagogy' (2007: 510/511).

Ricento and Hornberger (1996) addressed this lack of articulation between fields of study in an early article. Reviewing the state of the art of language policy research in the mid-1990s, they acknowledged some of the advances made through the development of the historical-structural and critical approaches, especially that of revealing the ideological underpinning of language policies. At the same time, they argued that more attention should be given to the different 'agents, levels and processes' (1996: 408) involved in language policy and planning and they introduced the now familiar 'onion' metaphor as a way of representing the multi-layered nature of language policy processes. They argued that research should take account of (or 'unpeel') the different layers of the 'policy onion', noting, quite rightly, that:

> Policies change as they move down through administrative levels, either explicitly in new written documents or through interpretation of existing documents. Only the most authoritarian political structures leave little room for variation in the implementation of official language policy. (1996: 417)

The different layers of policy-making are illustrated with comparative data from language policy in the US and in Peru. Again, as in earlier work by Nancy Hornberger, the classroom is seen as the core of policy-making processes. As Ricento and Hornberger put it: 'We place the classroom practitioner at the heart of language policy (at the center of the onion)' (1996: 417).

A decade later, Hornberger and Johnson (2007) put ethnography firmly on the language policy research agenda. Echoing Ricento and Hornberger (1996), and subsequent work by Canagarajah (2005) and by Stritikus and Wiese (2006), Hornberger and Johnson reiterate the critique of language policy research which focuses only on the global, national and institutional dimension of policy-making and on the political and ideological processes driving language education policies. As they put it: 'an (over)emphasis on the hegemonic power of policies obfuscates the potentially agentive role of local educators as they interpret and implement the policies' (2007: 510).

Hornberger and Johnson return to the 'onion' metaphor and call for multilayered, ethnographic research on language policy and planning (LPP), arguing for 'slicing the onion ethnographically' (2007: 509). They demonstrate, in compelling detail, why the study of language policy 'on paper' (i.e. the discourse analysis of policy documents) needs to be combined with ethnography to avoid giving only a partial account of the ways in which policy-making unfolds. They explain that:

> An ethnography of language policy can include textual and historical analyses of policy texts but must be based in an ethnographic understanding of some local context. The texts are nothing without the human agents who act as interpretive conduits between the language policy levels (or layers of the LPP onion). (Hornberger & Johnson, 2007: 528)

Thanks to the agency of Hornberger and Johnson (2007), epistemological space has been opened up at the interface between the tradition of interpretive classroom research in multilingual policy contexts and the field of language policy. Their intervention has generated considerable interest and research activity, including conference panels and publications (e.g. McCarty, 2011). The interface between these two fields of study is at last being more fully explored.

Biliteracy as a Lens on Educational Policy and Practice

Nancy Hornberger was the first to explore, in depth, the relationship between bilingualism and literacy, adopting the term 'biliteracy' (Hornberger, 1989, 1990, 2003). As García *et al.* (2007) noted in their review of research on biliteracy, she became 'its most perceptive scholar' (2007: 210). She provided the first systematic and detailed account of the multi-faceted nature of biliteracy, drawing attention to its significance in the education of bilingual learners and establishing valuable conceptual signposts for research, policy and practice in this area.

Building on Heath's (1983) seminal ethnographic research on literacy, Hornberger (1990) defined biliteracy as 'any and all instances in which communication occurs in two (or more) languages in and around writing' (1990: 213). In this early definition, it is already clear that the term encompasses multilingual literacies and instances where learners have lived experience of two or more languages along with the written forms of those languages. The *Continua of Biliteracy* framework, first proposed in Hornberger (1989), was designed to capture different facets of literacy acquisition and use in multilingual contexts and to identify the ways in which these facets were inter-related. As Cummins (2003) has put it: 'the initial *Continua* framework created an intellectual space for considering the phenomenon of biliteracy (and multiliteracy) in an integrated, comprehensive and interdisciplinary way' (2003: viii). In this framework, she unpacked some of the complexity of the relationship between bilingualism and literacy, taking account of the *development* of literacy, along with the *media* for biliteracy and the *contexts* in which biliteracy is acquired (Hornberger, 1989). The framework was further elaborated a decade or so later (Hornberger, 2003; Hornberger & Skilton-Sylvester, 2000) to incorporate a critical perspective and to foreground the asymmetrical relations of power that result in the privileging of particular languages, particular literacy resources (*media*) and particular ways of reading, writing and using texts (*contexts* and *content*).

As Nancy Hornberger herself has pointed out, there are clear resonances between the *Continua* framework and the ways in which Kathryn Jones and I have defined the notion of 'multilingual literacies' (Hornberger, 2000; Martin-Jones & Jones; 2000). García *et al.* (2007) have proposed yet another term, namely 'pluriliteracies'. With this term, they aim to account for the changing nature of the contemporary literacy landscape, for the changing relationship between verbal and other semiotic modes of communication, and for the prevalence of hybridised forms of spoken and written language in digital worlds of literacy. Articulating a broadly post-modern view of language and culture, they argue that: 'a pluriliteracies approach better captures the sociolinguistic realities of the current epoch' (2007: 217).

Far-reaching changes are, indeed, taking place in the contemporary communicative landscape, with the rapid development of digital literacies. With the advent of new technologies and the globalised spread of new technoscapes (Appadurai, 1990), we have seen the rapid diversification of communication media (e.g. computers, mobile phones), of digital artefacts (e.g. new forms of software) and of textual resources (e.g. new genres such as blogs and tweets) and we have seen the opening up of myriad new possibilities for literacy (Kress, 2003). Within the communicative landscape, different media, artefacts and textual resources are taken up and used in different ways to make meaning and people make diverse and creative use of these resources, particularly in relatively unregulated spaces (Sebba *et al.*, 2011), often blending and recasting language forms and specific features of writing systems.

However, the proposed concept of 'pluriliteracies' overlooks the ends of the *Continua* framework where the greatest power is vested. In education systems around the world, there is renewed emphasis, in language and literacy policies, on a skills-based view of literacy and on mastery of the monolingual, academic literacies. Even in bilingual education programmes, in different national and regional contexts, students are still evaluated primarily on their abilities to produce monolingual texts in two (or more) languages. The continued privileging of monolingual, academic and literary text production in languages, like English, that have a global reach, is also a crucial dimension of contemporary sociolinguistic realities; and these inequities are highlighted in the *Continua*. More precisely, the *Continua* model challenges the narrow, monolingual views of literacy that persist worldwide, in contemporary education systems, and lays the foundations for a pedagogy aimed at building on the language and literacy resources that all students bring to their learning in school.

Diverse Research Sites, Sustained Observation On-the-Ground and Then 'Bringing Anthropology Home'

It is difficult to think of a scholar, in the fields of language policy, bilingualism and literacy, who has had as wide an experience of research and practice in language and literacy education in multilingual settings as Nancy Hornberger has. She has been closely involved in research on Quechua-language education policy and practice for over 30 years, living for extended periods in local rural communities in Peru, learning Quechua and documenting the ways in which the uses of Spanish and Quechua mediate children's experience of schooling. Since the late 1990s, this involvement in Indigenous education has been extended and deepened through her long-term collaboration with Luis Enrique López and through participation in the

Programa de Formación en Educación Intercultural Bilingüe para los Países Andinos (PROEIB) (Programme for Professional Development in Bilingual Intercultural Education for the Andean Countries), based in Bolivia. PROEIB runs a Masters course (*Maestría*) for Indigenous students from across six Andean countries.

At the same time, Hornberger has also been engaged in research collaboration and dialogue with colleagues and research students in North and South America around their common concern with Indigenous education and language development. One of the fruits of this collaboration was a major edited volume entitled: *Indigenous literacies in the Americas.* In this volume, Hornberger reiterates her concern with grassroots initiatives and with the role of the researcher in providing an on-the-ground view of local efforts to reverse language shift by developing indigenous literacies. She aptly describes these efforts as 'language planning from the bottom up' (Hornberger, 1996: 357).

Nancy Hornberger teaches in the Graduate School of Education at the University of Pennsylvania, in a higher education context where, over the years, scholars like Dell Hymes and Fred Erickson have taken and made a place for ethnography in research in educational settings. She is now making her own distinguished contribution to the development of this tradition, establishing a vibrant environment for ethnographic research on education in multilingual settings, through her writing, through her teaching, through her work with doctoral researchers, through her research collaborations with educational practitioners in the city of Philadelphia and through her key role as organiser of the annual Ethnography and Education Forum.

In her work at the University of Pennsylvania and through her recent writing on language policy in the US (Hornberger, 2005a, 2005b; Hornberger & Hardman, 1994; Hornberger & Johnson, 2007), Hornberger has also been 'bringing anthropology home' in the Hymesian sense (Hymes, 1996) and making global and local comparisons. She has expressed deep concern about the significant policy shift that has taken place in the US, in the wake of the No Child Left Behind Act, passed in 2002, towards English-only education and towards the dismantling of resources for bilingualism in education (Hornberger, 2005a). At the same time, through her writing on language policy ethnography, she has offered a vision of how researchers and practitioners can work together to raise awareness of the ways in which top-down imposition of monolingual education policies are negotiated, challenged or actively resisted in local educational sites. As she noted, with considerable prescience, in the mid-1990s:

sociolinguistically-informed approaches to ethnographic research in the schools provide perspectives and methodologies which allow us not only to understand what's going on, but also to imagine and implement change. (Hornberger, 1996: 245)

References

Appadurai, A. (1990) Disjuncture and difference in the global cultural economy. In M. Featherstone (ed.) *Global Culture: Nationalism, Globalization and Modernity.* London: Sage.

Arthur, J. (1996) Codeswitching and collusion: Classroom interaction in Botswana primary schools. *Linguistics and Education* 8 (1, 2), 17–33.

Auer, P. (1984) *Bilingual Conversation.* Amsterdam: John Benjamins.

Blackledge, A. and Creese, A. (2010) *Multilingualism.* London: Continuum.

Bonacina, F. (2011) Ideology and the issue of access in multilingual school ethnography: a French example. In S. Gardner and M. Martin-Jones (eds) *Multilingualism, Discourse and Ethnography.* London: Routledge.

Bourdieu, P. (1991) *Language and Symbolic Power.* Cambridge: Polity Press.

Canagarajah, S. (1993) Critical ethnography of a Sri Lankan classroom: Ambiguities in opposition to reproduction through ESOL. *TESOL Quarterly* 27 (4), 187–212.

Canagarajah, S. (2005) *Reclaiming the Local in Language Policy and Practice.* Mahwah, NJ: Lawrence Erlbaum.

Chick, J.K. (1996) Safe-talk: collusion in apartheid education. In H. Coleman (ed.) *Society and the Language Classroom* (pp. 21–39). Cambridge: Cambridge University Press.

Chimbutane, F. (2009) The purpose and value of bilingual education: A critical, linguistic ethnographic study of two rural primary schools in Mozambique. Unpublished PhD thesis, University of Birmingham, UK.

Cincotta-Segi, A. (2009) 'The big ones swallow the small ones'. Or do they? The language policy and practice of ethnic minority education in the Lao PDR: A case study from Nalae Unpublished PhD thesis, Australian National University.

Creese, A. (2005) *Teacher Collaboration and Talk in Multilingual Classrooms.* Clevedon: Multilingual Matters.

Cummins, J. (2003) Foreword. In N.H. Hornberger (ed.) *Continua of Biliteracy: An Ecological Framework for Educational Policy, Research and Practice in Multilingual Settings* (pp. vii–xi). Clevedon: Multilingual Matters.

Erickson, F. and Shultz, J. (1982) *The Counselor as Gatekeeper: Social Interaction in Interviews.* New York: Academic Press.

Freeman, R. (1998) *Bilingual Education and Social Change.* Clevedon: Multilingual Matters.

García, O., Bartlett, L. and Kleifgen, J. (2007) From biliteracy to pluriliteracies. In P. Auer and L. Wei (eds) *Handbook of Multilingualism and Multilingual Communication* (pp. 207–228). Berlin: Mouton de Gruyter.

Garfinkel, H. (1986 [1972]) Remarks on ethnomethodology. In J.J. Gumperz and D. Hymes (eds) *Directions in Sociolinguistics: The Ethnography of Communication.* New York: Blackwell.

Gumperz, J.J. (1982) *Discourse Strategies.* Cambridge: Cambridge University Press.
Heath, S.B. (1983) *Ways with Words: Language, Life and Work in Communities and Classrooms.* New York: Cambridge University Press.
Heller, M. (1999) *Linguistic Minorities and Modernity: A Sociolinguistic Ethnography.* London: Longman.
Heller, M. and Martin-Jones, M. (eds.) (2001) *Voices of Authority: Education and Linguistic Difference.* Westport, CT: Ablex.
Hornberger, N.H. (1988) *Bilingual Education and Language Maintenance: A Southern Peruvian Quechua Case.* Berlin: Mouton de Gruyter.
Hornberger, N.H. (1989) Continua of biliteracy. *Review of Educational Research* 59 (3), 271–296.
Hornberger, N.H. (1990) Creating successful learning contexts for bilingual literacy. *Teachers College Record* 92 (2), 212–229.
Hornberger, N.H. (1995) Ethnography in linguistic perspective: Understanding school processes. *Language and Education* 9 (4), 233–248.
Hornberger, N.H. (ed.) (1996) *Indigenous Literacies in the Americas: Language Planning from the Bottom Up.* Berlin: Mouton.
Hornberger, N.H. (2000) Afterword: multilingual literacies, literacy practices, and the continua of biliteracy. In M. Martin-Jones and K. Jones (eds) *Multilingual Literacies: Reading and Writing Different Worlds* (pp. 353–367). Amsterdam: John Benjamins.
Hornberger, N.H. (ed.) (2003) *Continua of Biliteracy: An Ecological Framework for Educational Policy, Research and Practice in Multilingual Settings.* Clevedon: Multilingual Matters.
Hornberger, N.H. (2005a) Nichols to NCLB: Local and global perspectives on U.S. language education policy. In O.García, T. Skutnabb-Kangas and M. Torres-Guzmán (eds) *Imagining Multilingual Schools: Languages in Education and Globalization* (pp. 223–237). Clevedon: Multilingual Matters.
Hornberger, N.H. (2005b) Opening and filling up implementational ideological spaces in heritage language education. *Modern Language Journal* 89, 605–609.
Hornberger, N.H. and Hardman, J. (1994) Literacy as cultural practice and cognitive skill: Biliteracy in a Cambodian adult ESL class and a Puerto Rican GED program. In D. Spener (ed.) *Adult Biliteracy in the United States* (pp. 147–169). Washington, DC: Center for Applied Linguistics.
Hornberger, N. H. and Johnson, D.C. (2007) Slicing the onion ethnographically: Layers and spaces in multilingual language education policy and practice. *TESOL Quarterly* 41, 509–532.
Hornberger, N.H. and Skilton-Sylvester, E. (2000) Revisiting the continua of biliteracy: international and critical perspectives. *Language and Education* 14 (2), 96–122.
Hymes, D. (1974) *Foundations in Sociolinguistics: An Ethnographic Approach.* Philadelphia: University of Pennsylvania Press.
Hymes, D. (1996) *Ethnography, Linguistics, Narrative Inequality.* London: Taylor and Francis.
Jaffe, A. (1999) *Ideologies in Action: Language Politics on Corsica.* Berlin: Mouton de Gruyter.
Johnson, D.C. (2007) Language policy within and without the School District of Philadelphia. Unpublished PhD thesis, University of Pennsylvania.
Kress, G. (2003) *Literacy in the New Media Age.* London: Routledge.

Lin, A. (1996) Bilingualism or linguistic segregation? Symbolic domination, resistance and codeswitching. *Linguistics and Education* 8 (1), 49–84.

Lin, A. (2008) Codeswitching in the classroom: Research paradigms and approaches. In K.A. King and N.H. Hornberger (eds) *Encyclopedia of Language and Education: Vol. 10. Research Methods in Language and Education* (2nd ed.) (pp. 273–286). New York: Springer.

Martin, P.W. (1996) Codeswitching in the primary classroom: One response to the planned and unplanned language environment in Brunei. *Journal of Multilingual and Multicultural Development* 17 (2–4), 128–144.

Martin-Jones, M. (2000) Bilingual classroom interaction: A review of recent research. *Language Teaching* 33 (1), 1–9.

Martin-Jones, M. (2007) Bilingualism, education and the regulation of access to language resources: Changing research perspectives'. In M. Heller (ed.) *Bilingualism: A Social Approach* (pp. 161–182). Houndmills, Basingstoke: Palgrave Macmillan.

Martin-Jones, M. and Jones, K. (eds) (2000) *Multilingual Literacies: Reading and Writing Different Worlds*. Amsterdam: John Benjamins.

Martin-Jones, M. and Saxena, M. (1996) Turn-taking, power asymmetries, and the positioning of bilingual participants in classroom discourse. *Linguistics and Education* 8 (1), 105–123.

McCarty, T. (ed.) (2011) *Ethnography and Language Policy*. New York: Routledge.

Mejía, A-M. de (1998) Bilingual story-telling: Codeswitching, discourse control and learning opportunities. *TESOL Journal* 7 (6), 4–10.

Ndayipfukamiye, L. (1996) The contradictions of teaching bilingually in postcolonial Burundi: From *nyakatsi* to *maisons en étages*. *Linguistics and Education* 8 (1), 35–47.

Pennycook, A. (1989) The concept of method, interested knowledge, and the politics of language teaching. *TESOL Quarterly* 23, 589–618.

Pennycook, A. (2001) *Critical Applied Linguistics*. Mahwah, NJ: Lawrence Erlbaum.

Ricento, T.L. and Hornberger, N.H. (1996) Unpeeling the onion: Language planning and policy and the ELT professional. *TESOL Quarterly* 30 (3), 401–428.

Rubinstein-Avila, E. (2002) Problematizing the 'dual' in a dual-immersion program: A portrait. *Linguistics and Education* 13 (1), 65–87.

Sacks, H., Schegloff, E. and Jefferson, G. (1974) A simplest systematics for the organization of turn-taking in conversation. *Language* 50, 696–735.

Sebba, M., Mahootian, S. and Jonsson, C. (eds) (2011) *Language Mixing and Codeswitching in Writing*. New York: Routledge.

Stritikus, T.T. and Wiese, A. (2006) Reassessing the role of ethnographic methods in education policy research: Implementing bilingual education policy at local levels. *Teachers College Record* 108 (6), 1106–1131.

Tollefson, J. (1991) *Planning Language, Planning Inequality*. London: Longman.

Tollefson, J. (ed.) (2002) *Language Policies in Education: Critical Issues*. Mahwah, NJ: Lawrence Erlbaum.

Chapter 1

Language Teacher Education and Teacher Identity

MANKA VARGHESE

Language teacher education (LTE) and Language teacher identity (LTI) have become a significant topic in Educational/Applied Linguistics in the last 25 years. The early work of Freeman and Richards (1993, 1996) and Johnson (1992) placed this squarely as an important topic of scholarship in the discipline. Their scholarship helped move the notion of language teaching pedagogy as a set of behaviors and practices to a more complex and holistic understanding of language teaching (see Varghese, 2007). This new conception included teachers' prior belief and practices; professional socialization; and the classroom, school and policy context. Currently, the work in LTE and LTI spans at least the study of the following: language teachers' lives and professional work (Cahnmann, 2005; Creese, 2005; Johnston, 1997; Varghese, 2007); language teachers' decision-making processes (Borg, 2003; Tsui, 2003; Woods, 1998); language teachers as language policy-makers (Menken & García, 2010; Skilton-Sylvester, 2003; Varghese, 2008); language teachers in terms of their professional, racial, ethnic, linguistic, religious differences (Allexsaht-Snider, 1996; Benson, 2004; Cahnmann & Varghese, 2006; Galindo, 1996; Lemberger, 1997; Liu, 1996; Monzó & Rueda, 2003; Varghese & Johnston, 2007); language teachers and their professional development (Cahnmann-Taylor & De Souto Manning, 2010; Edge, 2001; Johnson & Golombek, 2002) as well as theoretical insights into language teacher education and identity (Johnson, 2009; Morgan, 2004; Varghese et al., 2005).

Although the topic of language teacher education and identity is not explicitly in the purview of Nancy Hornberger's scholarship, her work in different areas has been influential to my (and others') work on the topic. I will illustrate this here through discussion of Hornberger's application of her continua of biliteracy to bilingual educators' roles and practices. In the continua of biliteracy (see Cahnman-Taylor; Martin-Jones;

Skilton-Sylvester; and others this volume), Hornberger describes biliteracy in terms of four aspects, which are nested within the other and exist in the form of a continua rather than fixed points: the media, contexts, development and content of biliteracy. Hornberger and others after her have used it as a framework to examine teaching, research and students' literacy practices. Hornberger has raised questions, produced data and discussed issues specific to teacher education and teacher education in this piece as well as in several other manuscripts (e.g. Ricento & Hornberger, 1996). In this chapter, I bring to the forefront the essential points she has raised and also discuss how my work and that of my students on the topic of LTE and LTI relates to these three which are listed here. Of course, other aspects of Hornberger's scholarship, such as her work on intercultural education, ethnography and linguistic minority rights are also relevant to the research in language teacher education and identity, and that influence is also apparent in this chapter. Furthermore, as Creese expresses in the prelude of her chapter in this book, Hornberger's approach of being open and inclusive of different perspectives (theoretically and methodologically); her commitment to multilingual education both locally and globally; and her attention to vivid detail to make her case permeate the way I have carried out and documented my research in language teacher education and identity. These focii on inclusiveness, multilingualism and details in research are thus present throughout this chapter.

In a paper on the applications of the continua of biliteracy for bilingual educators and bilingual teaching, Hornberger (2004) uses vignettes to provide examples of the different aspects of the continua. Each of these aspects illuminates various dilemmas as Hornberger frames them, that are experienced by bilingual educators: the context aspect is used to explore the global/local dilemma; the media aspect to examine the standard/non-standard dilemma; the development of biliteracy to look at the language/content dilemma; and finally, the content of the continua to illuminate the language/culture/identity dilemma. In this chapter, I explore three of these dilemmas (all except the standard/non-standard dilemma) through examples from my past studies or those of my graduate students in a similar way that Hornberger (2004) did in her original chapter. Within the last dilemma, I discuss in detail how her work on language policy has shaped the understanding of language educators as policy-makers. The aim of presenting all of these as dilemmas is to show how Hornberger approaches the practice of language teaching as a set of dilemmas for teachers that depend deeply on their contexts of teaching as well as their professional identities.

The Global/Local Dilemma

The global/local dilemma is one where language educators experience how their local learning and teaching environments as well as their pedagogical goals are connected with the forces of globalization. Hornberger writes that 'the global/local dilemma ... is how we as bilingual educators can respond adequately and fully to both global and local pressures on our students' (2004: 69). In discussing this dilemma, I bring forth examples from my work on bilingual teachers in an international dual language school (Varghese & Park, 2010), my work on Evangelical Christians teachers (Johnston & Varghese, 2006; Varghese & Johnston, 2007), and my graduate student's dissertation work on non-native-speaker teachers (Huang, 2009). All of these studies show how local and global discourses simultaneously push on language educators in their work.

In both my dissertation study of bilingual teachers in Urbantown (Varghese, 2006) and my work on a dual language program in the Northwest of the US (Varghese & Park, 2010), bilingual teachers were caught in the middle of a discourse for bilingualism to serve their immigrant students locally and one to serve all students in terms of global cross-cultural understanding and the global economy. These discourses were sometimes compatible and at other times not. The literature on globalization and language teaching has identified three clear themes, mostly with regards to the spread of English but also in relation to the teaching of multiple languages. One is the tension between cultural and linguistic homogenization and heterogenization (Block, 2002; Cameron, 2002); the second is the neoliberal rationale for language teaching that positions it within a 'deregulated, hyper-competitive, post-industrial, globalized economy' (Cameron, 2002: 72), and the last is the tension between the communicative use of a language versus an academic emphasis on a language.

The dual language school with an international emphasis had an English-Japanese program as well as an English-Spanish program. At the time of the study, 27.3% of students received free or reduced-price meals and the student body's ethnicity was 47% Anglo, 24% and Latino/a with the remaining 30% from various other groups. The teachers we interviewed felt that overall the program did benefit Latino/a students although they also expressed concern about potential inequalities in the program. In one interview, the teacher noted, 'Being an international school has been a magnet for a lot of students who want to maintain their home language, Japanese or Spanish. But partly it's to keep the rich Anglo families in the public schools instead of sending their kids to private schools, so that's part of it too . . . So the families here value the diversity and like the diversity, like the opportunity the school provides'. Yet while diversity was valued for some students, one of the teachers noted that it was rare to find a Latino/a student who had a strong sense of self and pride in his or her home culture: 'I mostly see people being pressured to assimilate.' The critical questions of which languages serve which communities and how to approach this are one that teachers who are teaching in bilingual schools wrestle with, and are clearly related to the global and local demands of the languages and the communities. In this case, Spanish may be serving the global demands of Anglo students but the local usage of it as a heritage language and as the language of a group that has been positioned locally and nationally in a marginalized way has to be also be accounted for.

The intersections of religion and language teaching also raise profound questions related to how language educators respond to local and global pressures and demands. As we make clear in our study of Evangelical Christianity and English language teaching (Johnston & Varghese, 2006), there is a connection between the two that needs to be understood at a global scale and is significantly dependent on how it is put into practice locally by language educators. The Christian Evangelical English teachers we interviewed (Varghese & Johnston, 2007) displayed a range in terms of how they perceived the use of English to promote their religion. We contrasted two teachers, Elizabeth and David. David, as we describe, expressed great sensitivity about the impact the push and demand for English was having on linguistic diversity around the world and the need to integrate the perspectives of local communities. Elizabeth, on the other hand, saw English language teaching as an excellent 'platform' to promote and spread her religious views. The teaching of English in conjunction with spreading Christianity globally has been regarded as a contentious practice in many contexts. However, as our work has sought to show, some Christian English language teachers are more aware and concerned than others about this controversy and the need to integrate local perspectives.

The last example that elucidates the global/local dilemma of language educators is the study of four non-native-speaker English as a Second Language (ESL) teachers in two US high schools (Huang, 2009). In this study, Huang argues that although these teachers would be framed as non-native-speaker teachers of English in the global context, the extent they ascribe to this membership or affiliation depends on the way they are framed at the local level. For instance, in one school and school district, these teachers were highly valued and their non-native status was not emphasized by the other staff, administrators or families; thus, these teachers did not see this particular membership as preeminent for them. This example shows that the local and global characterizations of these teachers need to be simultaneously studied to understand how they view their roles.

The examples from these studies not only show that the decisions language educators make with regards to language pedagogy must be framed with a sense of global and local understandings and consequences for their students. The roles of language teachers need to be character-ized globally and locally. It is clear that the teaching of languages, and especially of English, is a profession perhaps more so than others (e.g. teaching Math) where the global and local needs and demands must more immediately be held together. The global perspectives of bilingual teaching as being primarily useful for the global workforce; Evangeli-cal Christianity's nefarious relationship with English language teaching; and the deficit framing of non-inner circle English language teachers as non-native-speaker teachers are widely circulating discourses which are altogether too simplistic. The study of language teachers' everyday practices and contexts at the local level add complexity to such blanket assumptions. They also reveal the decisions that language teachers need to wrestle with, amidst competing demands on themselves, their students and their families.

The Language/Content Dilemma

The language/content dilemma of how biliteracy develops asks lan-guage educators to focus on both the teaching of language and content. This dilemma is becoming the most pressing question for English lan-guage teachers and bilingual teachers across the globe and in many countries where English is the dominant language of academics (Evans, 2000; Wannagat, 2007; Yoon, 2001). Much has been written about how the teaching of language and content simultaneously is 'more than just good teaching' (DeJong & Harper, 2005; Gibbons, 2002, 2006; Lucas *et al.*, 2008); specifically, what must be central to the practice of a language educator is how language is taught (within content) and not only how content is mod-ified. At the same time, the importance for students to be able to access the content cannot be overlooked. In my teacher education classes where I help to prepare future elementary school teachers in teaching emerging bilinguals, we focus on modifying the content so that it can be accessible to emerging bilinguals, as well as finding ways to scaffold their development of academic language. This is no small feat for teachers who have multiple demands on their time and their practice as well as limited pre-service and in-service teacher preparation. Kaje (2009) examined the practices of two mainstream fourth-grade teachers who were viewed as exemplary teachers of their emerging bilingual students. She found that one significant feature that both teachers shared was the way they explicitly addressed language and its use in their classes; in addition, their content was not diluted but rather scaffolded for the students. For instance, Mrs. Hutchins (one of the teachers) in almost every class would ask students to come in front of the class and explain their thinking and why they did what they did. As the teacher explained in subsequent interviews, this exercise was not only about having the students explain the content of what they had learned and how they did so, but about compelling them to use more formal language for an audience. As Kaje (2009: 118) describes:

> In her first lesson, Mrs. Hutchins spent the class session introducing the concept of area by having students act out the difference between area and perimeter .... and discuss different applications for using area in real lie .... at the end of this first lesson as a formative assessment, Mrs. Hutchins had students write in their math journals to a third grader to explain area ....

However, Mrs. Hutchins, as Kaje explains, was still not convinced that several of her emerging bilinguals had secured the concept and the language and decided to have the students write their explanations to their fifth-grade teacher. Mrs. Hutchins explained her rationale in the following way:

> I changed the plan just a little bit, as far as having them explain. What I did was to have them explain in their journals to a third grader how you find area. So, now I've changed it a bit. Because now I want them to describe it to an adult. So, that I can bring that language up just a little bit more, just to see if they've really got it. (Kaje, 2009: 119)

Essential questions that I along with several of my graduate students are currently pursuing are the following: (1) what can different models of effective professional development for language educators that need to address language and content look like, (2) what institutional contexts can be supportive for these teachers, and (3) what professional identities should we be envisioning for these language educators? The simultaneous focus on language and content seems to be an exigent aspect of their professional role for the language educator in a high-stakes environment across the globe.

The Language/Culture/Identity Dilemma

This dilemma is described by Hornberger (2004: 75) as: 'how we as bilingual educators can respond adequately and fully to dynamic negotiations of cultures and identities and of overlapping language affiliations not necessarily linked to expertise or inheritance'. This approach frames the work of the language educator to be one of negotiating students' culture and linguistic identities and affiliations and that this process of negotiation is connected to language educators' cultural and linguistic identities/affiliations. Rather than being another independent dilemma, I view this dilemma as actually overlapping or embodying all the other dilemmas. This speaks directly to what I have referred to in my work as the professional identity of language teachers (Varghese, 2006, 2008; Varghese *et al.*, 2005) and how these are formed (or in the process of being formed). I also make the direct link between LTI and LTE by calling for the latter to be framed with a vision and the realities of professional identities and roles.

My early work from my dissertation on bilingual teachers revealed that these teachers were involved in seeking out and forming a professional identity rather than solely attempting to acquire a set of skills and knowledge (Varghese, 2006, 2008). I found that the two aspects of their professional identity that were most salient to them were advocacy and language policy-making (Varghese, 2006, 2008). These two findings underscored how language teaching is a more complex and multilayered profession than what has traditionally been the view.

In an earlier seminal piece, Ricento and Hornberger (1996) put forward the critical role that language teachers have as language planners and policy-makers as they use the metaphor of an onion to explain the interacting layers of agents and processes that influence language policy and planning (LPP). I situate my work on teachers as language policy-makers within what Menken and García (2010) refer to as research that focuses on how members from the 'so-called bottom of the educational policy structure' create/resist/negotiate language policies. This line of work has been followed up by other scholars such as Corson (1999), Skilton-Sylvester (2003), Ramanathan (2005) and most recently Menken and García (2010). This work has shown how language teachers can challenge entrenched monolingual or otherwise restrictive curriculum and pedagogy through their practices and policies. Skilton-Sylvester goes so far as to argue that 'much of language teaching can also be seen as language policymaking' (2003: 7). At the same time, my work (Varghese, 2008) has looked at how these practices and policies are mediated by teachers 'cultural models' or their ways of understanding the world that are influenced by their past and present personal and professional experiences. In a recent chapter in the edited volume by Menken and García (2010), doctoral student, Bonnie English and I also show how one teacher is an advocate for the English learners in her school because of her own personal and professional experiences as well as the resources in her school (English & Varghese, 2010). At the same time, at the end of the chapter we raise the point that although teachers can enact positive changes for their students, it is impossible to address systemic improvement by relying solely on individual teachers. The language/culture/identity dilemma, therefore, emphasizes how intertwined the changes that teachers can enact for their students are with their own roles and affiliations. Furthermore, these roles are deeply connected to structural affordances and challenges.

Conclusion

All of the examples above as well as the three dilemmas – the global/local, language/content, and language/culture/identity – clearly elucidate one of the critical points that Hornberger has made through much of her scholarship. Collectively, her work has shown how educators can enact positive changes in restrictive language policy environments and how the local practices of these educators need to be examined and described to show the openings that are created. At the same time, she has been unflinching in her criticism of policies in different countries that have restricted the aspirations and possibilities of multilingualism. Overall, the ability to keep an eye on the macro and the micro and document both simultaneously has been invaluable in studying language teacher education and identity. The different studies I have discussed in the chapter with the examples I provide show this clearly. In this chapter, I have also included the work of my graduate students since Hornberger has also served as an important model for me in how she has mentored her students, included and cited her students' work and significantly coauthored with her students. Several of my students, as I have mentioned earlier, are pursuing scholarship in teacher education and teacher identity; their topics include the professional lives of non-native-speaker teachers in K-12 US schools; the practices of mainstream teachers teaching culturally and linguistically diverse students; the beliefs and practices of foreign-language teachers in higher education; case studies of professional development models for English learners in school districts. All of these research studies embody a number of Hornberger's principles, such as her commitment towards equity and multilingualism, as well as her methodological approaches in qualitative research methods and ethnography. Ultimately, her ability to reveal the openings that language teachers create for themselves and their students is present in my work and that of my students.

References

Allexsaht-Snider, M. (1996) Windows into diverse worlds: The telling and sharing ofteachers' life histories. *Education and Urban Society* 29, 103–119.
Benson, C. (2004) Do we expect too much of bilingual teachers? Bilingual teachers in developing countries. In J. Brutt-Griffler and M. Varghese (eds) *Bilingualism and Language Pedagogy* (pp. 112–129). Clevedon: Multilingual Matters.
Block, D. (2002) 'McCommunication': A problem in the frame for SLA. In D. Block and D. Cameron (eds) *Globalization and Language Teaching*. New York: Routledge.
Borg, S. (2003) Teacher cognition in language teaching: A review of research on what language teachers think, know, believe and do. *Language Teaching* 36, 81–109.
Cahnmann, M. (2005) Translating competence in a critical bilingual classroom. *Anthropology & Education Quarterly* 36 (3), 230–249.
Cahnmann-Taylor, M. and Souto-Manning, M. (2010) *Teachers Act Up: Performing Lives, Enacting Change*. New York: Teachers College Press.
Cahnmann, M. and Varghese, M. (2006) Critical advocacy and bilingual education in the United States. *Linguistics and Education* 16 (1), 59–73.
Cameron, D. (2002) Globalization and the teaching of 'communication skills'. In D. Block and D. Cameron (eds) *Globalization and Language Teaching*. New York: Routledge.
Corson, D. (1999) *Language Policy in Schools: A Resource for Teachers and Administrators*. Mahwah, NJ: Lawrence Erlbaum.
Creese, A. (2005) *Teacher Collaboration and Talk in Multilingual Classrooms*. Clevedon: Multilingual Matters.
DeJong, E.J. and Harper, C.A. (2005) Preparing mainstream teachers for English language learners: Is being a good teacher good enough? *Teacher Education Quarterly*, Spring, 101–112.
Edge, J. (ed) (2001) *Action Research*. Alexandria, Virginia: Teachers of English to Speakers of Other Languages Inc.
English, B. and Varghese, M. (2010) Enacting language policy through the facilitator model in a monolingual policy context in the United States. In K. Menken and O. García (eds) *Negotiating Language Policies in Schools: Educators as Policymakers* (pp. 107–122). New York: Taylor and Francis.
Evans, S. (2000) Hong Kong's new English language policy in education. *World Englishes* 19 (2), 185–204.
Freeman, D. and Richards J.C. (1993) Conceptions of teaching and the education of second language teachers. *TESOL Quarterly* 27, 193–216.
Freeman, D. and Richards, J.C. (eds) (1996) *Teacher Learning in Language Teaching*. Cambridge: Cambridge University Press.
Galindo, R. (1996) Reframing the past in the present: Chicana teacher role identity as a bridging identity. *Education and Urban Society* 29, 85–102.

Gibbons, P. (2002) *Scaffolding Language, Scaffolding Learning: Teaching Second Language Learners in the Mainstream Classroom*. Portsmouth, NH: Heinemann.

Gibbons, P. (2006) *Bridging Discourses in the ESL Classroom: Students, Teachers, and Researchers*. London: Continuum.

Huang, I. (2009) Theorizing non/native dichotomy: Non/native teachers of English secondary ESL classrooms. Unpublished PhD thesis, Seattle: University of Washington.

Hornberger, N.H. (2004) The continua of biliteracy and the bilingual educator: Educational linguistics in practice. In J. Brutt-Griffler and M. Varghese (eds) *Bilingualism and Language Pedagogy* (pp. 63–79). Clevedon: Multilingual Matters.

Johnson, K.E. (1992) Learning to teach: Instructional actions and decisions of preservice ESL teachers. *TESOL Quarterly* 26, 507–535.

Johnson, K.E. (2009) *Second Language Teacher Education: A Sociocultural Perspective*. New York: Routledge.

Johnson, K.E. and Golombek, P.R. (eds) (2002) *Teachers' Narrative Inquiry as Professional Development*. Cambridge: Cambridge University Press.

Johnston, B. (1997) Do EFL teachers have careers? *TESOL Quarterly* 31, 681–712.

Johnston, B. and Varghese, M. (2006) Neo-imperialism, evangelism, and ELT: Modernist missions and a postmodern profession. In J. Edge (ed.) *(Re-)Locating TESOL in an Age of Empire* (pp. 195–207). Basingstoke, UK: Palgrave Macmillan.

Kaje, E. (2009) More than just good teaching: Teachers engaging culturally and linguistically diverse learners with content and language in mainstream classrooms. Unpublished PhD thesis, Seattle: University of Washington.

Lemberger, N. (1997) *Bilingual Education: Teachers' Narratives*. Mahwah, NJ: Lawrence Erlbaum Associates.

Liu, J. (1999) Nonnative English-speaking professionals in TESOL. *TESOL Quarterly* 33, 85–102.

Lucas, T., Villegas, A.M. and Freedson-Gonzales, M. (2008) Linguistically responsive teacher education: Preparing classroom teachers to teach English language learners. *Journal of Teacher Education* 58, 361–373.

Menken, K. and García, O. (eds) (2010) *Negotiating Language Policies in Schools: Educators as Policymakers*. New York: Taylor and Francis.

Monzó, L. and Rueda, R. (2003) Shaping education through diverse funds of knowledge: A look at one Latina paraeducator's lived experiences, beliefs, and teaching practice. *Anthropology & Education Quarterly* 34 (1), 72–95.

Morgan, B. (2004) Teacher identity as pedagogy: Towards a field-internal conceptualization in bilingual and second language education. In J. Brutt-Griffler and M. Varghese (eds) *Bilingualism and Language Pedagogy* (pp. 80–96). Clevedon: Multilingual Matters.

Ramanathan, V. (2005) Rethinking language planning and policy from the ground-up: Refashioning institutional realities and human lives. *Current Issues in Language Planning* 6 (2), 89–101.

Ricento, T.K. and Hornberger, N.H. (1996) Unpeeling the onion: Language planning and policy and the ELT professional. *TESOL Quarterly* 30 (3), 401–428.

Skilton-Sylvester, E. (2003) Legal discourses and decisions, teacher policymaking and the multilingual classroom: Constraining and supporting Khmer/English biliteracy in the United States. *International Journal of Bilingual Education and Bilingualism* 3, 4, 168–184.

Tsui, A.B.M. (2003) *Understanding Expertise in Teaching: Case Studies of Second Language Teachers*. Cambridge: Cambridge University Press.

Varghese, M. (2006) Bilingual teachers-in-the-making in Urbantown. *Journal of Multilingual and Multicultural Development* 27 (3), 211–224.

Varghese, M. (2007) Language teacher research methods. In K. King and N.H. Hornberger (eds) *Encyclopedia of Language and Education* (pp. 287–298). New York, NY: Springer.

Varghese, M. (2008) Using cultural models to unravel how bilingual teachers enact language policies. *Language and Education* 22 (5), 289–306.

Varghese, M. and Johnston, B. (2007) Evangelical Christians and English language teaching. *TESOL Quarterly* 41 (1), 5–31.

Varghese, M., Morgan, B., Johnston, B. and Johnson, K. (2005) Theorizing language teacher identity: Three perspectives and beyond. *Journal of Language, Identity and Education* 4, 21–44.

Varghese, M.M. and Park, C. (2010) Going global: Can dual language programs save bilingual education? *Journal of Latinos and Education* 9 (1), 72–80.

Wannagat, U. (2007) Learning through L2-content and language integrated learning and English as medium of instruction. *The International Journal of Bilingual Education and Bilingualism* 10 (5), 663–682.

Woods, D. (1998) *Teacher Cognition in Language Teaching*. Cambridge: Cambridge University Press.

Yoon, M. (2003) Content based instruction: Can it work in Korea? Unpublished PhD thesis, Korea: Dankook University.

Chapter 2

Terrorism, Nationalism and Westernization: Code Switching and Identity in Bollywood

VINITI VAISH

This chapter uses as its research site the cultural space of 'Bollywood.' 'Bollywood' – a tongue-in-cheek term created by the English-language press in India in the late 1970s – 'has now become the dominant global term to refer to the prolific and box-office-oriented Hindi-language film industry located in Bombay (renamed Mumbai in 1995)' (Ganti, 2004: 3). In the last decade or so, Bollywood has become a symbol of a globalizing India's 'soft power,' i.e. the power of culture. *Taal*, released in 1999 and starring former Miss World Aishwarya Rai, was the first Bollywood movie to become a top box office draw in the USA and UK, beating numerous Hollywood films that were released the same week (Power & Mazumdar, 2000). Since then, multiple Bollywood movies have collected revenues in excess of competing Hollywood movies, which has turned the gaze of the media to this new cultural export from India.

Though the audiences for Bollywood are mainly Indians, these include both Indians in India and the increasingly influential Indian diaspora. According to Ganti (2004), since 1998 the overseas market for Bollywood films has become extremely profitable, with some films making more money outside India than within the country. Thus the size of the audience for Bollywood movies is substantial. In India, which has a population of 1.3 billion, these movies are extremely popular amongst all social classes. The size of the Indian diaspora, according to the Ministry of External Affairs, is about 20 million, spread out over about 23 countries/regions (Ministry of External Affairs, 2000). Though small compared to the number of Indians in India, the diaspora has enormous purchasing power and contributes substantially not only to box office ticket sales, but also to the sales of live Bollywood shows which are increasingly held only outside India.

The matrix language of most Bollywood movies is Hindi (Myers-Scotton, 1993, 2006). The type of Hindi that is used in Hindi-language films is generally referred to as Hindustani (Ganti, 2004), which is a word popularized by Mohandas Karamchand Gandhi in the 1940s and 1950s when the national language of newly independent India was a highly contested topic in the nation-building endeavor. Gandhi strongly promoted his idea of 'Hindustani': a syncretic language in which the matrix language was Hindi but the lexicon would be derived from all the major languages of India. More specifically, Hindustani was a colloquial language spoken in North Indian bazaars and was a mixture mainly of Hindi and Urdu. However, due to fierce language loyalty among Indian's diverse language groups, Gandhi's idea of a syncretic language never caught the imagination of most Indians. Though Hindustani did not become the national language, it became the language of the Hindi film industry.

Trivedi (2006) challenges Ganti's (2004) contention that the language of Bollywood is Hindustani. His argument is that all types of Hindi are equally important in Hindi cinema, not just Hindustani. He shows that throughout the history of Bollywood, since its inception in the 1930s, there is a legacy of Urdu due to the influence of Urdu poets like Sahir Ludhianvi. Trivedi suggests, then, that Bollywood is equally influenced by Sanskritic Hindi. At the same time, what is known as dialect Hindi, or the type of Hindi that is spoken in rural north India, is also used in Hindi films. Another dialect of Hindi popular in Bollywood is 'Bambaiya Hindi' or the type of Hindi that is spoken in the city of Bombay (now called Mumbai). Finally, current Bollywood cinema has a high level of 'Hinglish' or Hindi and English in code-switched forms in keeping with the fact, highlighted earlier, that the audience of Hindi films includes diasporic Indians who tend to be English speaking bilinguals. Thus Trivedi emphasizes the pan-Indian nature of Bollywood as these films appeal to many linguistic groups amongst Indians and not just Hindi speakers. Though Trivedi's conclusion has merit, it is important to remember that India also has a parallel cinema based in Chennai called Kollywood, which makes hugely popular Tamil films. Many Indians in South India prefer to watch Tamil films and ignore Bollywood entirely.

Though Trivedi does not give the Urdu aspect of Bollywood much importance, the language and its affiliate cultures and religion need to be introduced as they are an extremely important part of Bollywood. Bhaskar and Allen (2009) refer to the 'Islamicate' nature of Bollywood films. Following the tradition in cultural studies they use the term Islamicate to refer not directly to the Islamic religion per se, 'but to the social and cultural complex historically associated with Islam and the Muslims, both among Muslims themselves and even when found among non-Muslims' (Bhaskar & Allen, 2009: 29). The Islamicate nature of Bollywood films is apparent in the genre of songs like the *nazm, ghazal* and *qawwali,* in the use of poetry or *shairi,* in the use of Urdu lexicon in dialogues 'and a whole range of ideas, mannerisms and emotions derived from a social and cultural complex that are identified with elite Muslim life' (Bhaskar & Allen, 2009: 7).

It is important to introduce the key words: terrorism, nationalism and Westernization, as I analyze the data on the basis of these codes. The expression of nationalism in Bollywood is usually through the use of pure Hindi. Bhatt (2008) analyzes code switching between English and Hindi in English-language newspapers in India and concludes that the increasing use of Hindi corresponds with the rise of the ultra conservative political party, the Bharatiya Janata Party. The Bharatiya Janata Party governed India from 1998 till 2004 on the basis of their 'Hindutva' ideology, a cultural ideology in which India is seen as a country mainly for Hindus, where Sanskrit is the most important language and where non-Hindu religions, specifically Islam, are not welcome. This political party practices a strict code of censorship in the media and believes that Indian media, specifically Bollywood movies, are becoming increasingly Western which is contaminating traditional Indian family values with Western depravity. Though the Bharatiya Janata Party is no longer in power, having lost the election to the currently ruling Congress Party, the idea of Hindutva is still part of the way India imagines its identity.

Terrorism has become a major theme in Bollywood movies in the last decade, taking the spot light from Westernization, which used to occupy the top spot in 'major themes.' In the last five years, i.e. from 2005 to 2010, there have been four box office hits on the theme of terrorism: *My Name is Khan* (2010), *Kurbaan* (2009), *New York* (2009) and *Fanaa* (2006). These box office hits must be acknowledged against the political backdrop of the Mumbai blasts that took place on 28–29 November 2008 in which numerous hotels and train stations were targeted by terrorists. According to newspapers in India, the blasts are attributed to the Lashkar-e-Taiba militants inside Pakistan. Westernization and its erosion of traditional family values is still an important theme in Bollywood as is illustrated in the box office hits: *Love Aaj Kal* (2009), *Namastey London* (2008) and *No Entry* (2006).

Motivations for Code Switching and Bollywood

There is little to no literature on motivations for code switching in Bollywood with the exception of Losch (2007) and Kachru (2006). Using the opposing theoretical frameworks of Myers Scotton's Markedness

Language Framework (MLF) and Peter Auer's Conversational Analysis (CA), Losch analyzes dialogue from Mira Nair's award-winning movie: *Monsoon Wedding* (2001). She shows how the interlocutors try to bridge or increase social distance by switching between Hindi and English. For each of the transcripts that Losch analyzes, she uses both MLF and then CA and finds that interlocutors switch from English to Hindi to establish closeness and kinship. Low-class characters in the movie, like Dubey and the police officers, switch from matrix language Hindi to English to show their desire for upward social mobility. I find Losch's use of CA puzzling because the conversation in a movie is not naturally occurring speech, however authentic it might be, and as such cannot really be subject to CA. The other concern I have about this dissertation is that since Losch is working with translated data, she misses the fact that in the transcripts the interlocutors also switch between Hindi and Punjabi.

Kachru (2006) comments on the humor, satire, irony and playfulness created by the use of English words and phrases in Hindi songs. She writes that 'mixing with English offers additional opportunities to express social and political commentary, employ fresh metaphors, imagery, and rhymes, and represent what is increasingly a familiar theme – that of the expatriate NRI (non-resident Indian) from the West visiting or returning to India with an affluent life style, and often skewed values' (227). Kachru finds that many Bollywood films portray the absurdities of NRI behavior and parody Western families, which is the same as the way Sanskrit and other Indian languages are used to caricature the traditional. For instance, in one of the songs that she analyzes, Kachru comments on the contrast between the lifestyles of affluent NRIs like parties, flirtations and fashion shows on the one hand and the miserable life of the poor in India represented by a queue to obtain basic necessities like rice and wheat.

In the field of cultural studies, there is substantial literature on Bollywood and identity. However, this does not usually have much to do with language except in a few cases like Dawson (2005), who analyzes the popularity of re-mixed Hindi film music amongst British Asian youth. The author notices that 'the lyrics of these songs tend to be based on the idealizing and pastoral romantic verse of the classical Persian and Urdu traditions' (163). This phenomenon that in its songs, the Hindi film leans heavily on Islamicate culture will be taken up again. Here I highlight Dawson's point that British Asian youth seek their identity in these film songs, especially in their re-mixed versions. What Dawson does not notice is that British Asians include a large number of Pakistanis, and the heavy use of Urdu, the national language of Pakistan, in Hindi film songs, could be one of the reasons why a sub-group amongst Asians are drawn to them.

What motivates switches between codes? The two most well-known theoretical foci that answer this question are the Markedness Model (Myers-Scotton, 1993, 2006) and Conversational Analysis (Auer, 1998; Wei, 2002). Though both foci are about how and why code switching happens, the former brings a priori assumptions about societal norms to the data whereas the latter prefers grounded analysis. Also, both approaches focus on the display of identity in code switching though in the first the researcher already knows a lot about the community from where the data are gathered whereas in the latter the researcher tries to derive every conclusion from the data itself even if he/she knows the community well. Finally, the former approach tends to take a broad overview of the data whereas the latter does a fine-grained microscopic analysis.

My concern with both these approaches is that both were developed in the 1990s on large corpora of conversational data, i.e. naturally occurring speech in everyday contexts like home, workplace, on buses, restaurants etc. Neither approach thus includes diverse text types related to literacy like advertisements, Web pages and film. In fact literacy is completely absent from the Nairobi corpus of Myers-Scotton and the Tyneside corpus of Li Wei. What then of biliteracy and the way that code switching happens in multimodal texts of the 21st century, in this case, film? These are not real conversations though in the movie the director is trying to make the dialogue look as authentic as possible. Though analyzing motivations in naturally occurring speech is far more complex, in a film script or song it is much easier to ascribe motivations to switches as the script writer desires a specific outcome not only in terms of the interlocutors in the movie, but also between the movie and the audience in the theater.

Given this theoretical background, I address the following research questions: What are the motivations behind switching from Hindi, which is the overall matrix language of the Bollywood movie, to Urdu or English? What kind of emotional outcomes does the script writer want to create in audiences within and without the movie (i.e., audience in the theatre is outside the movie per se)? And finally, what implications does code switching between Hindi, Urdu and English have for the key themes of Bollywood: terrorism, nationalism and Westernization?

Description of Data

The data consist of five extracts from five films that have been some of the biggest box office hits since 2005. The rationale for choosing extracts only from box office hits is to situate the data in mainstream cinema and not within 'art' films in Hindi that are only watched by the elite. The culling of extracts is still ongoing. In each of these films I am scanning the dialogues and songs with three main codes: westernization, terrorism and nationalism. Within these broad categories there are finer categories, for instance under 'terrorism' the film was also scanned for key words like Islam, Jihad (holy war), Kaum (community) and exclusion. At the time of writing this paper the film *My Name is Khan* (2010) has yielded more than 100 extracts on terrorism. For this chapter I have chosen five extracts that best highlight these three codes.

Methodologically I lean towards the markedness model, specifically towards the premise that speakers, and in turn script writers, choose marked or unmarked codes on the basis of which one will bring them the best outcome. Thus they weigh the costs and rewards of speaking one language rather than the other and make a rational choice about which language is best at this juncture in the movie. Myers-Scotton's (1993, 2006) recommendation about deciding which one is the matrix language in naturally occurring speech is based on the number of words in each of the languages and a decision about the grammatical bedrock of the sentence/utterance that is being analyzed. Following this recommendation, all the extracts, except Extract 2, use matrix language Hindi. This decision about which one is the matrix language between Hindi and Urdu is further complicated by the fact that the grammar of both languages is nearly identical, only the vocabulary differs.

At the same time, the term 'biliteracy' and Hornberger's definition of it: 'the use of two or more languages in and around writing' (Hornberger, 2003: xii), is central to this chapter. The biliterate text type I examine here is multimodal in nature, which means that it is a digital text with affordances like gesture, music, color and voice over (Vaish & Towndrow, 2010). However, it is not multimodality that is the focus here but biliteracy, and how and why Hindi, Urdu and English are code-mixed.

Data and Discussion

Extract 1 from *My Name is Khan* (2010)[1]

> *Noor e Khuda*
> *Noor e Khuda*
>
> Ajnabi mod hai
> *Khauf* har or hai
> Har *nazar* pe dhuan cha gaya
> Pal bhar mein jaane kya kho gaya

Aasmaan zard hai
Aaahen bhee *sard* hain
Tan se saaya judaa ho gayaa
Pal bhar mein jaane kya kho gaya

(Light of God
Light of God

This is an unfamiliar junction
There is terror everywhere
Each gaze is clouded with smoke
What has been lost in a mere instance?

The sky is pale
My sighs are cold
My shadow is separated from my body
What has been lost in a mere instance?)

Extract 2 from *Kurbaan* (2009)

Shukr Allah
Walhamdullillah
Shukr Allah
Walhamdullillah

Nazaron se *Nazaren* Milee to
*Janna*t see *mahekee phizayen*
Lab ne jo lab choo liyaa to
Aasmaan se barsee *duaen*
Esee apnee *muhabbat*
Esee *rooh e ibadat*
Hum pe *meherbaan* do *jahaan*

Shukr Allah
Walhamdullillah
Shukr Allah
Walhamdullillah

(Thanks be to Allah
Allah be praised

When our gazes met
The winds of paradise became fragrant
When our lips touched
Blessings showered from the heavens

Such is our love
Such is the prayer of our soul
That both the worlds are blessing us.
Thanks be to Allah)

Extract 3 from *Om Shanti Om* (2007)[2]

Ladies and Gentleman [*sic*]:
Itnee *shiddat* se meine tumhe pane kee *koshish* kee hai
Ke har *zarre* ne mujhe tumse milaane kee *sazish* kee hai
(With such devotion I have desired you
That every atom in the universe has conspired to bring me to you)

Extract 4 from *Namaste London* (2007)

Arjun Singh: Namaste. Sir mera naam hai Arjun Singh. Paanch *hazaar* saal puraani sabhyata kee vajeh se hum Hindustaani sabko aise hee jhuk ke pranaam karte hain.

Jazz: When we greet one another we fold our hands in Namaste because we believe that God resides in the heart of every human being.

Arjun Singh: Ek aisa desh jahaan ek Catholic aurat pradhaan mantri kee kursi ek Sikh ke liye chod deti hai aur ek Sikh pradhaan mantri kee shapath ek Muslim rashtrapati se letaa hai uss desh kee bagdor sambhaalne ke liye jis desh kee assi pratishat janta Hindu hai.

Jazz: We come from a nation where we allow a lady of Catholic origin to step aside for a Sikh to be sworn in as Prime Minister by a Muslim President to govern a nation of over 80% Hindus.

Extract 5 from *Love Aaj Kal* (2009)

Jai: Hey! Hi! See mein pile on nahin karnaa chahta par . . .
Meera: To mat karo. Chahte nahin ho to kyon kar rahe ho? Pile on. No reason.
Jai: That's a good point. Hmm. Nayaa angle hai. Hame isko aur discuss karna chahiye.
(Jai and Meera are shown dancing)
Jai: He says tum bahut hot ho.
Meera: I know. Yeah.
Jai: She knows. You don't have to bother.
Jai: Hey Hi! See I don't want to 'pile on' but . . .

Meera: Then don't. If you don't want to then why are you doing so? Pile on. No reason.
Jai: That's a good point. Hmm. It's a new angle. We should discuss this further.
Jai: He says you are very hot.)

Use of Urdu

As mentioned in the introduction, Islamicate culture, specifically the use of Urdu, has been part of Hindi films from their very inception in the 1930s. Though there have been Bollywood movies, for instance, *Sarfarosh* (1999), in which Urdu-speaking Muslims are shown as the main villains, current Bollywood movies on terrorism show a far more nuanced use of language. Extracts 1 and 2 are from movies which are about terrorism, and in which the lead actor is either a terrorist or suspected of being one. However, both heroes are depicted as middle-class Indians who code switch between Hindi and English and are not presented as Urdu speakers. The heavy dose of Urdu is mainly in the background songs. It is important to note that the traditional Bollywood movie in which the actors lip synchronize to playback songs is now no longer the norm and neither *My Name is Khan* (2010) nor *Kurbaan* (2009) follow this pattern of lip synching. The importance of the songs in these movies is that they carry the emotional weight of the themes. The fact that Urdu is heavily used in these songs points to the fact that when an extremely emotional or soulful expression has to be made, for instance, on the theme of love, racism or brotherhood between Hindus and Muslims, Urdu is deemed more appropriate than Hindi.

The song in Extract 1 refers specifically to a racist incident in an American school in which an Indian Muslim boy was killed by his white peers. This is set against the 9/11 political catastrophe in the US. The key words in the song are all in Urdu. For instance, the word for God is *Khuda*, fear is khauf and cold is *sard*. The Hindi words for these lexical items are 'Bhagwaan,' 'dar' and 'thanda' respectively. However, these Hindi words do not carry the emotional burden that the symbolic moment in the movie conveys. This is a marked choice on the part of the songwriter so as to bring out the complexity in the fact that the racist encounter in school happened because the father of the murdered boy is Muslim. The overuse of Urdu words conveys the pain of Muslims in America and other parts of the world who suffer without being party to terrorism only because they are adherents of Islam.

In Extract 2 the theme of the song is the love between a Hindu girl and a Muslim boy who later on in the movie turns out to be a terrorist. The theme of love is rarely expressed either in dialogue or songs in pure Sanskritized Hindi. In the language ideology of Hindi-Urdu speakers, it is the latter language that is more suitable for expressions of love. In this sense the use of Urdu for a love song is unmarked in Bollywood movies. In Extract 2 however, the repeated invocation of Allah is marked because that is not a word that one would commonly find in love songs. In this song the use of 'Allah' highlights the jihadist nature of the violence in this movie. It also problemetizes the love between the main characters, because the Muslim hero masterminds his relationship with the Hindu heroine, only to enter the US and join a gang of terrorists. Thus, the hero is motivated more by jihad than by love, though at the end of the movie the audience is left in quandary about his true motivations.

Even as a native Hindi speaker, who is also fluent in Urdu, I am unable to decide what the matrix language of this song is: Hindi or Urdu? I believe the inextricability of the matrix language in Extract 2 is a deliberate attempt on the part of the songwriter to convey the syncretic message of the film. Thus in some cases, e.g. Hindi and Urdu, it may not possible to decide which one is the matrix language on the basis of the number of words in each of the languages in an utterance. In Extract 3, the hero Shah Rukh Khan, who plays a struggling junior artist in Bollywood, is pretending that he has won a major film award and is giving an acceptance speech to an auditorium full of Bollywood personalities. In the movie he is drunk and is actually declaiming to a bunch of ragged street urchins. He starts in English using the singular form of 'gentlemen' thus revealing his lack of fluency. However, the use of English is this junior artist's attempt to display the identity of a well-educated middle-class actor. The character then switches codes from English to Urdu and recites a 'sher,' which is compact couplet. Though the couplet sounds as if it is being recited to a lover, in this case it is actually to a film award to which Omi, the character played by Shah Rukh Khan, aspires.

The switch from English to Urdu is marked because in the language ideology of Hindi-Urdu speakers, it is Urdu that expresses intense emotion which Omi wants to convey. At the same time the difficult Urdu words like *'shiddat,' 'zarre,' 'sazish'* are impenetrable to the uneducated urchins sitting in front of the declaiming Omi, a situation that has a comic sub-text. As in the case of the songs, the rational choice of using Urdu is based on creating a specific outcome in the audience: in all these uses of Urdu the desired outcome is an intense emotional engagement with the situation and characters. Some of the lexical items in this couplet are difficult even for an audience who knows Urdu; for instance, I had to look up the meaning of '*shiddat*' as I was unsure whether the word means 'longing' or 'devotion.' However, even if the audience does not know the meaning of all the Urdu words, they will sense that with this switch from English to Urdu the emotional epicenter of the movie has changed from the mundane to the mystical.

Use of English

In Extract 5 the young hero and heroine, Jai and Meera respectively, have just met in a bar in New York City. The title of the movie this is from, *Love Aaj Kal*, uses code switching between Hindi and English, much like the dialogue in Extract 5. The title means 'love now and in the past' and the movie contrasts the love story of two couples, one growing up in the US and the other, from the previous generation, growing up in India. More specifically the contrast in type of love is between the everlasting love of the older couple which is based on sacrifice and waiting, and the more sexual, selfish love of the younger couple in the US.

In this extract the matrix language is Hindi with generous lexical borrowing (nouns, adjectives and verbs) from English. The key lexical items to note are the use of 'pile-on' and 'hot.' The phrase 'pile-on' amongst youth in India is used specifically in a sexual way to refer to a man trying to 'pile on' to a woman. In some cases it is also used to refer to a person who is trying to take advantage of others. Though both 'pile on' and 'hot' have Hindi equivalents, these are not used to show that the two main characters are both highly educated Non-Resident Indians (NRIs). Also, the use of English gives the characters an upper-middle-class social status whereas the use of Hindi, specifically, for these words would not convey the impression of high social class.

The use of English in this way also sets the stage for the later development of the story. Jai and Meera are shown in a very 'Western' relationship by Indian standards, in that they neither want to get married nor do they have any plans about carrying the relationship into the future. This modern relationship is contrasted with that of an older Indian couple, also living in New York City, in which the couple believes in the Indian tradition of 'Janm Janm kaa saath,' which means being together through many lives. This idea of continuity and monogamy is very important in the Indian marriage ritual during which the couple walk seven times around a fire symbolizing that they wish to be together for the next seven lives. Thus the use of lexical borrowing from English in matrix language Hindi, in the speech of Jai and Meera, is indicative of their

Westernization, and in the context of this movie, incorrect approach to the idea of love.

Use of Hindi

Extract 4 is from *Namaste London* (2007) which, like *Love Aaj Kal* (2009), is also about young Indians growing up in the West, in this case London, and how parents are trying to teach them traditional Indian values. This interaction takes place during a boat party on the River Thames. During the party a white British minor character makes a racial slur against India and Indians to which Arjun Singh replies with the first speech in this extract. The translations for Arjun Singh's comments are made by Jazz, whose real name is Jasmeet. She is an Indian who has grown up in London and considers herself British. Her contact with Arjun Singh, who has been chosen by her father for an arranged marriage with his daughter, transforms Jasmeet's view of her own identity.

The language of Arjun Singh in Extract 4 is Hindi without any code mixing from English or Urdu. As such this kind of Hindi becomes marked in a movie in which most of the characters code switch between these three languages. In using words like 'sabhyata,' 'pranaam' and 'pratishat,' the language of Arjun Singh sounds Sanskritized. At the same time the script writer has not overdone the Sanskritic element in Arjun Singh's comments because the content of the speech is the pluralist nature of India. In the language ideology of India, Hindi is the national language of the country, though this is a highly contested notion of language and has been fiercely opposed by the South where Hindi is not widely spoken. However, in *Namaste London* (2007) in particular and in current Bollywood movies in general, slightly Sanskritized Hindi is used to express a national Indian identity.

Conclusions

The chapter has analyzed code switching between Hindi, Urdu and English in Bollywood movies to draw conclusions about the display of identity through language. Specifically I have commented on how terrorism, nationalism and Westernization are important themes in these movies and how language is used to express identities associated with these themes. The matrix language in Bollywood is Hindustani and the use of English and Urdu is usually in the form of borrowing, except in a few cases. The use of Urdu creates a connection with Islamicate culture, which is part of the history and imagination of India. Urdu also problemetizes the theme of terrorism in that current Bollywood movies show

terrorists not as outright villains, but as complex characters with contradictory motivations. Borrowing from English depicts middle-class NRIs
who are out of touch with Indian values. At the same time English is
not shown as a colonial imposition; it is very much part of the identity
of upper-class Indians.

Notes

1. Hindi is written in the Devanagari script and Urdu in Arabic. However in
   the cultural space of Bollywood both languages are Romanized. This is a
   bottom up approach and there is no linguistic commission that has standardized the Romanization of Hindi and Urdu. In this paper Hindi and Urdu are
   shown in Roman script. Urdu words are italicized. English translations are in
   parentheses.
2. This dialogue by Shah Rukh Khan can be seen on 'Youtube, award speech, Om
   Shanti Om': http://You Tube Om Shanti Om Dialogue.

List of Films

Ali, I. (Director) (2009) *Love Aaj Kal* [Motion Picture]. India: Illuminati Films.
Bazmee, A. (Director) (2005) *No Entry* [Motion Picture]. India: BSK Network and
Entertainment.
D'Silva, R. (Director) (2009) *Kurbaan* [Motion Picture]. India: Dharma Productions.
Ghai, S. (Director/Producer) (1999) *Taal* [Motion Picture]. India: Mukta Arts.
Gowarikar, A. (Director) (2008) Jodha Akbar [Motion Picture]. India: UTV Motion
Pictures.
Johar, K. (Director) (2010) *My Name is Khan* [Motion Picture]. India: Dharma
Productions.
Khan, F. (Director) (2007) *Om Shanti Om* [Motion Picture]. India: Red Chillies
Entertainment.
Khan, K. (Director) (2009) *New York* [Motion Picture]. India: Yash Raj Films.
Kohli, K. (Director) (2006) *Fanaa* [Motion Picture]. India: Yash Raj Films.
Shah, V.A. (Director) (2008) *Namaste London* [Motion Picture]. India: Eros
International.

References

Auer, P. (ed.) (1998) *Code-Switching in Conversation: Language, Interaction and
Identity*. London: Routledge.
Bhaskar, I. and Allen, R. (2009) *Islamicate Cultures of Bombay Cinema*. New Delhi:
Tulika Books.
Bhatt, R.M. (2008) In other words: Language mixing, identity representations, and
third space. *Journal of Sociolinguistics* 12 (2), 177–200.
Dawson, A. (2005) 'Bollywood Flashback': Hindi film music and the negotiation of
identity among British-Asian youths. *South Asian Popular Culture* 3 (2), 161–176.
Ganti, T. (2004) *Bollywood: A Guidebook to Popular Hindi Cinema*. Routledge Film
and Guidebook Series. New York: Routledge.
Hornberger, N.H. (ed.) (2003) *Continua of Biliteracy: An Ecological Framework for
Educational Policy, Research, and Practice in Multilingual Settings*. Clevedon:
Multilingual Matters.

Ministry of External Affairs (2000) The Indian diaspora – Online document: www.indiandiaspora.nic.in/contents.htm. Accessed 20 October 2010.

Kachru, Y. (2006) Mixers lyricing in Hinglish: Blending and fusion in Indian pop culture. *World Englishes* 25 (2), 223–233.

Losch, E. (2007) The construction of social distance through code-switching: An exemplary analysis for popular Indian cinema. Unpublished Master's thesis, Technical University of Chemnitz.

Mattan, J.M. (1999) *Sarfarosh* [Motion Picture]. India: Eros International.

Myers-Scotton, C. (1993) *Social Motivations for Codeswitching: Evidence From Africa*. Oxford: Clerendon Press.

Myers-Scotton, C. (2006) *Multiple Voices: An Introduction to Bilingualism*. Malden: Blackwell Publishing.

Power, C. and Mazumdar, S. (2000, February 28) Bollywood goes global. *Newsweek*.

Trivedi, H.K. (2006) All kinds of Hindi: The evolving language of Hindi cinema. In V. Lal and A. Nandy (eds) *Fingerprinting Popular Culture: The Mythic and the Iconic in Indian Cinema* (pp. 51–86). New Delhi: Oxford University Press.

Vaish, V. and Towndrow, P.A. (2010) Multimodal literacy in language classrooms. In N.H. Hornberger and S.L. McKay (eds) *Sociolinguistics and Language Education* (pp. 317–349). Bristol: Multilingual Matters.

Wei, L. (2002) 'What do you want me to say?' On the conversation analysis approach to bilingual interaction. *Language in Society* 31, 159–180.

Chapter 3
Making Local Practices Globally Relevant in Researching Multilingual Education

ANGELA CREESE

Prelude

I associate Nancy Hornberger's work with a commitment to studying the local practices of people engaged in implementing bilingual and biliterate educational programs around the world. Whether she is studying Indigenous peoples shaping and implementing policy or describing communities quietly challenging oppressive practices, her research accounts provide vivid descriptions and new insights into the 'real lives of real people' (Hornberger, 1992: 165). In her work, Hornberger makes connections across diverse sites around the world which retain the voices of participants in those contexts. She provides us with theoretical tools to step out and survey the bigger picture. She expertly uses ethnography to develop inductive theory, and her ecological perspective requires us to consider the complexity of the social scene. She introduces us to new ways of viewing familiar contexts, creating an epistemological lens which places minority and Indigenous experience at its heart, and shows how people's determination creates spaces for multilingual practices. She provides a pedagogic resource to view the complexity of biliteracy in all its dimensions, refusing to allow us shortcuts in the design, implementation and evaluation of educational policy.

Like many, I have found inspiration in this careful work which endeavors to build on what others have given. Hornberger not only meticulously crafts her work but also carefully builds on the scholarly work of others to produce research which is reliable, insightful and trustworthy. She is the very antipathesis of what Hammersely sees as a trend in the social sciences for 're-branding and relaunching' existing theory (2007: 690). Rather,

Hornberger seeks to extend and build, critique and develop and in making hitherto unnoticed links across arguments and theories, allows us to develop new perspectives and think anew. In her scholarly endeavors, she is inclusive of and responsive to the different standpoints offered. She has provided us with a detailed understanding of developments in educational linguistics (Hornberger & Hult, 2006); ecological perspectives on language and pedagogy (Hornberger, 2008); and described connections and lineages in linguistic anthropology (Hornberger, 1995, 2003). As a ' "believer" in bilingual education' (1992: 162), she has argued for a multilingual vision of society which views linguistic diversity as a strength and resource (Blackledge, 2005; Ruiz, 1984). This belief is predicated on years of research in the field, evidenced in her use of vivid and descriptive narratives of bilingual settings. Through these accounts we see how she reaches her conclusions and we come to trust in them through the details presented. The necessity of this methodological rigor in ethnography is the topic of this chapter. It is a worthy topic not only because Hornberger provides an excellent example of how knowledge construction is achieved in anthropological linguistics, but also because in the age of digital technology it is worth reminding ourselves of the importance of participation and relationships in the field.

Introduction

Technological advancement for recording linguistic data has introduced new levels of surveillance in research sites which allow us 'to transport selected and carefully focused slices of life out of the original nexus of activity for collegial, peer-reviewable examination in richer more multimodal formats' (Scollon & Scollon, 2007: 620). The Scollons point out that this must be balanced with the complex and sharper focus brought by the more 'unimodal transcriptions' of the ethnographer in the field (2007: 620). In essence, this means using the far-reaching linguistic and semiotic coverage brought by new technologies alongside the detailed and thick descriptions of the ethnographer. Since sociolinguistic ethnography is a focus on the linguistic and semiotic resources used in social activities, we use both 'new' and 'old' technologies for interpreting our participants' rationalities, meanings and actions.

The balancing of data sets within language-focused ethnographies is not without debate. Recently Rampton *et al.* (2004) have suggested that the authority of warrants made from onsite and unfolding (digital) interactional recordings should be seen as stronger than those made from fieldnotes. Rampton *et al.* argue for the interactional to be the first point of analysis in linguistic ethnography because interaction data is more 'easily accessible for counter-arguments and independent testing' (2004: 6). More explicitly, they argue, 'The testimony of fieldnotes may sound quite authoritative in reports on exotic locations which few westerners have ever visited, but evidentiary standards tend to be more demanding in social scientific accounts of social processes close to home.' However, this argument is countered by Blommaert (2007). He makes the point that linguistic anthropology has a long-established pedigree and tradition which sees research into language and culture as a single object, socially constructed in [linguistic] action. He appears to argue against a data hierarchy which sees interactional data as more important than fieldnote data. I interpret Blommaert to say that the study of interactional data cannot be privileged over fieldnote data as both are equally necessary in the study of language-in-culture and culture-in-language.

The ethnographic approach is one which sees the analysis of small phenomena as set against an analysis of big phenomena, and in which 'both levels can only be understood in terms of one another' (Blommaert, 2006: 16). McCarty reminds us that ethnography provides a particularly powerful 'way of seeing' both 'the fine-grained details of everyday discursive practices and their organization within larger cultural and historical frames' (2005: xxii). Erickson describes this movement between levels as an 'attempt to combine close analysis of fine details of behavior and meaning in everyday social interaction with analysis of the wider societal context' (1990: 80). Hornberger (1994) speaks of the value of ethnography in juxtaposing the emic and holistic views so that we are introduced to the local and situated understandings and actions of members alongside the wider social scene. Hornberger reminds us that it is through this emic/holistic 'creative tension' that ethnographic research emerges and that each 'refines and reforms the other' (1994: 688).

This chapter looks at fieldnotes as an analytical process which reveals the dialogic of small and large phenomena. Because fieldnotes are 'primordial' writings (Emerson *et al.*, 1995: 16) they are sources of data which record early interpretations and developing arguments. Fieldnotes are usually drafted and redrafted by the researcher as they move from scribbled notes to descriptive accounts to the polished analytic vignettes (Erickson, 1990) presented in published work. Fieldnotes are personal, academic and political. In this chapter, I focus on fieldnotes and analytic vignettes in Hornberger's ethnographies with the aim of discussing their scope for producing evidence-based, rigorous and analytic accounts of biliterate and bilingual contexts in our schools and educational contexts. I will discuss the use of fieldnotes and analytic vignettes in Hornberger's work to explore and report on 'local interpretations' and show how she uses these to 'pry open implementational and ideological space' (Hornberger & Johnson, 2007: 511) to argue for multilingual education policies and practices. I investigate how Hornberger uses her fieldnotes to detail, describe, evaluate, intervene and critique. I use this opportunity to reflect on the use of fieldnotes in my own recent work which has used team ethnography to research multilingualism in the UK over the last 10 years. I describe the relevance of fieldnotes in teams as a way of building consensus while also retaining particularity, complexity and contradiction. I again draw on Hornberger to describe tensions in ethnographic team research.

Fieldnotes: Presenting an Emic Perspective

Back in 1992, Hornberger asked herself the question, 'should the purpose of my ethnography be description, or should it also include, perhaps, evaluation, intervention, or critique?' (1992: 165). Participant observation produces observational accounts of people in their social contexts. These fieldnotes are typically resources which the researcher uses to question, examine and contemplate their developing analyses. The ethnographer's role in general and her use of fieldnotes in particular are critical in the interpretive processes of ethnography. It is here that close detail of local action and interaction is embedded in a consideration of the wider social world. Erickson argues that fieldwork is needed because of the invisibility of everyday life and the need to make the familiar strange (Erickson, 1990). Fieldnotes have a special place within ethnography because of their role in documenting participant observation. Through the use of fieldnotes, 'the units, criteria, and patterning of a community' are described (Hornberger, 1995: 238). Fieldnotes document details of practice. They are productions and recordings of the researchers' noticings with the intent of describing the research participant's actions emically.

Approaches in the ethnographic tradition emphasize the plurality of realities employed by the people being researched and the meaning they assign to objects as well as their notions of what is important and interesting (Hymes, 1968, 1980; Shaffif & Stebbins, 1991). Through fieldnotes, everyday events in the field setting are described and attempts are made to identify the significance of actions in the events from the various points of view of the actors themselves (Shaffif & Stebbins, 1991). In undertaking observations, in drafting and redrafting fieldnotes and in writing up analytic vignettes (Erickson, 1990), the researcher engages in making explicit the connections of local lives to social and political lives. Blommaert describes fieldnotes in the following way:

> I attach great importance to fieldnotes, if for nothing else because I still use and re-use my own field notebooks, some of which are now over two decades old. They still provide me with invaluable information, not only about *what* I witnessed in the field, but even more importantly about *how* I witnessed it – amazed, outraged, amused, factual and neutral, puzzled, curious, not understanding, confident about my own interpretations. They still tell me a story about *an epistemic process*: the way in which I tried to make new information understandable for myself, using my own interpretive frames, concepts and categories, and gradually shifting into new frames, making connections between earlier and current events, finding my way in the local order of things. (Blommaert, 2006: 34)

Participant observation requires following social action. Moreover it requires investing in social relationships rather than simply shadowing social action. As Hornberger records, 'it is not enough to enter the community simply by residing in it; rather, I enter it by establishing social relationships with its members' (1992: 160). In an early piece of work, Hornberger reflects on how she negotiated a relationship with two participants in a school-based project on literacy based in her own neighborhood. She describes how at the end of school, she walked with two students, Than and Noeun, through her familiar neighborhood with new eyes.

> As we walk the approximately 12 blocks there and 14 blocks back to the Noeun's house my eyes are opened to an entirely different neighborhood than the one I usually walk though. The streets and sidewalks are the same, but now I see them through the two children's eyes, particularly because they are very loquacious with me about what they observe as we go. (Hornberger, 1992: 163)

Here Hornberger sets the scene. We are told about the distances covered, we are given a flavor of the relationship between the three of them as they chat on the way to Than's house. Later in the same vignette Hornberger goes on to make an analytic point about their orientation to the environment as they navigate themselves home. This short extract shows three layers of observation. First the emic perspective of the two young women is described through recounting what they notice in their journey. Second the autobiographical declaration of the researcher herself in the field is also recorded as she is required to think anew about what she notices and what she misses. Third, she steps outside the vignette to make a methodological observation about the observer's paradox.

> As my neighborhood takes on a whole new look to me, I am forcibly reminded that part of a an ethnographer's task is to allow the familiar to become strange enough that we can describe it (Erickson, 1986: 121). My glimpse into Than and Nouren's view of our neighborhood allows me to discover an aspect of the Cambodian community's 'strangeness' in West Philadelphia – even in the midst of an urban environment, these farming people are visually oriented toward natural, and not print, signs around them. It is the 'observer's paradox' in reverse – not that my observation has an effect on their participation, but that their participation has an effect on my observation. (Hornberger, 1992: 164)

This rich paragraph makes substantive and analytical points about the community being researched as well as dealing with fundamental theoretical and methodological concerns. Fieldnotes are presented as data for others to scrutinize, allowing the reader to consider the credibility and dependability of these notes. The presentation of fieldnote data allows us to consider the autobiographical and subjective nature of the account as a strength. The fieldnotes represent not only the 'being there' (Geertz, 1988) of ethnographic research but provide evidence of the social relations formed in the field. This allows us, the readers, to make judgments about how dependable the data are.

Hornberger's attention to detail culminates in an account of her noticings, and it is in the detail that we are able to confirm the data as dependable. We see through her use of fieldnotes the machinery of knowledge making. Through Hornberger's vignettes we are provided with an account of the developing trust between her and her participants which also serves to develop trust between the author and the reader. In her fieldnotes, we are presented with not only the rigor of the research process but also her ongoing questions and concerns:

> As always, it strikes me that these questions include just about everything to do with literacy. In my observations, everything will surely seem relevant, and my field notes for the day will probably reflect that in their voluminousness, as they have every other day as well. I wish I could learn to frame narrower, more manageable questions, yet I am always confronted by the fact that I would not be satisfied with answers (or questions) that excluded any of the factors that might have a bearing on literacy for these children. (Hornberger, 1992: 161)

In these extracts, Hornberger describes the West Philadelphia scene but also simultaneously deals with epistemological debates in ethnography. In the extract below she provides a concrete example of making the familiar strange and the observer's paradox.

> 5.00 P. M. As I walk home, I am aware that the day has raised many more questions than it has answered. Methodological issues of generalizability, objectivity, validity, and ethics have surfaced amidst theoretical questions about biliteracy acquisition, maintenance, and attitudes. All are deeper questions about the real lives of real people around me. In the end, it is the last ones, that are of most interest. The opportunity to know, and make known, heroic human lives hidden all around us is what, for me, makes ethnographic research truly revealing and rewarding. (Hornberger, 1992: 165)

Throughout the substantial body of Hornberger's writings she uses her observations in the field to make connections between the emic and the holistic; the local and the global. A recent plenary paper is a further illustration of this approach in which Hornberger (2009) uses six vignettes (as well as interview transcripts) to argue for 10 certainties in multilingual education. She uses the vignettes to link local contexts to larger arguments. She achieves this through using fieldnotes developed into vignettes.

Erickson (1990) describes vignettes as rich descriptive narrative accounts which are drawn from fieldnotes. The writing of vignettes is part of the interpretive process of identifying the significant actions as seen by the actors themselves. According to Erickson (1990: 80), this involves 'being empirical without being positivist' as well as rigorous and systematic in adopting interpretive approaches. It is through interpretation that the corpus of materials collected in the field becomes data. Before the analytic process, they are resources for data but not data themselves:

> Fieldnotes, videotapes, and site documents are not data. Even interview transcripts are not data. All these are documentary materials from which data must be constructed through some formal means of analysis. (Erickson, 1990: 161)

Hornberger's use of analytic vignettes in much of her work exemplifies how fieldnotes are put to use to make the analytic argument. Below is a good example in which she uses fieldnote data to make a substantive and analytical point. Here she describes a bilingual classroom in Andean South America.

At Kayarani, a new school building was inaugurated last year and the rooms are nice, with tables and chairs that can be set up for group work. Berta, a native of Tarija, has been teaching here for three years, implementing bilingual education under the 1994 Bolivian National Education Reform. She began with her class from the start of their schooling; they are now in 2nd–3rd grade. The classroom is decorated with posters made by the teacher in Quechua, including models of a story, a poem, a song, a recipe, and a letter, as well as both the Quechua and the Spanish alphabets, which the students recite for me later. Also on the wall is the class newspaper, *Llaqta Qhapariy* [Voice of the People], featuring an article in Quechua, written by student Calestino about farmers' wanting better prices for their potatoes, which constitute their community's subsistence.

A key provision of the 1994 Reform is the establishment of a library in every primary classroom of the nation, each stoked with a collection of 80 books provided by the Ministry of Education under the auspices of UNESCO. Included are six Big Books in Spanish, three of the based on oral traditions in Quechua, Aymara, and Guarani, respectively. This classroom, too, has a library corner housing a small collection including a couple of Big Books, and the teacher class on a child to come to the front of the class to read from one of the Big Books aloud to his classmates. Later, after the class leaves for recess, a couple of children notice my interest in the Big Books and gleefully hold the books up for a photo (Kayarani, Bolivia, 14 August 2000). (Hornberger, 2009: 199)

The analytic vignette above is a hybrid text referencing earlier fieldnotes and critiquing policy documents including Bolivian national reform and international support through UNESCO. The vignette appears in a paper structured to list 10 certainties about multilingual education. In the structure of this paper, Hornberger uses the vignette above to illustrate two of these certainties. The first certainty focuses on policy and shows how policy opens up ideological and implementational spaces for multilingual education. She backs up this claim through using additional historical and statistical information. The second certainty made in the use of the vignette focuses on the participants themselves and how their agency opens up but similarly closes down spaces for multilingual education. She uses the focus on their social action and particularly their linguistic action around literacy practices to help us understand the educational possibilities of the Kayarani classroom. In other words, she uses the vignette to show not only how policy is put creatively into practice by teachers and students but also how it meets resistance. Hornberger expertly uses the vignette to reveal the tensions, contradictions and alternative perspectives in this set of social and linguistic practices.

Her fieldnotes also mirror her theoretical commitment to developing an ecological perspective on studying multilingualism and one which best represents bilingual and biliterate lives (Hornberger, 2008). For Hornberger, an ecological perspective on multilingualism involves a dialectic between the local interactional and the social ideological. In the Kayarani classroom observations above we see how she moves between the emic and the holistic, been the micro-interactional and macro-political, historical and social. As pointed out earlier, it is in the creative relationship between the two that new understandings are reached. An ecological perspective also warns against too easily reaching comprehensive, tidy findings. It is through the contrasting dimensions of observations in her fieldnotes that Hornberger achieves a multilayered description. In the next section, I look at an additional approach to capturing the multiple perspectives and shared knowledge of participants in the field.

Fieldnotes in Team Ethnography

Many of us in the academy today engaging in ethnographic work are encouraged by the research funding councils to work in teams. Describing the US context, Mitteness and Barker (2004) show how North American research councils explicitly require collaborative research through their funding arrangements and the desire to see research meaningfully applied. In Europe and the UK, there is a similar imperative to work in teams to build an interdisciplinary approach to problem solving. Behind this call is the belief that the research problems of today demand the varied expertises and skills which only collaborative and multidisciplinary teams can bring. Within ethnography, too, there is an acknowledgment that the use of teams can provide complexity in representations, allowing for more nuanced, richer and contradictory accounts of researched and researcher. Eisenhart (2001a, 2001b) has argued that ethnography needs to use collaborative teams to broaden insights and perspectives. Diverse teams, Eisenhart argues, will help us adjust our conceptual orientations and methodological priorities to take into account changing human experiences and priorities. However, team research is not without its tensions (Erickson & Stull, 1998). Working in teams produces a different set of concerns from those of the lone ethnographer working in the field (Creese, 2008a).

In her first experience of team ethnographic inquiry, Hornberger described facing a new set of issues:

> The problem for team ethnographic inquiry rests, however, in the paradox that the primary research instrument in ethnographic research is the researcher(s), and yet an ethnography seeks to present *a* picture, *one* picture, one whole, interpretive picture. How can the pieces of understanding residing in multiple researchers be brought together to present one holistic, emic view? (1992: 162)

She explains how her research team fell mistakenly into deductive approaches and the use of a priori codes and categories. She describes how the introduction of these categories ended up paralyzing the team with indecision as they struggled to code data in ways which did not capture the complexity and variability of the local context. In the team's search for a unified framework, Hornberger warns how 'assigning literacy events and acts to a priori categories, even though they had evolved out of early fieldwork stages, simply did not allow for the multiple realities and perspectives that were emerging' (Hornberger, 1992: 162). This quote illustrates Hornberger's awareness of the productive and constructed nature of building categories in ethnographic research (Sipe, 2004). However, it also illustrates the process of 'finding' data through repeatedly searching, defining and identifying (Erickson, 2004: 486). Hornberger describes how the team readjusted their practices and switched to adopting a primarily inductive approach to analyzing their fieldnotes. This involved individual team members inferring their own headings without abandoning the quest of holistic integrated picture.

Hornberger's approach is fundamentally a paradigmatic one. Like Hymes (1974) and Erickson (1990, 2004), her interest is in discovering the dimensions of co-occurrence and contrast. Rather than starting with the identification of 'parts', 'moves', 'categories' in an approach which would analytically map from bottom to top, she looks at the whole. Erickson describes a process of following the examples of his mentors which involves looking for 'the biggest shifts in activity within the interactional occasion as a whole, then for the next biggest shifts, and so on ... [L]ooking continually for lines of contrast' (Erickson, 2004: 491). Hornberger is part of this genealogy. Her ethnography is democratic in the sense that her analysis works with whole to the part, mapping out how her participants themselves experience their social contexts. Her approach is to show us the patterns across all her data resources which, as Erickson suggests, involves parsing 'analytically from whole to the part and then down again and again, successively identifying subsequent next levels and their constituents' (2004: 491).

Hornberger's description of managing data collection and analysis in the team resonates with many of the issues facing our recent experience of working in a multilingual team (Blackledge & Creese, 2010; Creese *et al.*, 2008a).[1] In a study which investigated the linguistic repertoires of young people and teachers, we were a team of nine researchers each with a different linguistic, ethnic, gendered, age and social class backgrounds. We also had different relationships with those we researched as well as different levels of experiences in engaging in research. We found that our fieldnotes were central in processes of team knowledge building and have argued that they can be used to build consensus as well voice dissent (Creese *et al.*, 2008b). In addition, we have investigated how team players with their different social and linguistic capitals use fieldnotes to record how they build relationships both in the field and also within the research team (Creese *et al.*, 2009). We have adopted these measures to be more explicitly reflexive in our research accounts.

In the team ethnographic process representation issues need to be explicitly addressed. Geertz points out that within anthropology, 'explicit representations of authorial presence tend to be relegated, like other embarrassments, to prefaces, notes or appendixes' (1988: 16), and he describes the tension of simultaneously finding a place in the text which achieves both 'an intimate view and a cool assessment' (1988: 10). In team ethnography, we found that we had to face up to these decisions regularly. This happened through the sharing of observations often conducted in pairs or threes and written up and shared amongst the team. In these accounts, we noted how each one differently and similarly represented what we had seen. We also saw how we brought our own perspectives into the frame.

We engaged in weekly readings of one another's fieldnotes to develop themes; we not only looked for recurring themes in these fieldnotes but also looked for differences; we referred to the expertises of other members of the team; we talked about researcher positionings and developing arguments and asked questions of one another in our fieldnotes. We also used our fieldnotes to develop arguments and ideas within team discussion. In these discussions we highlighted not only analytic issues central to our developing arguments on multilingualism but we also commented on the issues we noticed and related these to our own lives. We were interested not only in what we were all noticing but also in what we individually noticed. We focused on the iterative, patterned and common place. But we also noticed the exceptional and occasional. These processes are all common place in ethnography; however, team ethnography forced them to be made explicit.

We found that our team ethnography increased the number of voices brought into the frame. Understanding how a multilingual research team builds relations with those they are researching in multilingual settings opens up opportunities for dialogue and debate. Our perspective is richly informed by the voices, experiences, knowledges and noticings of a diverse team of ethnographers brought together to investigate the context of multilingualism in community-based education. Without this team diversity we would have been unable to achieve either the coherence or the diversity necessary in our four case study educational linguistic research design. Of course, this team work was not devoid of tension and issues of power and status. Some voices were heard more loudly than others. We found the emic perspectives gained through researchers' social investment with participants was crucial to detailing of the case studies (Blackledge & Creese, 2010). However, the team processes also made explicit our knowledge building to one another and required us to move between the emic and the etic to look for bigger theoretical and methodological contributions to multilingual education.

Conclusion

In this chapter I have used Nancy Hornberger's work to reconsider the importance of fieldnotes and vignettes as 'evidence' in linguistic anthropological research. I have shown how Hornberger achieves a balance between the study of local practice while making a commitment to broaching global, political and social issues. She achieves this through presenting a multilayered perspective which shows shared knowledge and thereby attaining an emic view.

I have focused predominantly on the data set of analytic vignettes to show how she achieves complex, detailed, illustrative and realistic accounts of research participants. My focus has been on the methodological insights that can be gleaned from a study of Hornberger's ethnographies. In highlighting fieldnotes and analytic vignettes I do not wish to suggest that the other interactional and interview data Hornberger uses in her work is not of value. Rather, I have argued that it is precisely in the combination of data sets in which that richness in argument is achieved. In emphasizing the voices of those she researches, Hornberger provides an immensely rich account of multilingual educational contexts not so easily available in other sources of data (Creese, 2010). It is through these fieldnotes that the local is made ideological. Through the fieldnotes and analytic vignettes, the variability, nuance and detail are revealed. Fieldnote accounts are also put to work to reveal oppressive educational policies and illustrate transformative forces. Through the representation of participants in her analytic vignettes, we see Hornberger establish a long-term commitment to educational change.

Hornberger adopts an ecological perspective which seeks complexity. Such a perspective reaches for balance and consensus in looking for overlap and shared lineages. It builds on what has gone before. This allows her to develop theory and methodology which is grounded in and reflects the circumstances of real people in a real world. Her vignettes, like all vignettes, are indeed autobiographical and capture her humility and respect for those she researches, teaches and works with in her untiring energy to address the challenges and inequities of many educational settings around the world.

Note

1. Creese, Angela, Taşkin Baraç, Arvind Bhatt, Adrian, Blackledge, Shahela Hamid, Li Wei, Vally Lytra, Peter Martin, Chao Jung Wu and Dilek Yağcıoğlu-Ali (2008b) *Investigating Multilingualism in Complementary Schools in Four Communities.* Final report to ESRC (RES-000-23-1180).

References

Blackledge, A. (2005) *Discourse and Power in a Multilingual World.* Amsterdam: John Benjamins.

Blackledge, A. and Creese, A. (2010) *Multilingualism: A Critical Perspective.* London: Continuum.

Blommaert, J. (2006) *Ethnography Fieldwork: A Beginner's Guide* – Online document: http://www.jyu.fi/hum/laitokset/kielet/fidipro/en/courses/fieldwork-text. Accessed 22 October 2010.

Blommaert, J. (2007) Commentaries: On scope and depth in linguistic ethnography. *Journal of Sociolinguistics* 11 (5), 682–688.

Creese, A. (2010) Linguistic ethnography. In E. Litosseliti (ed.) *Research Methods in Linguistics* (pp. 138–154). London: Continuum.

Creese, A., Bhatt, A., Bhojani, N. and Martin, P. (2008a) Fieldnotes in team ethnography: Research complementary schools. *Qualitative Research* 8 (2), 223–242.

Creese, A., Baraç, T., Bhatt, A., Blackledge, A., Hamid, S., Li Wei, Lytra, V., Martin, P., Wu, C. J. and Yağcıoğlu-Ali, D. (2008b) *Investigating Multilingualism in Complementary Schools in Four Communities.* Final Report to ESRC RES-000-23-1180.

Creese, A., Bhatt, A. and Martin, P. (2009) Multilingual researcher identities: Interpreting linguistically and culturally diverse classrooms. In J. Miller, M. Gearon and A. Kostogriz (eds) *Culturally and Linguistically Diverse Classrooms: New Dilemmas for Teachers* (pp. 215–233). Bristol: Multilingual Matters.

Eisenhart, M. (2001a) Educational ethnography past, present and future: Ideas to think with. *Educational Researcher* 30 (8), 16–27.

Eisenhart, M. (2001b) Changing conceptions of culture and ethnographic methodology: Recent thematic shifts and their implications for research on teaching. In V. Richardson (ed.) *Handbook of Research on Teaching* (4th ed.) (pp. 209–225). Washington DC: American Educational Research Association.

Emerson, R.M., Fretz, R.I. and Shaw, L. (1995) *Writing Ethnographic Fieldnotes.* Chicago: Chicago University Press.

Erickson, Frederick G. (1986) In M.C. Wittrock (ed.) *Handbook of Research on Teaching* (pp. 119–162). New York: Macmillan.

Erickson, F. (1990) Qualitative Methods. In R.L. Linn and F. Erickson (eds) *Research in Teaching and Learning* (Vol. 2). New York: MacMillan Publishing Company.

Erickson, F. (2004) Demystifying data construction and analysis. *Anthropology and Education Quarterly* 35 (4), 486–493.

Erickson, K. and Stull, D (1998) *Doing Team Ethnography: Warnings and Advice.* London: Sage.

Geertz, C. (1988) *Works and Lives: The Anthropologist as Author.* Cambridge: Polity Press.

Hammersley, M. (2007) Reflections on linguistic ethnography. *Journal of Sociolinguistics* 11 (5), 689–695.

Hornberger, N.H. (1992) Presenting a holistic and an emic view: The literacy in two languages project. *Anthropology & Education Quarterl* 23, 160–165.

Hornberger, N.H. (1994) Ethnography. *TESOL Quarterly* 28 (4), 688–690.

Hornberger, N.H. (1995) Ethnography in linguistic perspective: Understanding school Processes. *Language and Education* 9 (4), 233–248.

Hornberger, N.H. (2002) Multilingual language policies and the continua of biliteracy: An ecological approach. *Language Policy* 1, 27–51.

Hornberger, N.H. (2003) Linguistic anthropology of education (LAE) in context. In S. Wortham and B. Rymes (eds) *Linguistic Anthropology of Education* (pp. 245–270). West Port, CT: Praeger

Hornberger, N.H. (2008) Continua of biliteracy. In A. Creese, P. Martin and N.H. Hornberger (eds) *Encyclopedia of Language and Education* (2nd ed., Vol. 9: Ecology of Language) (pp. 275–290). New York: Springer Science+Business Media LLC.

Hornberger, N.H. (2009) Multilingual education policy and practice: Ten certainties (grounded in Indigenous experience). *Language Teacher* 42 (2), 197–211.

Hornberger, N.H. and Hult, F.M. (2006) Educational linguistics. In K. Brown (ed.) *Encyclopedia of languages and Linguistics* (2nd ed.) (pp. 76–81). Amsterdam: Elsevier.

Hornberger, N.H. and Johnson, D.C. (2007) Slicing the onion ethnographically: Layers and specs in multilingual language education policy and practice. *TESOL Quarterly* 41 (3), 509–532.

Hymes, D. (1968) The ethnography of speaking. In J. Fishman (ed.) *Readings in the Sociology of Language* (pp. 99–138). The Hague: Moulton.

Hymes, D. (1974) *Foundations in Sociolinguistics: An Ethnographic Approach.* Philadelphia, PA: University of Pennsylvania Press.

Hymes, D. (1980) Language in education: Forward to fundamentals. *Language in education: Ethnolinguistic Essays.* Washington, D.C.: Center for Applied Linguistics.

McCarty, T.L. (ed.) (2005) *Language, Literacy, and Power in Schooling.* Mahway, NJ: Lawrence Erbaum.

Mitteness, L.S. and Barker, J.C. (2004) Collaborative and team research. In C. Seale, G. Gobo, J. Gubrium and D. Silverman (eds) *Qualitative Research Practice* (pp. 276–294). London: Sage.

Rampton, B., Tusting, K., Maybin, J., Barwell, R., Creese, A. and Lytra, V. (2004) UK Linguistic Ethnography: A Discussion Paper – Online document: www.ling-ethnog.org.uk.

Ruiz, R. (1984) Orientations in language planning. *NABE Journal* 8 (2), 15–34.

Scollon, R. and Scollon, S.W. (2007) Nexus analysis: Refocusing ethnography on action. *Journal of Sociolinguistics* 11 (5), 608–625.

Shaffif, W.B and Stebbins, R.A. (eds) (1991) *Experiencing Fieldwork.* Newbury Park: Sage.

Sipe, L.R. (2004) Developing conceptual categories in classroom descriptive research: Some problems and possibilities. *Anthropology & Education Quarterly* 35 (4), 472–485.

Section II

Continua of Biliteracy

Thematic Overview II
New Literacy Studies and the Continua of Biliteracy

BRIAN STREET

In offering support and praise for Nancy Hornberger's work as a colleague in the UK (though I have also been a Visiting Professor in her department at UPenn for many years) I will consider the ways in which her major contribution to literacy studies – via the concept of the 'Continua' – potentially relates to the ideas prevalent in the field of New Literacy Studies (NLS). In working towards bringing these two perspectives together and clarifying the similarities and differences can, I hope, make a contribution that builds appropriately on Hornberger's work.

I begin with a summary of a chapter that Hornberger wrote in a book for which I was co-editor on Latin American literacy studies (Kalman & Street, 2010). The volume addresses new directions in research and theory in the field of literacy studies, and the opening chapter by Hornberger puts many of the subsequent pieces into theoretical and international perspective. She locates the discussion of Indigenous languages in Latin America in a broader context by reviewing three cases of multi-language policy in the Andes, in Paraguay and in Aotearoa / New Zealand. Her chapter, 'Voice and biliteracy in the revitalisation of Indigenous languages: Continuous practices in a Quechua, Guarani and Māori context', provokes two key questions: (1) What are the best educational approaches for children from linguistic minorities (Indigenous and immigrant)? (2) What policies, programs and circumstances support or promote the preservation and revitalisation of minority languages? These central questions frame her chapter, but also reflect her long-standing interests and decades of scholarship. She reflects on these questions through the analysis of three cases of multilingual language policy made from an ecological perspective of language (see Wang, this book). This perspective poses the reciprocity between language and its environment, focusing on the description of the social and psychological context in which the language is situated, as well as the effect of such contexts on practice and policy. Taking this as a background landscape, the ecological exploration presented in her chapter takes three tracks: biliteracy, revitalising languages and voice. This approach, as many chapters in this book discuss, defines biliteracy as any instance in which communication takes place in two (or more) languages around a written text; revitalising languages can be understood as an attempt to add new linguistic forms or social functions into a threatened minority language to increase its use or users; voice is analyzed from a Bakhtinian perspective, which considers the individual in active dialogue with their surroundings. In light of the issues associated with Bakhtinian voice and the concept of continuous local practices, four instances of biliteracy are analysed to understand how the use of Indigenous languages as the medium of instruction in Indigenous communities can contribute to better learning by children and the revitalisation of the language. Hornberger, then, adds further dimensions to the 'Continua' model for which she is well known, and my chapter here continues this process by adding a New Literacy Studies (NLS) dimension to the accounts of literacy in multilingual contexts with which we are all concerned. I will firstly, then, outline what I take to be the main contribution of NLS.

New Literacy Studies

What has been referred to as 'New Literacy Studies' (Barton & Hamilton, 1998; Gee, 1999; Heath, 1983; Street, 1993) involves an understanding of literacy practices in their social and cultural contexts. This approach has been particularly influenced by those who, like Hornberger, have advocated an 'ethnographic' perspective, in contrast with the experimental and often individualistic character of cognitive studies, and the textual, etic perspective of linguistic-based studies of text. Much of the work in this tradition focuses on the everyday meanings and uses of literacy in specific cultural contexts and links directly to how we understand the work of literacy programmes, which themselves then become subject to ethnographic enquiry (Robinson-Pant, 2004; Rogers, 2005).

In trying to characterise these new approaches to understanding and defining literacy, I have referred to a distinction between an 'autonomous' model and an 'ideological' model of literacy (Street, 1984). The 'autonomous' model of literacy works from the assumption that literacy in itself – autonomously – will have effects on other social and cognitive practices. The model, I argue, disguises the cultural and ideological assumptions that underpin it and that can then be presented as though they are neutral and universal. Research in the social practice approach challenges this view and suggests that in practice dominant approaches based on the autonomous model are simply imposing Western (or urban, etc.) conceptions of literacy on to other cultures (Street, 2001). The alternative, ideological model of literacy offers a more culturally sensitive view of literacy practices as they vary from one context to another. This model starts from different premises than the autonomous model. It posits instead that literacy is a social practice, not simply a technical and neutral skill and that it is always embedded in socially constructed epistemological principles. The ways in which people address reading and writing are themselves rooted in conceptions of knowledge, identity and being. Literacy, in this sense, is always contested, both its meanings and its practices, hence particular versions of it are always 'ideological', they are always rooted in a particular world-view and a desire for that view of literacy to dominate and to marginalise others (Gee, 1999). The 'autonomous' model is, then, itself a strongly ideological perspective, since it takes a firm view on what counts as literacy, its consequences for human social development. The argument about social literacies simply makes explicit what remains implicit in the autonomous model: that engaging with literacy is always a social act even from the outset, even where educational policy perspectives attempt to describe such learning and practices as 'neutral'. The ways in which teachers or facilitators and their students interact is already a social practice that affects the nature of the literacy being learned and the ideas about literacy held by the participants, especially the new learners and their position in relations of power. It is not valid to suggest that 'literacy' can be 'given' neutrally and then its 'social' effects only experienced or 'added on' afterwards.

For these reasons, as well as because of the failure of many traditional literacy programmes (e.g. Abadzi, 2003), academics, researchers and practitioners working in literacy in different parts of the world are beginning to come to the conclusion that the autonomous model of literacy, on which much of the existing practice and programmes have been based, was not an appropriate intellectual tool, either for understanding the diversity of reading and writing around the world or for designing the practical programmes this required which may be better suited to an ideological model (e.g. Aikman, 1999; Canieso-Doronila, 1996; Heath, 1983; Hornberger, 1997, 2002). The question this approach raises for policy makers and programme designers is, then, not simply that of the 'impact' of literacy – to be measured in terms of a neutral developmental index – but rather of how local people 'take hold' of the new communicative practices being introduced to them, as Kulick and Stroud's (1993) ethnographic description of missionaries bringing literacy to New Guinea villagers makes clear.

Literacy, in this sense, is, then, already part of a power relationship and how people 'take hold' of it is contingent on social and cultural practices and not just on pedagogic and cognitive factors. This raises questions that need to be addressed in any literacy programme: What is the power relation between the participants? What are the resources? Where are people going if they take on one literacy rather than another literacy? How do recipients challenge the dominant conceptions of literacy?

This approach has implications for both research and practice. Researchers, instead of privileging the particular literacy practices familiar in their own culture, now suspend judgement as to what constitutes literacy among the people they are working with until they are able to understand what it means to the people themselves, and which social contexts reading and writing derive their meaning from. Many people labelled 'illiterate' within the autonomous model of literacy may, from a more culturally sensitive viewpoint, be seen to make significant use of literacy practices for specific purposes and in specific contexts. For instance, studies suggest that even non-literate persons find themselves engaged in literacy activities so the boundary between literate and non-literate is less obvious than individual 'measures' of literacy suggest (Canieso-Doronila, 1996). Academics have, however, often failed to make explicit the implications of such theory for practical work. In the present conditions of the world, such ivory-tower distancing is no longer legitimate. But likewise, policy makers and practitioners have not always taken on board such 'academic' findings, or have adopted one position (most often that identified with the autonomous model) and not taken account of the many others outlined here. These findings, then, raise important issues both for research into literacy in general and for policy in adult basic education and training in particular.

Key concepts in the field of New Literacy Studies that may enable us to overcome these barriers by applying these new conceptions of literacy to specific contexts and practical programmes include the concepts of *literacy events* and of *literacy practices*. Shirley Brice Heath characterised a 'literacy event' as 'any occasion in which a piece of writing is integral to the nature of the participants' interactions and their interpretative processes' (1983: 50). I have employed the phrase 'literacy practices' (Street, 1984: 1) as a means of focusing upon 'the social practices and conceptions of reading and writing', although I later elaborated the term both to take account of 'events' in Heath's sense and to give greater emphasis to the social models of literacy that participants bring to bear upon those events and that give meaning to them (Street, 1988). David Barton, Mary Hamilton and colleagues at Lancaster University have taken up these concepts and applied them to their own research in ways that have been hugely influential both in the UK and internationally (cf. Barton *et al.*, 1999). The issue of dominant literacies and non-dominant, informal or vernacular, literacies is central to their combination of 'situated' and 'ideological' approaches to literacy.

There has, however, recently, been a critique of this position in turn: Brandt and Clinton (2002) refer to 'the limits of the local'. They and others (e.g. Collins & Blot, 2003) question the 'situated' approach to literacy as not giving sufficient recognition to the ways in which literacy usually comes from outside of a particular community's 'local' experience, a feature common in adult literacy programmes. Street (2003) summarises a number of these texts and the arguments they put forward and offers some counter arguments from an ethnographic perspective. Maddox (2001, 2007) has attempted to bring together the 'situated' approach with that of 'New Literacy Studies', using his own ethnographic field research in Bangladesh to explore the relationship. For instance, he critiques NLS for its 'reluctance . . . in examining the role of literacy capabilities and practices in progressive forms of social change and the production of agency' (Maddox, 2007: 257). Like Brandt and Clinton (2002), Maddox (2007) wants to recognise the force of 'outside' influences associated with literacy, including the potential for helping people move out of 'local' positions and take account of progressive themes in the wider world. For instance, the desire to keep 'keeping accounts of household expenditure' (2007: 261) was not just a technical issue, but one of authority, gender relations and kinship; literacy (and numeracy) could play a catalytic role in such women's breaking free from traditional constraints. Maddox wants, then, to 'shift away from the binary opposition of ideological and autonomous positions that has dominated . . . debates in recent years' and develop a 'more inclusive theory that can link the local and the global, structure and agency and resolve some of the theoretical and disciplinary tensions over practice and technology' (2007: 266–267). Stromquist (2006) also critiques aspects of the 'social' perspective on literacy from the perspective of someone wishing to build upon literacy interventions for equity and justice agendas. She accepts the arguments put by NLS against the strong version of the cognitive consequences of literacy, but does not believe that means entirely abandoning recognition of where literacy and cognition are associated: 'Understanding the contributions of literacy does not mean that one needs to see literacy functions as the only way to develop cognitive ability and reasoning powers, but rather that there be acknowledgement that literacy does enable people to process information that is more detailed, deliberate and coherent than oral communication' (2006: 143). For instance, 'literacy enables people to participate in modern life processes such as reading newspapers and maps, following instructions, learning the law, and understanding political debates' (2006: 143). Without returning to the now discredited claims of the autonomous model, she and others in the field of adult literacy want to hold on to some of the powers of literacy associated with it.

This account links closely with that by Sen (2002) and Nussbaum (2006), who both argue for an equity and justice approach that places string emphasis on the positive 'good' offered by acquiring literacy. Nussbaum (2006) is very critical of social practice approaches to inequality and literacy based in ethnography, which she criticises as 'relativist'. Rather, she sees literacy as a universal good along with other 'concepts of a good life that are valued across diverse cultural contexts' and argues that 'these virtues provide a basis for human development and social justice' (Nussbaum, 2006; cited in Maddox, 2008: 191). Literacy is included in her list of 10 'central human capabilities' under a category related to 'senses, imagination and thought'. Like the early exponents of the autonomous model, such as Goody and Ong (cf Street, 1984), she sees literacy as enabling the ability to use the sense, to imagine, to think and to reason as though those classified by literacy indicators as lacking literacy were somehow unable to do these things. Such qualities are, she believes, universal rights:

> The capabilities approach is fully universal; the capabilities in question are held to be important for each and every citizen, in each and every nation, and each is to be treated as an end. (Nussbaum, 2006: 78)

Likewise Sen locates literacy within a larger list of basic capabilities and argues that it is a 'necessary condition for well being' (1990: 126). As Maddox notes, 'Sen also notes the incompatibility of inequalities in basic capabilities with effective human development' (2008: 189). Using census data, Sen claims that literacy is not only correlated with such public goods as child mortality, gainful employment etc. but is actually causal of effects that overcome such conditions. As in the autonomous model, correlation and cause are being confused here with respect to international goals and, as Goody points out, a single factor is being proposed where theoretical approaches suggest multiple causality: 'Sen's concern for literacy appears to be informed by a consequentialist concern with the achievement of freedoms and agency and an awareness of the impact of unequal distribution' (Maddox, 2008: 190). He lists six ways in which schooling and literacy (as Scribner and Cole pointed out in 1981, many such commentators continue to confuse these two categories) help to 'reduce human insecurity', overcoming deprivation, unemployment and the like, and leading to political participation and peace. Bryan Maddox's account of the work of Nussbaum (2006) and of Sen (2002) on which I have drawn here attempts to use his own field work as an example of how such a 'Capabilities Approach' can be reconciled with ethnography (Basu *et al.*, 2009; Maddox, 2001, 2008).

The positions and arguments outlined here, whether just the privileging of the 'local' evident in some early NLS positions or the recognition of 'outside' and global as well as cognitive influences, as in Brandt, Maddox, Stromquist and others, imply different approaches to what counts as 'literacy' and to how programmes for the extension and enhancement of adult literacy may be conceptualised and designed. The implications of these scholarly debates for these strands are not that we abandon work in this field – despite the occasional tendency in that direction as researchers question many of the supposed gains associated with literacy – but rather that we put it into perspective and recognise the limitations and constraints imposed by the different theoretical positions we adopt.

Continua of Biliteracy

This, then, brings us back to Hornberger's work and the Continua of Biliteracy. How far and in what ways does that theoretical position engage with the ideas discussed above within the New Literacy Studies perspective? And in what ways does the Continua handle or resolve the dilemmas and problems raised above? It is evident that the Continua deals with literacy as social practice, much as do researchers in NLS. The four nested sets of intersecting continua characterising the contexts, media, content and development of biliteracy (Hornberger, 2003; also Skilton-Sylvester, this book) can be linked closely with the attention to social context in the NLS approach. But how might Hornberger and her colleagues address the critiques raised by Brandt and Clinton, regarding the local and the global? And what are the implications of the position for policy programmes in adult literacy? How does it deal with the justice and equity issues raised by Stromquist and by Senn and Nusbaum and their claims that literacy does in fact 'contribute' to cognitive and social development, despite the NLS critique of the autonomous model? And does it address the concerns raised by Maddox and others regarding the apparent 'dichotomy' between autonomous and ideological models and the need to reconcile these positions in active policy programmes? These questions all suggest further directions for the approach that Hornberger and her colleagues have been developing and I look forward to a future engagement with her ideas as fruitful as the last two decades have been.

References

Abadzi, H. (2003) *Improving Adult Literacy Outcomes: Lessons from Cognitive Research for Developing Countries*. Washington, DC: World Bank.

Aikman, S. (1999) *Intercultural Education and Literacy: An Ethnographic Study of Indigenous Knowledge and Learning in the Peruvian Amazon*. Amsterdam: Benjamins.

Barton. D. and Hamilton, M. (1998) *Local Literacies: Reading and Writing in One Community*. London: Routledge.

Barton. D., Hamilton, M. and Ivanič, R. (eds) (1999) *Situated Literacies: Reading and Writing in Context*. London: Taylor and Francis.

Basu, K., Maddox, B. and Robinson-Pant, A. (eds) (2009) *Interdisciplinary Approaches to Literacy and Development*. London: Routledge.

Brandt, D. and Clinton, K. (2002) Limits of the local: Expanding perspectives on literacy as a social practice. *Journal of Literacy Research* 34 (3), 337–356.

Canieso-Doronila, M.L. (1996) *Landscapes of Literacy: An Ethnographic Study of Functional Literacy in Marginal Philippine Communities*. Hamburg: UNESCO Institute of Education.

Collins, J. and Blot, J. (2002) *Texts, Power and Identity*. London: Routledge.

Gee, J. (1999) The new literacy studies: From 'socially situated' to the work of the social. In D. Barton, M. Hamilton and R. Ivanic (eds) *Situated Literacies: Reading and Writing in Context* (pp. 180–196). London: Routledge.

Heath, S.B. (1983) *Ways with Words*. Cambridge: Cambridge University Press.

Hornberger, N. (2003) *Revisiting the Continua of Biliteracy: A Framework for Educational Research, Policy and Practice in Multilingual Settings*. Clevedon: Multilingual Matters.

Hornberger, N. (ed.) (2002) *The Continua of Biliteracy: An Ecological Framework for Educational Policy, Research and Practice in Multilingual Settings*. Clevedon: Multilingual Matters.

Hornberger, N. (1997) Indigenous literacies in the Americas. In N. Hornberger (ed.) *Indigenous Literacies in the Americas* (pp. 3–16). Berlin: Mouton de Gruyter.

Kalman, J. and Street, B. (eds) (2010) *Literacy in Latin American; Local and International Perspectives*. Madrid: Siglo XXI Editores and CREFAL.

Kulick, D. and Stroud, C. (1993) Conceptions and uses of literacy in a Papua New Guinean village. In B. Street (ed.) *Cross-cultural Approaches to Literacy* (pp. 30–61). Cambridge: Cambridge University Press.

Maddox, B. (2008) What good is literacy? Insights and implications of the capabilities approach. *Journal of Human Development* 9 (2), 185–206.

Maddox, B. (2007) What can ethnographic studies tell us about the consequences of literacy? *Comparative Education* 43 (2), 253–271.

Maddox, B. (2001) Literacy and the market: The economic uses of literacy among the peasantry in north-west Bangladesh. In B. Street (ed.) *Literacy and Development* (pp. 137–151). Routledge: London.

Nussbaum, M (2006) *Frontiers of Justice: Disability, Nationality, Species Membership.* Cambridge, MA: Belknap Press.

Robinson-Pant, A. (ed.) (2004) *Women, Literacy and Development: Alternative Perspectives.* London: Routledge.

Rogers, A. (ed.) (2005) *Urban Literacy: Communication, Identity and Learning in Urban Contexts.* Hamburg: UNESCO Institute for Education.

Scribner, S. and Cole, M. (1981) *The Psychology of Literacy.* Cambridge, MA: Harvard University Press.

Sen, A.K. (2002) *Rationality and Freedom.* Cambridge, MA: Harvard University Press.

Sen, A.K. (1990) Gender and cooperative conflicts. In I. Tinker (ed.) *Persistent Inequalities: Women and World Development* (pp. 123–149). Oxford: Oxford University Press.

Street, B. (2003) What's 'new' in new literacy studies? Critical approaches to literacy in theory and practice. *Current Issues in Comparative Education* 5 (2), 77–91.

Street, B. (2001) Literacy and development: Challenges to the dominant paradigm. In A. Mukherjee and D. Vasanta (eds) *Rethinking Literacy: Dominant and Alternative Discourses.* Sage: London.

Street, B. (ed.) (1993) *Cross-Cultural Approaches to Literacy.* Cambridge: Cambridge University Press.

Street, B. (1988) Literacy practices and literacy myths. In R. Saljo (ed.) *The Written Word: Studies in Literate Thought and Action* (pp. 59–72). Heidelberg: Springer-Verlag Press.

Street, B. (1984) *Literacy in Theory and Practice.* Cambridge: Cambridge University Press.

Stromquist, N. (2006) Women's rights to adult education as a means to citizenship. *International Journal of Educational Development* 26, 140–152.

Chapter 4

Continuing the Continua: Why Content Matters in Biliterate Citizenship Education

ELLEN SKILTON-SYLVESTER

It is hard to believe that it has been 20 years since I began graduate studies with Nancy Hornberger at the University of Pennsylvania. Interestingly, these same two decades of my development as a scholar/teacher also include key points on the developmental trajectory of the Continua of Biliteracy. In many ways, I have grown up as a biliteracy researcher with the continua as a companion and as I have stretched and grown, it has as well. Hornberger's publication of the original 'Continua of biliteracy' article in *Review of Educational Research* in 1989 (Hornberger, 1989) appeared just before my first year of graduate school. I remember reading the article twice before coming to class to discuss it and feeling humbled and confused by its complexity, attention to detail and comprehensiveness. What did it mean for me as a teacher and future scholar think in terms of continua of biliterate contexts, media and development? As time when on, I realized just how powerful the model could be not only for describing what was happening in homes, classrooms, school districts and courthouses, but also in providing a vision for education that addresses the needs and talents of all learners, especially those who know more than one language. By including both domestic and international contexts beyond the immediate moment-to-moment interactions of people (but not ignoring specific instances of face-to-face interaction), by dismantling the traditional dichotomy between oral and written contexts and language development and by acknowledging the way that literacy is both a cultural practice and a cognitive skill, she had, in one elegantly crafted and meticulously researched article, powerfully illustrated that the intellectual battles that force us to choose sides in academic debates fail to account for the lived realities of bilingual learners, language teachers and educational policy makers. To be honest, it took me many readings of the article after that first-class discussion to feel as though I could wrap my head around it, but once I did, I could not let it go.

A key element of Hornberger's emphasis on context included the idea that I first heard Rebecca Freeman Field articulate: 'It's always more than language' (Freeman, 1996). As I did my own dissertation research (Skilton-Sylvester, 1997) exploring local language in education policies and the biliteracy practices and identities of Cambodian women and girls in Philadelphia, these non-linguistic elements of biliteracy became increasingly visible and important to my analysis. In the end, I proposed adding the continua of biliterate content to the continua of biliteracy model (much to the chagrin of students who would read about the continua for the first time in my courses and realize it originally had three rather than four continua). As evidence of Hornberger's gift for collaborating with and nurturing her students, she embraced this additional continua (that includes literary–vernacular, majority–minority and contextualized–decontextualized content continua) as part of the model. Including the continua of biliterate content and an explicit analysis of the traditional power weighting of the endpoints on each of the continua, the original continua article was followed a decade later with the article, 'Revisiting the continua of biliteracy,' in *Language and Education* (Hornberger & Skilton-Sylvester, 2000).

Now, another decade later, it is useful to re-examine the power of this model to illuminate what matters in bilingual and biliteracy education and to highlight the urgency of these perspectives in a pedagogical and policy context in the US that seems to get more restrictive each day. As Hornberger explains:

> With enactment of *No Child Left Behind* in 2002, bilingualism and bilingual education vanished (Wiley & Wright, 2004: 155), indeed were banished, from US educational policy vocabulary, closing up with one fell swoop both ideological and implementational spaces that had been created by the Bilingual Education Act. (Hornberger, 2005: 9)[1]

In the past 10 years, the country as a whole has seen diminished official support for bilingual education under *No Child Left Behind* Act (NCLB), and particular states (California, Arizona and Massachusetts) have enacted legislation that explicitly limits or eliminates bilingual instruction in schools. Because of this history, and the current educational and political climate in the US, state legislative actions and re-interpretations of NCLB during the Spring of 2010 make the Arizona case a particularly valuable one to consider in thinking about the relevance and urgency of Hornberger's vision for education in multilingual communities in the US.

This chapter utilizes the continua of biliteracy – and particularly the continua of biliterate content – to analyze four legislation-based policies in Arizona that seek to eliminate or ignore the value of particular kinds of biliterate content in educational contexts. These three decisions include the 2000 enactment of Proposition 203 (Arizona Revised Statutes, 2000) mandating English-only education for English Language Learners (ELLs), and two 2010 educational decisions that have come on the heels of the much publicized and debated new immigration law that criminalized undocumented residents of the state (SB1070, Arizona Revised Statutes, 2010a): (1) the new ban on ethnic studies (HB2281, Arizona Revised Statutes, 2010b), and (2) a much less publicized but equally restrictive re-interpretation of NCLB in the Spring of 2010, focusing on teacher fluency in English, that will have an impact on many native-Spanish-speaking teachers in Arizona. The primary analysis in this chapter focuses on the July 2010 ethnic studies ban (HB2281), an aggressive attempt to eliminate or greatly restrict minority and contextualized content through state law. However, my analysis also includes these two other Arizona decisions that seek to ignore and/or de-emphasize content in language instruction and instead focus on requiring unaccented English for teachers without attention to teacher skill, preparation or curriculum implementation (re-interpretation of NCLB), and English-language instruction without attention to curricular content or pedagogy (Proposition 203). As a petition by Stanford faculty recently stated:

> The *Wall Street Journal* (4/30/10) points out that Arizona's English 'fluency' initiative is particularly troubling if read within the context of the state's extremely tense debate over immigration (SB1070), and we would further add, its recent ban on Ethnic Studies (HB2281). Both policies have been widely interpreted as harmful to Latinos directly and to other non-dominant groups by extension. Ironically, these policies may inadvertently serve to further the very social divisions they purport to eradicate, and they may deepen the educational rift between Latina/o students and their white counterparts. (21 June 2010)

In analyzing these legislative directives in Arizona, I argue that the continua of biliteracy not only asks us to pay attention to less powerful – and often overlooked – ends of the continua as a means to create equitable and meaningful education for all, but that the continua also embraces (perhaps indirectly) a definition of multicultural citizenship and belonging (e.g. Banks, 2008; Flores & Benmayor, 1997) that is critical to creating full participation for all in a multilingual and multicultural society.

Highlighting the Continua of Biliterate Content

In the continua of biliteracy model (Hornberger & Skilton-Sylvester, 2000), the continua of biliterate content include three intersecting continua: literary–vernacular, majority–minority and contextualized–decontextualized. Several scholars (including Gordon, this volume) have meaningfully addressed these content continua in diverse research contexts with young children, teenagers and adults (Lincoln, 2003; Schwinge, 2003; Skilton-Sylvester, 2008). With varied data and analysis, we have proposed that the traditionally powerful ends of the continua typically include literary texts (e.g. published literature) that focus on mainstream/majority topics (e.g. the US Revolutionary War), and decontextualized facts (e.g. the year that Bill Clinton was elected). We have stressed that curriculum for linguistically and culturally diverse students should also include attention to the less powerful ends of the continua, by including vernacular texts (e.g. informal student writing from out-of-school contexts), minority/culturally relevant topics (e.g. Chicano history) and contextualized content (e.g. personal connections to and thoughts about policies enacted by Bill Clinton).

Hornberger's discussion of ideological and implementational spaces for supporting bilingualism (Hornberger, 2005), even in the context of restrictive state and national policies, has been very useful for imagining close-to-the ground possibilities for meaningful biliterate pedagogies and curriculum development that includes biliterate content in the 21st century. In particular, because the content of biliteracy has been only indirectly regulated in most educational policy (e.g. by focusing exclusively on high stakes tests, content is often restricted, see Menken, 2008 or via decisions by state boards of education to emphasize particular versions of American History or social studies, see Shapiro, 2010), inclusion of biliterate content has often been possible even in the context of the most restrictive legal provisions for English-only instruction. That is, because educational policy decisions have typically not explicitly banned biliterate content and have focused only on language of instruction or the required social studies curriculum, it has often been possible to teach in an English-only environment while still addressing the minority, vernacular and/or contextualized ends of the biliterate content continua. Not all continua of biliterate content will be emphasized equally in the analysis that follows, but it is very clear that the ban on Ethnic Studies in Arizona (HB2281) is an attempt to systematically restrict contextualized minority content in Arizona schools.

Ignoring biliterate content in AZ: Proposition 203 and 'Accented English' restrictions

In order to understand the context in which the Ethnic Studies ban was passed and its position relative to contextualized, minority content, it is useful to look at two other key legislative influences on biliterate content in the state of Arizona. Passed in 2000, Proposition 203 or 'English for the Children' sought to eliminate bilingual education in the state and was modeled after Proposition 227 in California (Wright, 2005a). Wright's (2005a, 2005b) detailed and critical analyses of Proposition 203 and its intersection with NCLB illuminate the fact that there has been almost no emphasis on pedagogy or content in analyzing its implementation. As Wright (2005b: 12) explains, '[The] definition [of Sheltered English Immersion] merely emphasizes the language of instruction. To date, the state has failed to provide a working definition of SEI other than just teaching ELLs in English.' The law itself says:

> Children in Arizona public schools shall be taught English by being taught in English and all children shall be placed in English language classrooms. Children who are English learners shall be educated through sheltered English immersion during a temporary transition period not normally intended to exceed one year. (A.R.S. §15–752)

> [Sheltered (or structured) English immersion (SEI) is] an English language acquisition process for young children in which nearly all classroom instruction is in English but with the curriculum and presentation designed for children who are learning the language. Books and instructional materials are in English and all reading, writing, and subject matter are taught in English. (A.R.S. §15–751) (in Wright, 2005b: 12)

Tellingly, when state officials visited classrooms to see if the law was being implemented, their checklists included no criteria about effective pedagogical tools or meaningful content, but only ones concerning the use of English at all times (Wright, 2005a). The content of the lessons observed was completely irrelevant.

In an even more narrow perspective on language and instruction, the state of Arizona recently interpreted NCLB's provision that highly qualified teachers should have facility in English to mean that the English of teachers of ELLs should be 'unaccented' (Jordan, 2010). In addition to the Stanford faculty who circulated a petition contesting this decision, the National Council for Teachers of English (NCTE) has also issued a statement condemning this policy and emphasizing research that indicates that teacher quality has more to do with 'understanding students and the dynamics of language teaching.' An excerpt from the full statement says:

> The effects of a new Arizona Department of Education policy are reverberating in the literacy education community. According to numerous reports, the Department has told school districts that teachers whose spoken English it deems to be heavily accented or ungrammatical must be removed from classes for students still learning English. This edict is dangerously misguided. Confirmed by research and by policy positions adopted by the National Council of Teachers of English, what matters most in teaching non-native English language learners is not elocution or adherence to a single dialect or speech pattern. What matters most is understanding students and the dynamics of language learning. Teachers who have deep roots in the culture and linguistic experiences of their students are well equipped for success in teaching English, regardless of their spoken dialect or accent. A recent NCTE position paper on 'The Role of English Teachers in Educating English Language Learners (ELLs)' emphasizes the importance of empathy, connections to ELL students' families and culture, and innovative teaching methods. (NCTE, 2010)

In her ethnographic study of working-class children and literacy teaching and learning, Hicks (2002) posits something quite similar in relation to all students – that 'what is required for critical literacy teaching is not just the right kinds of discourses, but the right kinds of relationships ... students' searches for social belonging are as much a part of learning in school as anything that might be described as cognitive or even discursive' (ix, 1).

This example illustrates the potential power of states to interpret federal law in restrictive ways, and highlights the state's emphasis on the English language per se rather than the linguistic and educational needs of children and the potential benefits of a bilingual staff. A recent *Wall Street Journal* article (Jordan, 2010) describes this shift in policy concerning the accents of teachers in relation to NCLB. The deputy superintendent of the state's schools said 'We know districts that have a fluency problem.' However, one principal disagreed with the state's definition: 'Teachers should speak grammatically correct English. ... I object to the nuance of

punishment for accent.' The article goes on to say: 'Arizona's enforcement of fluency standards is based on an interpretation of the federal
NCLB. That law states that for a school to receive federal funds, students
learning English must be instructed by teachers fluent in the language.
Defining fluency is left up to each state....' In this case, the fuzziness
of the law is creating ideological and implementational spaces that run
counter to the insights of Hornberger's continua of biliteracy model
and research on effective instruction for bilingual students by restrict-
ing language, ignoring content and diminishing positive and effective
community relationships between teachers and students.

   In this example, as in the state law banning bilingual instruction, a
narrow de-contextualized perspective on language is embraced with no
attention to pedagogy, the content of instruction (even in relation to access
to the mainstream curriculum) or the contexts of students' lives in and
out of school. Each of these policy decisions fly in the face of the complexity and language-as-resource orientation (Ruiz, 1984) of the continua
of biliterate contexts, content, development and media. As Wright (2005a:
668) points out, these policies are based on an 'oversimplification of language learning that is not supported by research [and fail] . . . to acknowledge the social and educational contexts of second language acquisition.'
He concludes that they end up being more about political spectacle than
about sound language in education policy, but they continue to have
profound implications on the students and teachers of Arizona.

Restricting cultural content and cultural citizenship: Banning ethnic studies through Arizona HB 2281

   With the above-stated disregard for the content of the curriculum, it
may seem to be contradictory that Arizona is in the news this spring for
banning particular kinds of content in public schools. In particular, this
new state law disallows courses that:

(1) Promote the overthrow of the US government
(2) Promote resentment toward a race or class of people
(3) Are designed primarily for pupils of a particular ethnic group
(4) Advocate ethnic solidarity instead of the treatment of pupils as
     individuals.

In reading the actual law, it is impossible not to think about Wright's
discussion of Proposition 203 and the ways that it is a tool for political
spectacle (Wright, 2005a). The particulars of these guidelines are vague yet

incendiary, seemingly designed to draw a line in the sand about appropriate pathways for being and becoming American (Abu El-Haj, 2007,
2010; Gordon, 2010). While the law highlights classes that 'promote the
overthrow of the US government,' it would prohibit classes offered by
Tuscon Unified School District's Mexican American Studies Department,
that in a completely different frame, are 'working towards the invoking
of a critical consciousness within each and every student.' Here, developing skills to critique the US government has been reframed as promoting
an overthrow. As one educator stated, 'If we think critically about U.S.
policies, would that be considered anti-American?' (Fernández, 2010). The
law was designed to target the Tuscon district but 'critics argue that the
bill was designed without any review of the program it was attempting
to target...Educators from the Tuscon Unified District...say they are in
compliance with the law, that their classes are open to all students and
their curriculum does not promote resentment' (Fernández, 2010).

It is the next three elements of restrictions on ethnic studies programs
in Arizona that I will focus on most directly because it is in these elements, particularly the final one that emphasizes a ban on courses that
promote 'ethnic solidarity instead of the treatment of pupils as individuals,' where we see a very particular version of what it means to be an
American that conflicts quite strongly with the underlying tenets of the
continua of biliteracy, with what research says about what helps language
minority students succeed in school (Hornberger, 1989; Hornberger &
Skilton-Sylvester, 2000; Lincoln, 2003; NCTE, 2010), and with what assists
all students in developing civic participation (Kahne & Sporte, 2008).

If we look first at the continua of biliteracy as a whole, Lincoln's (2003)
description is particularly helpful. As she writes,

> The continua model predicts that, for language minorities to have
> agency and voice, planners and educators must pay more attention
> to the typically less powerful ends of the content and media continua,
> that is, minority ways of knowing, vernacular ways of speaking and
> writing, and contextualized language use, as well as non-standard or
> 'mixed' language varieties and orthographies. (155)

Although not explicitly stated, the continua (and particularly the continua
of biliterate content) implicitly frame participation and belonging in
schools and society as linked to what Flores and Benmayor (1997) call
cultural citizenship:

> Cultural citizenship can be thought of as a broad range of activities
> of everyday life through which Latinos and other groups claim space

in society, define their communities, and claim rights. It involves the
right to retain difference, while still attaining membership in society.
It also involves self-definition, affirmation, and empowerment. (262)

By banning ethnic studies in this way, the state of Arizona is not only
influencing students' engagement and success in school by not allowing
the curriculum to draw on minority, vernacular and contextulized ends
of the continua, but they are also limiting the ways that students in these
schools may see themselves as active citizens in the future.

Collectively – the ethnic studies ban, the ban on bilingual education
and the elimination of teachers with accents (who often have ties to the
communities of ELLs) – create a context in which language learning and
content learning are much less likely to happen. Even more, they create a
context in which it is hard to imagine that the less powerful ends of the
continua of biliterate content (minority, contextualized, vernacular) will
be addressed at all. As a consequence, real engagement as citizens may
be much less likely if students' histories and experiences – and their affiliation to both a particular ethnolinguistic group and to this multicultural
society – have not been recognized in the curriculum (Skilton-Sylvester,
2009). As Kahne and Sporte (2008) suggest:

Theorists like John Dewey (1900) and reformers such as Deborah
Meier (1995, 2002) link experiencing a sense of belonging to a caring
and supportive school community with the development of commitments and capacities for democratic ways of living . . . . When students
expressed more of a sense of belonging to the school, they reported
higher levels of commitments to civic participation. (743)

In looking at the details of the ban on ethnic studies, one sees a vision of
our country in which individuals are primary and affiliations with others are secondary. What Hornberger's continua model suggests, however,
is that building a multicultural society involves many languages, many
experiences and connections to those who speak in ways that you do and
those who do not.

Beyond the Individual: Building a Future for the Common Good

Continuing the continua involves continuing to use this powerful lens
to look at new bilingual and biliterate situations with fresh eyes. My latest readings of Hornberger's work, my recent research on citizenship,
care and belonging (Skilton-Sylvester, 2009) and my investigation in this

chapter about what the continua could tell us about the current situation in Arizona have highlighted the ways that the continua continues to be a useful and powerful model for understanding what is and for imagining what can be. The analysis here illustrates the ways that this model envisions forms of citizenship and participation – what Hornberger calls voice and agency (Hornberger & Skilton-Sylvester, 2000) – that are possible when all points of the continua are addressed. Perhaps even more importantly, the continua model provides a structure for challenging policies and practices and for creating ideological and implementational spaces for biliteracy and belonging in the face of restrictive policies that deny voice and agency. In looking closely at the Arizona ban on Ethnic studies in relation to the continua of biliterate content, I am most struck by the contrasting views of what it means to be a member of US society that surface in HB2281 and in the Continua of Biliteracy.

The Arizona laws highlighted in this article, and particularly HB2281, seem to have as an underlying assumption the idea that our rights are primarily individual in nature and that our affiliations with particular ethnolinguistic groups are counter-productive and perhaps even dangerous. In addition to the language of individualism found in HB2281, the idea that ELLs should 'soar academically as individuals' appeared often in 2000 in the Arizona campaign to ban bilingual education through Proposition 203 (Wright, 2005a: 681). This assumption that rights and achievements are solely individual in nature is not unique to Arizona, however. As Abu El-Haj (2010) states:

> The ideal of individual freedom is commonly considered an enduring commitment of American democracy. This ideal, which has been characterized as an expression of the 'American creed,' holds that the United States is a land where individuals from all over the world can come to remake themselves through the opportunities afforded by the nation's political commitments to equality and liberty of all people (Gerstle, 2001; Smith, 1988). Dominant discourses define American national identity in relation to citizens who are treated as *free* and *equal* and who, as democratic subjects, should act not out of predetermined group allegiance but from individual conscience and conviction.... The national ideal of individual freedom derives from a commitment to the primacy of individuals over groups.... (250)

The continua of biliteracy assume a powerful connection to a group with which one shares a language and culture and groups with which one does not. Knowing, learning and/or teaching multiple languages require us to maintain meaningful affiliations with more than one group and to develop solidarity within and across those groups. One of the most hope-ful things that I saw recently at a hearing with Philadelphia government officials about collaborations between law enforcement and immigration authorities was that so many different ethnolinguistic groups were repre-sented in that crowded church basement. Simultaneous translation was happening in English and Spanish and there was a real sense that all were welcome and that all – even those of us who didn't live in that particular neighborhood and who didn't speak Spanish or English very well – had a stake in the outcome. In times of fear and despair about the kinds of laws being enacted across the US to create physical and emotional barriers between people of different languages and nations of origin, I am reminded of something that Nancy Hornberger taught us in her scholarship and by example. Official rules and restrictions are only part of the story. Human connection, curiosity and creativity are often able to seep in between the official pronouncements to find 'ideological and implementational spaces' for supporting biliterate development and for imagining educational policies and practices for tomorrow that do not seem possible today.

Note

1. The Bilingual Education Act – Title VII of the Elementary and Secondary Edu-cation Act was originally passed in 1968. It was re-authorized many times since 1968 and varied in its support of bilingual education depending on the current US presidential administration. Although it was more restrictive at some points than others, it did not eliminate the possibility of supporting bilingual programs in the same way that NCLB has.

References

Abu El-Haj, T. (2007) 'I was born here, but my home, it's not here': Educating for democratic citizenship in an era of transnational migration and global conflict. *Harvard Educational Review* 77 (3), 285–316.

Abu El-Haj, T. (2010) The beauty of America: Nationalism, education and the war on terror. *Harvard Educational Review* 80 (2), 242–274.

Arizona Revised Statutes, Title 11, Chapter 7, Article 8; Title 13, Chapter 15, §13–1509, §13–2319; Title 13, Chapter 29, §13–2928, §13–2929, §23–212, §23–212.01, §23–214, §28–3511; Title 41, Chapter 12, Article 2, §41–1724; Relating to Unlawfully Present Aliens (2010a) – Online document: http://www.azleg.gov/legtext/49leg/2r/bills/sb1070s.pdf.

Arizona Revised Statutes, Title 15, Chapter 1, Article 1, §15-111-15-112 (2010b) – Online document: http://www.azleg.gov/legtext/49leg/2r/bills/hb2281p.pdf.

Arizona Revised Statutes, Title 15, Article 3.1, §15-751-17-755 (2000) – Online document: http://www.azleg.gov/FormatDocument.asp?inDoc=/ars/15/00751.htm&Title=15&DocType=ARS.

Banks, J.A. (2008) Diversity, group identity, and citizenship education in a global age. *Educational Researcher* 37 (3), 129–139.

Fernández, V. (2010, May 28) Arizona's ban on ethnic studies worries more than Latinos. La Prensa San Diego. www.laprensa-sandiego.org.

Flores, W.V. and Benmayor, R. (1997) (eds) *Latino Cultural Citizenship: Claiming Identity, Space and Rights*. Boston, MA: Beacon Press.

Freeman, R.D. (1996) Dual-language planning at Oyster Bilingual School: 'It's much more than language.' *TESOL Quarterly* 30, 557–582.

Gerstle, G. (2001) *American Crucible: Race and Nation in the 20th Century*. Princeton, NJ: Princeton University Press.

Gordon, D. (2010) Disrupting the master narrative: Global politics, historical memory, and the implications for naturalization education. *Anthropology and Education Quarterly* 41 (1), 1–17.

Hicks, D. (2002) *Reading Lives: Working-class Children and Literacy Learning*. New York: Teachers College Press.

Hornberger, N.H. (1989) Continua of biliteracy. *Review of Educational Research* 59 (3), 271–296.

Hornberger, N.H. (2005) Nichols to NCLB: Local and global perspectives on U.S. language education policy. *Working Papers in Educational Linguistics* 20 (2), 1–17.

Hornberger, N.H. and Skilton-Sylvester, E. (2000) Revisiting the continua of biliteracy: International and critical perspectives. *Language and Education: An International Journal* 14 (2), 96–122.

Jordan, M. (2010, April 30). Arizona grades teachers on fluency: State pushes school districts to reassign instructors with heavy accents or other shortcomings in their English. *Wall Street Journal*. www.wsj.com 23. Accessed October 2010.

Kahne, J. and Sporte, S. (2008) Developing citizens: The impact of civic learning opportunities on students' commitment to civic participation. *American Educational Research Journal* 45 (3), 738–766.

Lincoln, F. (2003) Language education planning and policy in middle America: Students' voices. In N.H. Hornberger (ed.) *Continua of Biliteracy* (pp. 147–165). Avon: Multilingual Matters.

Meier, D. (1995) *The Power of their Ideas: Lessons for America from a Small School in Harlem*. Boston, MA: Beacon.

Meier, D. (2002) *In Schools We Trust: Creating Communities of Learning in an Era of Testing and Standardization*. Boston, MA: Beacon.

Menken, K. (2008) *English Learners Left Behind: Standardized Testing as Language Policy*. Clevedon: Multilingual Matters.

National Council of Teachers of English (NCTE) (2010, June) NCTE Speaks Out on Arizona Department of Education Ruling on Teacher Speech: *Evaluate Teachers on Their Competence, Not on Their Accents* – Online document: www.ncte.org.

Ruiz, R. (1984) Orientations in language planning. *NABE Journal* 8 (2), 15–34.

Schwinge, D. (2003) Enabling biliteracy: Using the continua of biliteracy to analyze curricular adaptations and elaborations. In N.H. Hornberger (ed.) *Continua of Biliteracy* (pp. 248–268). Clevedon: Multilingual Matters.

Shapiro, A. (2010) *The Texas Social Studies Controversy* – Online document: www.teachablemoment.org.

Skilton-Sylvester, E. (1997) Inside, outside and in-between: Identities, literacies and educational policies in the lives of Cambodian women and girls in Philadelphia. Unpublished PhD dissertation, University of Pennsylvania.

Skilton-Sylvester, E. (2008) Academic biliteracies for adults in the United States. In K.M. Rivera and A. Huerta-Macias (eds) *Adult Biliteracy: Sociocultural and Programmatic Responses* (pp. 131–153). Lawrence Erlbaum Associates.

Skilton-Sylvester, E. (2009) 'Who cares?': Relationships, recognition and rights in the democratic education of three Cambodian sisters in the United States. *Inter-American Journal of Education for Democracy* 2 (2), 274–294.

Smith, R. (1988) The 'American creed' and American identity: The limits of liberal citizenship in the United States. *Western Political Quarterly* 41 (2), 225–251.

Wright, W.E. (2005a) The political spectacle of Arizona's Proposition 203. *Educational Policy* 19 (5), 662–700.

Wright, W.E. (2005b) English language learners left behind in Arizona: The nullification of accommodations in the intersection of federal and state policies. *Bilingual Research Journal* 29 (1), 1–29.

Wiley, T.G. and Wright, W.E. (2004) Against the undertow: Language-minority education policy and politics in the 'Age of Accountability.' *Educational Policy* 18 (1), 142–168.

Chapter 5

Literacy in Two Lands: Refugee Women's Shifting Practices of Literacy and Labor

DARYL GORDON

Introduction

As Laotian refugee women adapt to radically different cultural landscapes in the US, they redefine their identities and develop new literacy practices. Many entered the US with little native language literacy, having received little or no formal education in their homeland. Laotian women were not expected to develop school-based literacy practices, as demonstrated in the following quotation from a mother who, like many parents in rural Laos, chose not to send her daughter to primary school. Explaining her reasoning, she said, 'All the things we need for use in our daily lives are dependent on our fields. Even if we don't study literacy, we can still eat rice' (Guttal, 1993: I–3). On entering the US, female refugees confronted a society with radically different expectation of school-based literacies and different expectations of skilled workers. In the US, Laotian women were required to use literacy in new contexts, including paying bills, completing forms, taking the US citizenship exam and passing standardized tests required to enter good-paying jobs.

This chapter investigates changing literacy practices for Laotian women in the US using Hornberger's continua of biliteracy as a heuristic to explore the shifts in women's cultural constructions of literacy, focusing on literacy practices in the context of refugee women's work. This focus responds directly to Luke's (2004) call to ethnographers of literacy to 'gauge and document the material consequences of social practices' and to question 'which languages and literacies, sanctioned by which state educational systems and globalised institutions, have which kinds of material consequences in people's lives' (2004: 332–334). The relationship between English literacy and labor is of particular importance for refugee women. Most Laotian refugee women work in low-paying jobs in non-union factories which require little or no English language or literacy. Immigrant women are one of the lowest paid sectors of the work force; 53% of immigrant women earn less than or near minimum wage (Gatta, 2005: 21).

Access to better paying jobs is particularly difficult for refugee women, as jobs traditionally held by women, such as beautician, medical assistant or secretary, require higher proficiency in English language and literacy and career training. While immigrant and refugee men may have access to better-paying jobs in heavy industry which are dependent on their manual labor, women's access to higher paying jobs is predicated upon their acquisition of English literacy. Examining the predominant occupations of men and women reveals that typically women's jobs in pre-primary education, nursing and midwifery, and secretarial work require higher literacy skills than typically men's jobs as miners, trades workers and ship deck workers (OECD, 2005). Sticht (2002) writes that men in the workforce have lower literacy levels than women workers and are more likely to self-report that they do not read well, but less likely to sign up for adult literacy classes.

This chapter begins with a review of the literature in the area of transnational literacy followed by methods of data collection and analysis. In order to provide background on the situation of female Laotian refugees, I offer a brief history of women's literacy in Laos and the migration experiences of Laotian refugees. I move then to explore ethnographic data demonstrating the dramatic shifts in literacy practices for women refugees. The data focus on the experiences of Ouma, a principal participant in this research study, as she moved from rural Laos to literacy classes in refugee camps in Thailand and the Philippines, awaiting final resettlement in the US, and finally to the world of literacy and work in the US. The chapter concludes with an analysis of the connections between literacy and labor for refugee women and the 'literacy myths' surrounding literacy and upward mobility for refugee women.

Ideological Perspectives on Biliteracy Content and Context

The analysis of literacy practices in this chapter draws heavily on the work of Brian Street and the New London School (Gee, 2000; Street, 1984, 1993, 2000, 2003). Street (1984) makes a distinction between autonomous and ideological notions of literacy. Autonomous literacy refers primarily to literacy as a set of cognitive skills and abilities and their generic use. In contrast, ideological literacy refers to the social conceptions and uses of literacy. In this view, literacy is what society does with literacy and represents a shift away from viewing literacy as simply the isolated skills of reading and writing. Rather, the focus is on how individuals understand and use text and images as part of their identities and their membership in schools, families and communities; as employees in workplaces and as citizens in public life. The ideological view represents literacies as plural and as complex and multifaceted social and cultural practices. Regarding literacy practices of Gujarati-speaking women in Britain, Martin-Jones writes that 'ways of speaking and ways of reading and writing serve as a powerful means of making statements about identity. They therefore merit close attention in ethnographic accounts of the ways in which women redefine their identities in the context of migration' (2000: 153).

Street notes that literacy is 'always embedded in social practices, such as those of a particular job market or a particular educational context and the effects of learning that particular literacy will be dependent on those particular contexts' (2003: 78). Investigating the connection between literacy and labor throughout the migration process shows how the context of labor in Laos and the US radically shifts the need for women's formal literacy and affects women's literacy practices. The movement from a rural economy based on subsistence agriculture to an urban environment based on wage labor caused dramatic shifts in refugee women's literacy practices. Additionally, the public perception of the dwindling literacy skills of US workers in the midst of a changing economy created a workplace literacy campaign which affected the context of literacy acquisition for immigrant workers.

Hornberger, employing a sociolinguistic perspective, points out that literacy practices encompass uses of and attitudes toward language and literacy, including underlying norms, values and conventions associated with these uses. Hornberger's continua of biliteracy, a comprehensive framework proposed to situate research, teaching and language planning in multilingual settings, offers a useful heuristic for examining shifts in literacy practices experienced in transnational migration. The framework describes biliteracy in terms of four nested sets of continua characterizing the media, contexts, development and content of biliteracy (Hornberger, 1989, 2003, 2007; Hornberger & Skilton-Sylvester, 2000). In my analysis of the shifts in literacy practice experienced by Ouma and other Laotian refugee women, I focus on the context and content dimensions of the continua.

The context dimension encompasses micro- to macro-levels and a range of monolingual–bilingual and oral–literate continua. An important consideration in contexts of biliteracy is society's tendency to weight power towards the macro, literate and monolingual ends of the continua. The context dimension is closely linked to the research of Brian Street and the New London School. This research has drawn 'attention to these kinds of contestations of macro-level, dominant, monolingual literacy practices, with their documentation of "multiple literacies" – the multiple social and cultural constructions of literacy in practice' (Hornberger & Skilton-Sylvester, 2000: 104).

The content dimension allows for an examination of the kinds of meanings expressed in particular biliterate contexts and includes majority to minority perspectives and experiences, literary to vernacular styles and genres and decontextualized to contextualized language texts (Hornberger, 2003; Hornberger & Skilton-Sylvester, 2000). Traditionally, formal literacy study has been weighted toward the majority, literary and decontextualized ends of this continua. However, Hornberger and Skilton-Sylvester (2000) have argued for the importance of including minority, vernacular and contextualized whole language texts within learner's literacy experiences. The content continua links biliteracy with bicultural literacy. Hornberger writes that the consideration of the content dimension is crucial for bilingual educators 'as they negotiate issues of cultural stereotyping, intercultural respect, and conflicting or overlapping cultural traditions and particularities' (Hornberger, 2004: 167–168). Of particular interest in this dimension is the decontextualized–contextualized continuum, which is closely linked to Street's (1984) distinction between autonomous and ideological literacies (Hornberger & Skilton-Sylvester, 2000). While refugees were exposed to the decontextualized end of this continuum in refugee camps, they experienced more contextualized content as whole language methods became more popular in US adult education classes.

Methodology

Data presented in this chapter were collected between 1997 and 2000 as part of a larger ethnographic research project focusing on women's second-language socialization (Gordon, 2004, 2009). Data collection methods included participant observation and interviewing in the homes and workplaces of research participants and at the Lao Temple in Philadelphia, a religious and cultural center of the Laotian-American community. Additional data were collected during a 3-month period of intensive Lao language study and a year of research and teaching in Laos, which allowed me to visit the family of Ouma and another principal participant in the study and to gain a more comprehensive understanding of Laotian literacy and cultural practices.

In 1999, the director of the Lao Assistance Center asked me to initiate an ESL and citizenship class at the center. This year-long class, along with interviews and participant observation with students, provided the main source of data for this chapter. Sixteen students attended the evening class, 14 of whom were women. Students ranged in age from mid-thirties to mid-fifties and all had entered the US as adults after 1980. Most had limited formal education in Laos and struggled with native language literacy. Most worked in non-union factory jobs in the US, where they had little contact with native speakers of English.

Background on Laotian Migration and Education

Laotian refugees settled in the US as part of a massive influx of nearly one million Southeast Asians from Vietnam, Cambodia and Laos, who sought refuge in the US after the end of the Vietnam War in 1975. Approximately 198,000 Lowland Lao individuals currently reside in the US (Niedzwiecki & Duong, 2004). The war, which lasted over a decade, effectively destroyed village life in Laos, as Laotian people fled their villages and the farms which provided their livelihoods to seek refuge in caves or in the jungle (Evans, 1998; Stuart-Fox, 1997).

The war interrupted formal schooling in many areas. However, women's access to formal education had historically been limited. Prior to the advent of public schooling instituted during the French colonial period, Laotian tradition dictated that boys received schooling in Buddhist temples while girls were taught domestic skills from their mothers at home. During the French colonial period (from 1893 to 1950) primary schooling, in which French was the language of instruction, was available only in a few provincial capitals. Limited to urban areas, education was available to an elite few and centered on boys' education.

Stuart-Fox (1997), in his comprehensive history of Laos, reports the illiteracy rate for men and women pre-revolution as 85%. Ngaosyvathn (1995) writes that in 1975, 95% of Lao women over 45 years of age were illiterate. In 1975 after the Lao revolution, the newly installed Pathet Lao government instituted policies which mandated basic education for both boys and girls. However, there continues to be a significant gender gap in education and learning opportunities across the Lao PDR, which is more pronounced in rural areas and among ethnic minority groups. While the rates of enrollment of girls have increased since the revolution, the disparities remain vast, especially in rates of completion. Nationally, girls make up 47% of first-grade students, but only 10% of secondary students are girls (Guttal, 1993). In her ethnographic study of girls' literacy in Laos, Guttal found that 75% of the parents who sent their daughters to school planned to stop their education after the second grade so that they could help with housework and agricultural production.

In rural areas where village schools commonly have only two grades, children must travel to a larger village to continue their education. This involves costs for travel, clothing and lodging which are significant given villagers' extremely limited resources. While in southern Laos, I became acquainted with a family who chose to stop their daughter's education after the two years she received in the village school because they had no bicycle by which she could make the four-mile trip to the neighboring village school. The lack of published material in the Lao language constitutes yet another impediment to literacy for youth and adults. The rural development organization with which I worked established small libraries in villages in order to increase the availability of books available in Lao language – most of the books were printed and donated by non-governmental organizations, such as UNICEF.

Ouma's Literacy Practices

Ouma, whose literacy practices form the basis of this chapter, entered the US in 1985 at the age of 26 with her husband and four children. The family had escaped from Laos in 1981 and lived in refugee camps in Thailand and the Philippines for four years before final resettlement. Ouma had received approximately two years of formal education in her rural village in southern Laos. However, her schooling was sporadic, because her family was displaced for most of her childhood because of wartime violence.

I first met Ouma in 1998, when she came to the Lao Assistance Center carrying a worn-looking paper bag filled with bills. She had come to request help from the Center's bilingual staff in understanding the bills, as she was confused about past due amounts and how much she was required to pay. After addressing her immediate concerns, she was referred to my ESL class. Ouma's goals for learning English included studying for the US Citizenship exam, being able to understand bills and forms more easily, and obtaining a better job. While Ouma's communicative abilities in English were sufficient to perform most routine interactions, reading and writing were her greatest concerns. Her needs assessment form indicated that she wanted to develop her literacy ability in order to complete job applications and forms at the doctor's office and her children's school.

Ouma attended the class I taught two evenings a week at the Lao Assistance Center. Because of her irregular work schedule, which often required evening work with little prior notice, she could not attend class regularly. When she did attend class, she was a vibrant, motivated and enthusiastic student. On occasions when she could not attend class, she studied independently, using textbooks and materials from previous ESL classes and a bilingual dictionary. She had enjoyed her limited formal education opportunities in Laos and learning English in the refugee camp and in the US and regretted that she had not been able to study more continuously.

Changing Contexts and Content of Literacy: ESL Classes in Refugee Camps and the US

Like Ouma, many Laotian refugees spent years in refugee camps in Thailand and the Philippines as they petitioned for permanent resettlement. The ESL classes in the refugee camps represented a dramatic shift in women's access to formal literacy, as both men and women were required to attend daily classes. In the Philippine camps, refugees received 4–6 months of ESL and work-orientation classes as well as American cultural-orientation instruction in their native language. English instruction focused on competency-based approaches that stressed the importance of learning the language for real-life tasks (also known as life skills or survival skills), such as completing applications, reading schedules and asking for information (Seufert, 1999).

These courses which emphasized English literacy for life skills and for work demonstrated a significant shift on the context dimension toward the macro, literate and monolingual ends of the continua. While the cultural-orientation course was provided in the native language, the intent was not to maintain or develop the first language, but to effectively transition refugees to English language and American cultural values. Hornberger and Skilton-Sylvester discuss this tendency to emphasize English-language acquisition at the expense of minority language maintenance within the US educational system, critiquing programs which 'used minority languages only to embed the more powerful English literacy' and which serve to 'pull students' biliterate development toward English' (2003: 101).

Ouma's description of the work orientation clearly demonstrates the courses' orientation toward the macro-end of the continuum. Hornberger defines the micro-end of the continuum as literacy which serves 'intrapersonal and interpersonal contexts' and the macro as connected to the interests of society or the larger social unit (2003: 10). When asked about what she learned in the Philippine refugee classes, Ouma spoke about learning about American culture, how to find a job and appropriate behavior in the American workplace. She learned that Laotian women should 'wear pants when go to work, no *sinn* (traditional Laotian skirt).' She also emphasized learning about time orientation in American work culture:

> Like go work on time.... If you don't walk faster, you will miss the bus and be late for work. If you late one minute, they will cut five minutes off.

The course content and focus on how Laotian refugees would be transformed into dutiful, punctual workers demonstrates how the courses in the refugee camps served the macro-level, government-level interests for workers who would suit the expectations of American corporations. Buck describes a similar orientation toward punctuality and the production of willing, obedient workers within a course for female Somali refugee newcomers in the US. Analyzing how local and national discourses around immigrants and refugees have shaped policies for newcomer education, she finds 'an emphasis upon the production of low skilled workers; an invoking of authoritarian relations between newcomers and longer term residents ... and an exclusion of newcomers from decision making regarding their schooling' (2008: 50).

Ouma's description of English literacy classes in the refugee camp demonstrates a clear preference toward literacy instruction in the content dimension, predominantly in the majority language using decontextualized texts. English literacy instruction centered on reading and writing to the exclusion of listening or speaking and with little context-embedded instruction. Ouma describes a decontextualized approach which progressed from individual letters to decoding words:

Daryl: What did you learn?
Ouma: Oh! The first thing, the first time, I didn't know any, even ABCD. Study about that.
Daryl: So, first you learned the alphabet (ABCD)?
Ouma: And then ... after that, try to learn, like book, chair, table, bird.
Daryl: Did you learn listening and speaking or did you learn more reading and writing?

Ouma: Read and write together because one hour a day, not take long time.

Daryl: So, let me make sure I understand. You learned reading and writing, but not listening and speaking? You learned mostly reading and writing.

Ouma: Yeah, because my class not high, still low. If I learn about listening, still don't know anything because still learn the first step like book, chair, table.

Ouma's description of learning English literacy demonstrates her acceptance that this method of instruction was appropriate and, in fact, necessary because of her beginning proficiency in English. Her last statement reveals her belief that the incorporation of listening skills and more contextualized instruction was not possible due to her limited proficiency in English. The absence of contextualized literacy instruction, she believed, was not the failure of the educational system, but rather a result of her low literacy ability. Ouma perceived that her limited English literacy required a decontextualized literacy approach which did not acknowledge the considerable experience, first-language literacy ability and interests she brought to the process of English literacy acquisition. The use of the decontextualized approach encouraged her already existing belief that she did not bring skills or resources into the process of literacy acquisition.

Hornberger and Skilton-Sylvester (2003) highlight the close and complex connection between the decontextualized–contextualized continuum and learner power (or lack thereof) in the educational process, a relationship which is also crucial to Street's (1984) distinction between autonomous and ideological perspectives on literacy. Using the content and context dimensions to analyze the literacy instruction of the refugee camps demonstrates an orientation toward decontextualized content, majority perspectives and experiences, and a macro-orientation toward the governmental and corporate needs of the American workforce. The refugee camp's focus on autonomous literacy and decontextualized literacy instruction along with instruction on labor oriented toward unskilled factory work reflects a belief that instructing refugees through a decontextualized approach will transform them into workers with high levels of contextualized literacy, resulting in refugee workers who will contribute to the American work force.

When Ouma entered the ESL class I taught at the Lao Assistance Center, she was exposed to a greater use of contextualized texts and writing activities on the micro-end of the continuum. Hornberger and Skilton-Sylvester point out that contextualized whole texts and vernacular texts are often absent from the school contexts. However, with greater focus on whole language approaches, more contextualized texts are used. They write that 'if students' whole contextualized texts, with all their imperfections, could be used as a starting point, meaning would be ensured and students could intrinsically see the links between decontextualized and contextualized language, and between the literary and the vernacular literacies' (2000: 111). In Ouma's ESL class, I used a series of readings about the experiences of newcomers in the US. One story involved a Southeast Asian woman in the US who was experiencing problems with her teenage daughter, who had rapidly acculturated to American cultural and gendered norms and begun dating. This type of reading was quite different from the content Ouma had been exposed to in the refugee literacy classes, which had focused on bills and job application forms. In a dialogue journal response to this writing, Ouma was able to communicate complex ideas in English:

> Thursday, February 25, 1999
> Her mothe doesn't want Nok to go out side because she so afraid of her daughter will get some problem like If she go out mabe she will go have some drug, bad friend, bad boy friend will distroy her future.
> I gess Nok will not listen to her mom right now. she will go out side with her boy friend as much as she wants. She doesn't care what is happen to her life. doesn't care about her mom's telling. but her mom try to tell and tell about the good things little by little, steps by steps. No matre where and what country. we have to do the good thing at all!
> Fanally! Nok will listen to her mother. she won't go out very often lik before. She will stay home, as much as she can.

The reading and Ouma's response were closely connected to the context of her experience as a refugee woman raising children in an American context with familial and gender roles which differed radically from her native Laos. Ouma's journal entry demonstrates her ability to articulate a clear response to the problem posed in the text about what will happen regarding the argument between Nok and her mother. Ouma details the reasons behind her mother's fears, based on Ouma's own fears for her own teenage children, growing up in a low-income neighborhood of urban Philadelphia. She uses complex sentences with conjunctions and demonstrates her familiarity with conventions of English writing through use of punctuation and paragraphs.

The reading selection, a published account of a female refugee, acknowledged the rich experience and knowledge adult refugees bring with them to the literacy class. This literacy event demonstrated the use of a text from the vernacular and minority ends of the content continuum and was connected to Ouma's background experience. As the class progressed, however, I questioned whether this approach helped Ouma achieve her stated goal of locating a better paying job. Despite Ouma's acquisition of more developed literacy skills, she continued to labor in a low-income job and experienced difficulties locating employment at a decent wage that could support herself and her children. Ouma, like most immigrant women, was required to pass a standardized test in order to gain entrance into more secure employment. I began to doubt whether the incorporation of micro- context and vernacular and minority content was a mismatch for her stated goals for literacy instruction. The following section explores the world of work for female refugees, focusing on the expectations for school-based literacy for skilled employment.

Labor and Literacy

Like many Laotian refugee women, Ouma was employed in a small, non-unionized factory, where there was little need for English language or literacy. Obtaining a better job which would allow her to support her four children was a constant source of anxiety for her, especially as she decided to leave her abusive husband and needed to support her children on her own income. The English language and literacy ability she would have to develop in order to obtain a better job, as well as the gendered nature of jobs available to her, played a principal role in her search for more secure and better-paid employment. She considered asbestos removal, a well-paid job held by many Southeast Asian refugee men, but was dissuaded from this job because it was considered 'men's work.' Her other job prospect, to become a manicurist, was a common job for Southeast Asian women.

When Ouma and I investigated the requirements for licensing of manicurists in the state of Pennsylvania, we found that candidates had to complete 200 hours in a licensed cosmetology school, have a 10th-grade education or equivalent, and pass a State Board examination consisting of both theoretical and practical questions (Pennsylvania Department of State Board of Cosmetology, 2006). While Ouma would be able to perform the required tasks of a manicurist, and in fact did nails informally for women in the Laotian community, the requirement of an equivalent of 10th-grade reading skills, her lack of familiarity with the specialized vocabulary of the exam and the format of a standardized test prevented her from certification.

Warriner (2007) demonstrates the increasingly important role of standardized testing in newcomer's search for employment, noting that refugees are required to obtain a certain score before refugee resettlement agencies will advocate on their behalf to potential employers. The focus on standardized testing works to shift pedagogical practices within ESL classes, privileging test-based literacies even among teachers who state a preference for a more communicative and authentic approach. She writes that 'a great deal of class time is spent on helping students fill out worksheets with the correct vocabulary or verb tense; respond to known-answer comprehension questions; write resumes; transfer answers to standardized test questions to an answer key (by filling in the circle next to the appropriate number)' (Warriner, 2007: 319). Despite a preference for more authentic, contextualized literacy instruction, the goals of the standardized test influence literacy practices which tend toward what Hornberger (2003) terms the 'traditionally more powerful' ends of the continua of biliteracy.

In addition to the exam, a number of other factors prevented Ouma from reaching her goal of obtaining a job which would support herself and her family. These include the very limited pool of jobs she learns of within the Laotian community, and those for which she deems herself qualified. She was also thwarted from her goal due to her husband's unwillingness to recognize her education as a priority, and lack of adequate, affordable childcare which would enable her to study. Ouma found herself caught between society's view that English language and literacy skills are instrumental to obtaining good-paying jobs and the lack of support which would enable women to gain the literacy skills necessary to obtain these jobs.

While developing greater proficiency in English language and literacy might indeed help Ouma locate a better-paying job, it is important to realize that improved literacy skill is only one factor which prevents her from obtaining a better job. Hull's critique of workplace literacy programs warns practitioners and researchers of the potential to 'mischaracterize literacy as a curative for problems that literacy alone cannot solve' (1997: 11). Similarly, Auerbach (2005) writes of the literacy myths that are reproduced seemingly in the service of learner empowerment. She urges literacy researchers to consider the ways that community empowerment and social change, rather than individual competencies, shape learner's life possibilities.

A close examination of literacy and labor for refugee women and their shifting transnational literacy practices will offer literacy researchers and educators greater perspective into their instructional needs. The continua of biliteracy provides a powerful heuristic for investigating the literacy abilities and needs of female refugees in the workforce. In this era of high stakes testing for adult immigrant and refugee workers and schoolchildren, researchers need to investigate the ways in which standardized testing and workplace expectations shift educational practices toward more decontextualized, macro and monolingual ends of the continuum. Researchers utilizing the continua to investigate women's literacy and labor will benefit from Luke's (2004) suggestion to investigate how literacy practices are used to shape access to material and discourse resources. Investigating the material consequences of literacy will provide not only a close description of literacy events and practices, but offer insight into 'how literate practices have convertible exchange value as forms of capital' (Luke, 2004: 333).

References

Auerbach, E. (2005) Connecting the local and global: A pedagogy of not-literacy. In J. Anderson, M. Kendrick, T. Rogers and S. Smythe (eds) *Portraits of Literacy Across Families, Communities and Schools* (pp. 363–379). Mahwah, NJ: Lawrence Erlbaum.

Buck, P. (2008) Becoming American in time?: The educational implications of binary discourse on immigration. In D. Stevick and B. Levinson (eds) *Advancing Democracy through Education?: U.S. Influence Abroad and Domestic Practices* (pp. 29–51). Charlotte, NC: Information Age Publishing.

Evans, G. (1998) *The Politics of Ritual and Remembrance: Lao since 1975.* Chiang Mai, Thailand: Silkworm Books.

Gatta, M. (2005) *Not Just Getting By: The New Era of Flexible Workforce Development.* Lanham, MD: Lexington Books.

Gee, J. P. (2000) The new literacy studies: From 'socially situated' to the work of the social. In D. Barton, M. Hamilton and R. Ivanic (eds) *Situated Literacies: Theorizing Reading and Writing in Context* (pp. 177–194). London: Routledge.

Gordon, D. (2004) 'I'm tired. You clean and cook.' Shifting gender identities and second language socialization. *TESOL Quarterly* 38 (3), 437–457.

Gordon, D. (2009) 'She's American now, I don't like that': Gendered language ideologies in a Laotian American community. *Journal of Southeast Asian American Education & Advancement* 4, 1–17. http://jsaaea.coehd.utsa.edu/index.php/JSAAEA/article/view/65/62. Accessed 22 October 2010.

Guttal, S. (1993) *Strategies for the Promotion of Basic Education for Women and Girls.* Unpublished manuscript, Lao PDR: World Education.

Hornberger, N.H. (1989) Continua of biliteracy. *Review of Educaitonal Research* 59 (3), 271–96.

Hornberger, N.H. (ed.) (2003) *Continua of Biliteracy: An Ecological Framework for Educational Policy, Research, and Practice in Multilingual Settings.* Clevedon: Multilingual Matters.

Hornberger, N.H. (2004) The continua of biliteracy and the bilingual educator: Educational linguistics in practice. *Bilingual Education and Bilingualism* 7 (2&3), 155–171.

Hornberger, N.H. (2007) Biliteracy, transnationalism, multimodality and identity: Trajectories across time and space. *Linguistics and Education* 18, 325–334.

Hornberger, N.H. and Skilton-Sylvester, E. (2000) Revisiting the continua of biliteracy: International and critical perspectives. *Language and Education* 14 (2), 96–122.

Hornberger, N.H. and Skilton-Sylvester, E. (2003) Revisiting the continua of biliteracy: International and critical perspectives. In N.H. Hornberger (ed.) *Continua of Biliteracy: An Ecological Framework for Educational Policy, Research, and Practice in Multilingual Settings* (pp. 35–70). Clevedon: Multilingual Matters.

Hull, G. (1997) *Changing Work, Changing Workers: Critical Perspectives on Language, Literacy, and Skills*. Albany, NY: State University of New York Press.

Luke, A. (2004) On the material consequences of literacy. *Language and Education* 18 (4), 331–335.

Martin-Jones, M. (2000) Enterprising women: Multilingual literacies in the construction of new identities. In M. Martin-Jones and K. Jones (eds) *Multilingual Literacies: Comparative Perspectives on Research and Practice* (pp. 149–169). Philadelphia: John Benjamins.

Niedzwiecki, M. and Duong, T. C. (2004) *Southeast Asian American Statistical Profile*. Washington , DC: Southeast Asian Resource Action Center (SEARAC).

Ngaosyvathn, M. (1995) *Lao Women: Yesterday and Today*. Vientiane, Lao PDR: State Publishing Office.

Organization for Economic Co-operation and Development (OECD) (2005) *OECD Employment Outlook*. Paris: OECD.

Pennsylvania Department of State (2010) State Board of Cosmetology Licensure Information – Online document: http://www.portal.state.pa.us/portal/server.pt/community/state_board_of_cosmetology/12507/licensure_information/572014#exam. Accessed 22 October 2010.

Seufert, P. (1999) *Refugees as English Language Learners: Issues and Concerns*. CAELA digest. Washington, DC: Center for Applied Linguistics. http://www.cal.org/caela/esl_resources/digests/Refugee.html. Accessed 4 April 2010.

Sticht, T.G. (2002, March) Adult basic skills: How many need it? How many want it? *Basic Skills*, 26–29.

Street, B. (1984) *Literacy in Theory and Practice*. Cambridge: Cambridge University Press.

Street, B. (ed.) (1993) *Cross Cultural Approaches to Literacy*. Cambridge: Cambridge University Press.

Street, B. (2000) Literacy events and literacy practices. In M. Martin-Jones and K. Jones (eds) *Multilingual Literacies: Comparative Perspectives on Research and Practice* (pp. 17–29). Philadelphia: John Benjamins.

Street, B. (2003) What's new in new literacy studies? Critical approaches to literacy in theory and practice. *Current Issues in Comparative Education* 5 (2), 77–91.

Stuart-Fox, M. (1997) *A History of Laos*. New York: Cambridge University Press.

Warriner, D.S. (2007) 'It's just the nature of the beast': Re-imagining the literacies of schooling in adult ESL education. *Linguistics and Education* 18, 305–324.

Chapter 6

Poetic Anthropology and the Lyric Continua between Science and Art

MELISA CAHNMANN-TAYLOR

Introduction

Since first publishing her influential article on the continua of biliteracy in 1989, Nancy Hornberger has revisited this framework (Hornberger & Skilton-Sylvester, 2000), added to its dimensions, and illustrated its applications to cases of biliteracy around the world (Hornberger, 2003). From Korean church schools in Philadelphia (Pak, 2003) to Welsh-English curriculum development in Wales (Baker, 2003), Hornberger, her students and colleagues have carried out research with bilingual communities living in monolingually dominant contexts around the globe, illuminating the various, interlocking dimensions of what it means to speak, listen, read and write in two or more languages, almost always where one language has more social power and prestige than the other.

The interdisciplinary expanse of the framework and its refusal of finite either/or ends marks a new kind of scholarship, one which aspires to be 'epistemologically humble' (Barone, 2008: 35), honoring the complexity and ambiguity of literacy in more than one language. Surrounded by scholarly and political debates over what forms of research 'count' as scientific and valid (Shavelson & Towne, 2002), I take this opportunity to honor the framework's fluidity by expanding it to include empirical dimensions.

Building upon Street's (1988) arguments against the false oral-literate divide proposed in the fifties as well as Edelsky's (1986) and Hudelson's (1984) arguments against neat, linear progressions in second-language acquisition from speaking and listening to reading and writing, Hornberger (1989) and later Hornberger and Skilton-Sylvester (2000) proposed a framework that encompassed the multifaceted and overlapping dimensions of biliteracy, including the process of language 'development' as it occurs in numerous 'contexts' through a variety of 'media' related to varying 'content.'

There are four dimensions of biliteracy with three continua, each 'embedded in a historical and contemporary matrix of intergroup power relations' (Hornberger, 2003: ix). The focus on continua rather than binaries acknowledges opposite ends (*e.g.* reception-production, oral-written), while highlighting the transformative potential of working between the ends, resisting the implicit privileging of one end over the other (*e.g.* policies that solely promote and affirm written, monolingual, decontextualized, and standardized practices). This draws attention to the way English educators may or may not resist existing power structures that tend to privilege standard English monolingualism in classrooms where a diversity of linguistic practices can either be silenced or given voice.

In the spirit of the existing framework, here I discuss the continua in epistemological terms, what it means to empirically and artfully come to know (e.g. document, analyze, and/or represent) something about the context, development, content and media of biliteracy. I provide three continua for consideration, emphasizing dimensions of power in terms of what is considered valid and valuable research (see Figure 6.1). A growing community of scholars, of which I am a part, have long sought to disrupt the exclusive privilege of utilizing 'scientific' tools to document and understand the 'Other' in certain, knowable and so-called 'objective' terms. Focus on the continua of empirical choices will, I hope, strengthen the right to conduct biliteracy inquiry in ways that emphasize ambiguity, that acknowledge the researcher's identity as focal and/or relational to studying the bilingual 'other,' and that expand our methodological toolbox to include techniques from the literary, visual, and performing arts.

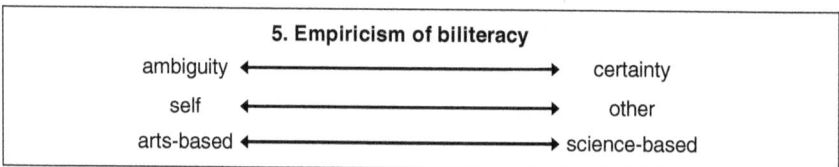

Figure 6.1 A fifth dimension of the continua of biliteracy

Ambiguous Answers vs. Certain Truths about Biliteracy

As I have written elsewhere (Cahnmann-Taylor, 2008a; Maynard & Cahnmann-Taylor, 2010), postmodern approaches to language research in the last few decades have shifted the conversation regarding what counts as knowledge and what methods constitute linguistic and ethnographic inquiry. Although the social sciences have traditionally privileged positivistic approaches, those emulating '(however imperfectly) the methods of turn-of-the-century physics and natural science' (Brady, 1991: 4), postmodern scholars have increasingly questioned the pursuit of absolute knowledge and reframed research endeavors as those which seek to write more refined and critical questions rather than result in finite answers (Barone, 2008). The outcome is an empiricism that places value on ambiguity over certainty, aiming to question the taken for granted and propose answers that are tentative, contradictory and/or those which lead to more questions.

This shift encourages biliteracy scholars to move away from linear research questions that identify 'best' bilingual education practices which lead directly to student achievement (e.g. Ramirez *et al.*, 1991) or the unidirectional transfer of L1 structures onto L2 (see Ellis, 1994: 341; Corder 1967; Dulay & Burt, 1973). Rather, the empirical continua of biliteracy disrupts linearity, viewing biliteracy practices at the individual and social levels as a constant 'zig-zag' (Hornberger, 1989: 286), where answers are socially situated and cyclical. Thus, biliteracy researchers continue to refine and expand methods which allow us to document and understand ambiguity and instability. Fishman's (1991; Hornberger & Pütz, 2006) lifetime work on language revitalization and Pavlenko's (2006) research on the interplay between emotions and multilingual language choices represent two examples of biliteracy research unafraid to delve into the messy and uncertain social worlds of language use – worlds where communication gets 'done' even in instances where that communication appears grammatically or cognitively impossible and/or socially inappropriate (Hymes, 1972). In the bilingual world nothing is stable – fluencies, identities, policies, contexts, attachments, motivations, even the languages themselves. To study bilingualism, a researcher must exchange the need for absolute certainty for the pursuit of qualified ambiguity where the only certainty is change itself.

The Biliterate Self and Biliterate Others

Nested within the continua between ambiguity and certainty is the question of the researcher's relative presence or disguise in a study. Social sciences modeled on 'standardized techniques and reporting formats' (Van-Maanen, 1988: 34) have privileged rational and systemic thinking, encouraging the researcher to use language which distances themselves from the objects or participants under study as a 'pretext of clinical distance' (Brady, 2000: 950). Just as the postmodern turn has questioned the search for absolute certainty, so too 'the relations of power whereby one portion of humanity can select, value, and collect the pure products of others needs to be criticized and transformed' (Rose, 1991: 284).

One often falsely assumes that the biliteracy researcher's focus is external: one conducts interviews and surveys, participates and observes or immerses oneself in the world of the bilingual/biliterate 'Other.' New turns in social science inquiry encourage researchers to explicitly state their subjectivity, acknowledge their own linguistic and cultural identities and pursue inquiry along the self-other 'hyphen' (Fine, 1994).

It is increasingly more common that researchers begin with their own biographies, narratives of their own experience that were previously suppressed in the name of an objective tradition. Feminist scholars have led the way, acknowledging the relationships qualitative researchers cultivate with their participants, and focusing empirical attention on the influences participants have upon the researcher (Stacey, 1991). For example, Abu-Lughod (1995: 347) documents the shift that occurred in her ethnography of Bedouin women when years later she returned to the field while struggling with her own fertility, finding 'constructions of [the researcher's] personal experience' (specifically fertility and motherhood) were shaped by knowledge of the Bedoin women's lives in her study. Rosaldo (1989, 2001) and Behar (1993, 1995, 1996, 2007, 2008) may be two of the best-known anthropologists to share the risks and vulnerabilities associated with research practices exposing the self-other continua. Documenting the Ilongot's violent mourning practices, Rosaldo (1989) lyrically and boldly wrote about his identification with the tribal 'head hunters' rage' after his own wife's unexpected death. Behar (2007) wrestled with risks on the hyphen when her memoir-based scholarship about leaving Jewish Cuba offended her own father. She asks, 'What do you do when your parents are "the other"? [and] they actually read what you write?' (1996: 67).

These and other researchers among multilingual and multicultural world communities illustrate a turn toward scholarship that breaks the divide between researcher Self and the participant Other, asking new questions and turning questions outward as well as inward. Researchers interested in the study of bilingualism are often (always?) attentive to how they themselves, in addition to bilinguals in their study context, navigate multiple linguistic and cultural worlds. Exposing the writer-researcher's connections and identifications amplifies and humanizes biliteracy knowledge.

Arts-based and Scientifically-based Approaches to Research

Ultimately, as I have written about extensively elsewhere (Cahnmann, 2003; Cahnmann-Taylor, 2008a; Cahnmann-Taylor & Siegesmund, 2008), a shift away from absolute certainty and objectivity frees the researcher to explore creative and transformative methodologies that capture nuance, uncertainty and multiplicity. One relatively new methodological approach to these two previously discussed continua has been to integrate tools from the literary, visual and performing arts into research designed to understand bilingual-biliterate experience. In the last two decades, there has been an explosion of social science researchers utilizing the arts in some aspect of the empirical process from data collection, to analysis and representation of findings (c.f. theatre [Kondo, 1995; Saldana, 2005; Cahnmann-Taylor & Souto-Manning, 2010], poetry [Brady, 2000; Maynard, 2001, 2002; Maynard & Cahnmann-Taylor, 2010; Cahnmann, 2003], visual arts [Springgay, 2008]; fiction [Gosse, 2008; Stoller, 2005], and memoir [Behar, 2007]). Scholars increasingly turn toward the continua between 'art' and 'science' as a means to engage artfully with participants and data (e.g. theater-based focus groups); to cultivate a 'leaping mind' (Bly, 1975) open to fast associations and new understandings about cultural and linguistic borderlands (e.g. taking poetic fieldnotes); to expand the multiple ways in which we represent those with whom we work (e.g. writing up findings in the form of portraiture, poems, short stories and plays); and to help us to be more attentive to how form can convey meaning (Maynard & Cahnmann-Taylor, 2010).

In language research there is a long and revered tradition of blurring the divide between scholarship and the arts, most notably the field of *ethnopoetics*, which began with scholars such as Dell Hymes, Stanley Diamond, Paul Friedrich and Ivan Brady, among others. Seeking textual means to accurately represent the oral arts of Indigenous communities under study, these scholars also wrote their own anthropological poems alongside lyrical approaches to ethnographic prose (c.f. Diamond, 1982; Brady, 2003; Maynard, 2001; Hymes, 1981, 1998, 2003). My own work has continued in this tradition, seeking the 'craft, practice, and possibility of poetry' (Cahnmann, 2003) to understand the chaos of fieldwork, to capture the feeling of 'being there' in bilingual schools and communities and to interpret shades of meaning rather than unambiguous findings. It is no surprise that Nancy Hornberger encouraged my early explorations of arts-based methodologies as approaches to understanding biliteracy phenomenon. The same year she published the first version of the Continua

(Hornberger, 1989), Hornberger became a member of the University of
Pennsylvania Choir and Choral Society and has enthralled audiences with
her trained singing voice ever since. I can only speculate the extent to
which Nancy's experiences and expression as a singing artist have influenced her expansive thinking as a scholar. There is no question that she
guides students and colleagues alike by an artistically informed, scholarly example – one which embraces all points along the continua between
ambiguity and certainty; research that connects the 'Self' to the 'Other'
under study; and 'scholARTistry' (Cahnmann, 2006; Neilsen, 2001, 2005)
which merges social science inquiry with artistic explorations.

The Poet-Scholar Visits the Chicken Plant

To illuminate ways an arts-based scholarship can render the complexity
of bilingual experience, I present three recent ethnographic poems from
research with public school teachers in Georgia, home to increasingly
large numbers of Spanish-speaking immigrant communities (McClure,
2010). Following other educational anthropologists who believe teachers' approaches to curriculum and instruction benefit from ethnographic
fieldwork in their students' lives (Moll & Greenberg, 1990; Tharp &
Gallimore, 1988), I began the F.U.N.D. (Finding UNity in Diversity) Project
with American-born Georgia teachers experiencing sudden and dramatic
increases in the immigrant, Latino populations in their classrooms. After
school and on weekends, we visited places where immigrant students
and their families lived, worked, prayed and played as a stepping stone
to develop engaging and culturally relevant approaches to curriculum
(Cahnmann *et al.*, 2003). One of these places was the local poultry plant
just down the street from a participating F.U.N.D. Project school. The
poultry plant smell was unmistakable, assailing students' and teachers'
noses on many warm schoolyard days. At the time this project took place,
none of the participating teachers had ever been to a poultry plant, an
industry that employed a large number of local and regional Latino students' parents. The poultry plant welcomed our group; donned teachers
in company smocks and hair nets; and walked us through each phase of
the poultry process. Certainly, we learned more about what many Latino
parents did during the day and night shifts, but we also learned something more about our complicated community relationships, something
I had not been able to articulate without the constraints and craft of
poetry.

The artist/teacher/researcher (Irwin & de Cosson, 1994) in me
immediately recognized the import of this shared experience, but it
wasn't until years later when I attended the Dodge Poetry Festival

(www.dodgepoetry.org) in New Jersey that I was able to make a poetic and scholarly leap to new understanding. After several rainy days at the poetry festival, I found myself in a shoe store to replace my badly soaked sneakers. The store clerk asked why I was visiting from out of town and thought I had said I was attending the 'Poultry Festival' happening the same weekend at a nearby location. That poetry and poultry were linguistic bedfellows was reinforced again later when searching for information on the poultry industry; I learned poultry, like poetry and language teaching generally, was not 'exact science,' resonant with the inexactness of biliteracy education for social transformation, and my endeavors as a researcher-poet to document student and teacher change. The three poems that follow this text reflect on several experiences the teachers and I shared through the F.U.N.D. project – the poultry plant tour (Cahnmann-Taylor, in press), a visit to the local flea market (Cahnmann-Taylor, 2008b, 2010) and an invited Latin dance instructor who spent an afternoon teaching teachers and students basic steps in Salsa, Cumbia and Cha-Cha. Each of these three poems helped me engage in the layered, uncertain meanings and intersections between home and school, researcher and researched, art and science. My hope is that by sharing poetic renderings of biliteracy research, I can render an aesthetic interpretation of some of the many challenges and possibilities of biliteracy education in the Southeast and the United States more generally.

GOLDKIST POULTRY, ATHENS, GEORGIA

So cold it could be Alaska on the plant floor
where body heat, endurance, and speed

shelter those with same social security names,
same blue hairnets and gloves. They've moved

from Huehuetenango to Georgia and Texas,
smuggled with them *pupusas* and *discotecas*.

They're indentured to where Leonel can make $7.75
to slice chicken legs: wage enough for a small *piñata*,

a quarter tank of gas. I came South to teach
poetry but the guidance counselor misheard me, reached

a hand to where the wind blows, said the smell
first strikes the throat. *Poetry* and *po' try*, neither one

exact science to measure what's good or done.
So I decided to tour the plant

to learn how families worked while I hurled
children to defiance in verse.

I hoped they'd use words
like *feathers in flight over mud*,

not *shackled* or *smocked* in couplets of *blood*.

ASKING SECOND GRADE TEACHERS TO DANCE

And they move against the wall,
     say *can't, prefer not to, another time*.
          Inside whirls a little girl with tight braids,

pink bulbs tied to each end,
     a boy's arms like banners outstretched in wind,
          feet rustling like fall leaves

across school blacktop,
     screams like seabirds,
          hips like kites in marine breeze.

Inside, each grownup's
     a room with yellow light, shiny
          hardwood, dark felt walls.

Inside, each prances barefoot
     in a flowing white shirt and pants.
          A sweet riff guides them from corners,

takes shape in blue
     taka-taka-tak, back
          to see-saw and swing,

water hose spray and laughter
     tumbling like waves to sand,
          falling down, standing up again

to a drumbeat clap
     till boys' cheeks dimple and girls' bangs flap –
          iridescent pigeons in the park

catching notes of music-bread
     in beaks and wonder
          how they could ever stop

          dancing.

TEACHING POETRY IN GEORGIA SCHOOLS

My house is like a pond, she says. *Is so pretty.*
I ask her to say it again.
Can you say that again?
Did you say 'pond'?

Round body of water behind a house in Vermont
where a white girl skinny dips and geese
make merry with picnics:
How can a house be like a pond?

She tells me Grandmom bakes custard pies.
She has a green carpet in the kitchen.
Her daddy likes candy. There's a waterfall by the door.

I ask her to say it again.
Can you say that again?
Did you say 'waterfall by the door'?

I don't know if there is water by her house,
a splashing image in a cheap frame from the flea market,
or the sound of a neighbor's pipes
flushing through the wall.

She writes about rainbows and spells rain *rian* and *bow*
as a separate word and *door* with two r's and one o
and she sits next to a boy who writes that he is from *Mixeco.*

Her skin is the color of pine bark; eyes framed in small
gold globes like two ponds filled with a life made visible
through close looking. I know how to live in this school trailer,
but I'm from a house like a jewel box.

She asks me to say it again.
Can you say it again?
Did you say 'jewel box?' Tha's nice.

References

Abu-Lughod, L. (1995) A tale of two pregnancies. In R. Behar and D.A. Gordon (eds) *Women Writing Culture* (pp. 339–349). Berkeley: University of California Press.

Baker, C. (2003) *Foundations of Bilingual Education and Bilingualism* (3rd edition). Clevedon: Multilingual Matters.

Barone, T.E. (2008) How arts-based research can change mind. In M. Cahnmann-Taylor and R. Seigesmund (eds) *Arts-based Research in Education: Foundations for Practice* (pp. 28–49). London: Routledge.

Behar, R. (1993) *Translated Woman: Crossing the Border with Esperanza's Story*. Boston: Beacon.

Behar, R. (1995) Writing in my father's name: A diary of Translated Woman's first year. In R. Behar and D.A. Gordon (eds) *Women Writing Culture* (pp. 339–349). Berkeley: University of California Press.

Behar, R. (1996) *The Vulnerable Observer: Anthropology that Breaks Your Heart*. Boston: Beacon.

Behar, R. (2007) *An Island Called Home: Returning to Jewish Cuba*. Rutgers, NJ: Rutgers University Press.

Behar, R. (2008) Between poetry and anthropology: Searching for languages of home. In M. Cahnmann-Taylor and R. Seigesmund (eds) *Arts-based Research in Education: Foundations for Practice* (pp. 55–72). London: Routledge.

Behar, R. and Gordon, D.A. (eds) (1996) *Women Writing Culture*. Berkeley: University of California Press.

Bly, R. (1975) *Leaping Poetry*. Boston: Beacon Press.

Brady, I. (ed.) (1991) *Anthropological Poetics*. Savage, MD: Rowman and Littlefield.

Brady, I. (2000) Anthropological poetics. In N.K. Denzin and Y.S. Lincoln (eds) *Handbook of Qualitative Research* (2nd edition) (pp. 949–979). London: Sage Publications.

Brady, I. (2003) *The Time at Darwin's Reef: Poetic Exploration in Anthropology and History*. Lanham, MD: Alta Mira.

Cahnmann, M. (2003) The craft, practice, and possibility of poetry in educational research. *Educational Researcher* 32 (3), 29–36.

Cahnmann, M. (2006) Reading, living, and writing bilingual poetry as schol-ARTistry in the language arts classroom. *Language Arts* 83 (4), 341–351.

Cahnmann-Taylor, M. (2008a) Introduction. In M. Cahnmann-Taylor and R. Seigesmund (eds) *Arts-based Research in Education: Foundations for Practice* (pp. 3–15). London: Routledge.

Cahnmann-Taylor, M. (2008b) Teaching poetry in Georgia schools. *Rio Grande Review*.

Cahnmann-Taylor, M. (2010) Teaching poetry in Georgia schools. *English Journal* 100 (2), 109.

Cahnmann-Taylor, M. (in press) Goldkist poultry, Athens, Georgia. *Pilgrimmage Magazine*.

Cahnmann-Taylor, M. and Souto-Manning, M. (2010) *Teachers Act Up! Creating Multicultural Learning Communities through Theatre*. New York: Teachers College Press.

Cahnmann-Taylor, M. and Siegesmund, R. (2008). *Arts Based Research in Education: Foundations for Practice*. London: Routledge.

Cahnmann, M., Aaron, J. and Ragsdale, L. (2003, January) *Taking Ourselves to Mexico and Bringing Transformative Introspection Back to Class*. Paper presented at the annual meeting of Qualitative Research (QUIG), Athens, GA.

Corder, S.P. (1967) The significance of learners' errors. *International Review of Applied Linguistics* 5, 161–169.

Diamond, S. (1982) *Totems*. Barrytown, NY: Open Book/Station Hill.

Dulay, H.C. and Burt, M.K. (1973) Should we teach children syntax? *Language Learning* 23, 245–258.

Ellis, R. (1994) *The Study of Second Language Acquisition*. Oxford: Oxford University Press.

Fine, M. (1994) Working the hyphens: Reinventing the self and other in qualitative research. In N. Denzin and Y. Lincoln (eds) *Handbook of Qualitative Research* (pp. 70–82). Newbury Park, CA: Sage Publications.

Fishman, J.A. (1991) *Reversing Language Shift*. Clevedon: Multilingual Matters.

Gosse, D. (2008) Queering identity(ies) and fiction writing in qualitative research. In M. Cahnmann-Taylor and R. Seigesmund (eds) *Arts-based Research in Education: Foundations for Practice* (pp. 182–193). London: Routledge.

Hornberger, N. (1989) Continua of biliteracy. *Review of Educational Research* 59 (3), 271–296.

Hornberger, N. (ed.) (2003) *The Continua of Biliteracy: An Ecological Framework for Educational Policy, Research, and Practice in Multilingual Settings*. Clevedon: Multilingual Matters.

Hornberger, N. and Pütz, M. (eds) (2006) *Language Loyalty, Language Planning, and Language Revitalization: Recent Writings and Reflections from Joshua A. Fishman*. Clevedon: Multilingual Matters.

Hornberger, N. and Skilton-Sylvester, E. (2000) Revisiting the continua of biliteracy: International and critical perspectives. *Language and Education* 14 (2), 96–122.

Hymes, D. (1972) Editorial introduction to 'Language in Society'. *Language in Society* 1, 1–14.

Hymes, D. (1981) *'In vain I tried to tell you': Essays in Native American Ethnopoetics*. Philadelphia: University of Pennsylvania Press.

Hymes, D. (1998) When is oral narrative poetry? Generative form and its pragmatic conditions. *Pragmatics* 8 (4), 475–500.

Hymes, D. (2003) *Now I Know Only So Far: Essays in Ethnopoetics*. Lincoln: University of Nebraska Press.

Irwin, R. and de Cosson A. (2004) *A/r/tography: Rendering Self through Arts-based Living Inquiry*. Vancouver: Pacific Educational Press.

Kondo, D.K. (1995) Bad girls: Theatre, women of color, and the politics of representation. In R. Behar and D.A. Gordon (eds) *Women Writing Culture*. Berkeley: University of California Press.

Maynard, K. (2001) *Sunk Like God behind the House*. Kent, OH: Kent State University Press.

Maynard, K. (2002) An imagination of order: The suspicion of structure in anthropology and poetry. *Antioch Review* 60 (2), 220–243.

Maynard, K. and Cahnmann-Taylor, M. (2010) Anthropology at the edge of words: Where poetry and ethnography meet. *Anthropology and Humanism* 35 (1), 2–19.

McClure, G. (2010) Pushing back and pulling away: Coteaching English language learners in the new Latino South. PhD thesis, University of Georgia, Athens, GA.

Moll, L.C. and Greenberg, J.B. (1990) Creating zones of possibilities: Combining social contexts for instruction. In L.C. Moll (ed.) *Vygotsky and Education: Instructional Implications and Applications of Sociohistorical Psychology* (pp. 319–348). New York: Cambridge University Press.

Neilsen, L. (2001) Scribbler: Notes on writing and learning inquiry. In L. Neilsen, A. Cole and G.J. Knowles (eds) *The Art of Writing Inquiry* (pp. 253–272). Toronto: Backalong Books.

Neilsen, L. (2005) *Homepage* – Online document: http://www.iirc.mcgill.ca/collaborators/collabln.html.

Pak, H.R. (2003) When MT is L2: The Korean church school as a context for cultural identity. In N.H. Hornberger (ed.) *Continua of Biliteracy: An Ecological Framework for Educational Policy, Research, and Practice in Multicultural Settings.* Clevedon: Multilingual Matters.

Pavlenko, A. (2006) *Bilingual Minds: Emotional Experience, Expression, and Repression.* Clevedon, England: Multilingual Matters.

Ramirez, J.D., Yuen, S.D. and Ramey, D.R. (1991) *Executive Summary: Final report: Longitudinal Study of Structured English Immersion Strategy, Early-exit and Late-exit Transitional Bilingual Education Programs for Language-minority Children* (Contract no. 300-87-0156). Washington, DC: US Department of Education.

Rosaldo, R. (1989) *Culture and Truth: The Remaking of Social Analysis.* Boston: Beacon.

Rosaldo, R. (2001) El angel de la guarda: Lessons of writing poetry. *Rhetoric Review* 20(3&4), 359–367.

Rose, D. (1991) In search of experience: The anthropological poetics of Stanley Diamond. In I. Brady (ed.) *Anthropological Poetics* (pp. 219–233). Savage, MD: Rowman and Littlefield.

Saldana, J. (2005) *Ethnodrama: An Anthology of Reality Theatre.* Walnut Creek, CA: AltaMira Press.

Shavelson, R.J. and Towne, L. (eds) (2002) *Scientific Research in Education.* Washington, DC: National Academy Press.

Springgay, S. (2008) Nurse-In: Breastfeeding and a/r/tographical research. In M. Cahnmann-Taylor and R.Seigesmund (eds) *Arts-based Research in Education: Foundations for Practice* (pp. 137–141). London: Routledge.

Stacey, J. (1991) Can there be a feminist ethnography? In. S.B. Gluck and D. Patai (eds) *Women's words: The Feminist Practice of Oral History* (pp. 111–120). New York: Routledge.

Stoller, P. (2005) *Gallery Bundu: A Story about an African Past.* Chicago: University of Chicago Press.

Tharp, R. and Gallimore, R. (1988) *Rousing Minds to Life: Teaching, Learning, and Schooling in Social Context.* New York: Cambridge University Press.

Van-Maanen, J. (1988) *Tales of the Field: On Writing Ethnography.* Chicago: The University of Chicago Press.

Policy and Planning for Linguistic Diversity in Education

Thematic Overview III

Unpeeling, Slicing and Stirring the Onion – Questions and Certitudes in Policy and Planning for Linguistic Diversity in Education

TERESA L. McCARTY

Readers familiar with Nancy Hornberger's work will recognize immediately the significance of key words in this chapter title for the field of language policy and planning (LPP). In a 1996 theme issue of *TESOL Quarterly* devoted to the role of English language teaching professionals in LPP, Nancy Hornberger and Thomas Ricento introduced the metaphor of 'unpeeling the onion' to represent a 'schema of agents, levels, and [LPP] processes ... that together make up the LPP whole' (Ricento & Hornberger, 1996: 408). Like an onion, all layers of the policy process – national, institutional, intergroup and interpersonal – intersect and conjoin. In a 2007 *TESOL Quarterly* revisitation of local enactments of language policy (Ramanathan & Morgan, 2007), Hornberger and David Cassels Johnson elaborated the metaphor, showing the power of ethnography to 'slice through the layers of the LPP onion ... to reveal agentive spaces in which local actors implement, interpret, and perhaps resist policy initiatives in varying and unique ways' (2007: 509). More recently, Kate Menken and Ofelia García extended the onion metaphor, urging us to attend more closely to education practitioners as '*stirrers* of the onion, producing the dynamism that moves the performances of all of the actors' (2010: 259, emphasis added).

In this chapter, I examine the metaphorical LPP onion, first tracing its genesis and maturation as a field of study and practice, then focusing on present 'disciplinary reorientations' (Canagarajah, 2005a: xvi) that investigate grounded manifestations of policy processes in practice. These reorientations, which Nancy Hornberger's research has spurred, lead me to pose twin questions for the field. Developing themes from her plenary speech at the 2008 Annual Meeting of the American Association of Applied Linguistics (AAAL) (Hornberger, 2009), I consider these questions in light of what we know – 'certainties,' as Hornberger described them in that speech – rooted in the experiences of Indigenous/minoritized communities.

Seeds, Roots, and Sprouts of the LPP Onion[1]

As an informal activity, LPP 'is as old as language itself,' writes Susan Wright, and is integral 'in the distribution of power and resources in all societies' (2004: 1). As a formal field of study, however, LPP is relatively young, having grown out of pragmatic concerns with solving language 'problems' in decolonizing multilingual states during the second half of the 20th century. As Wright recounts, 'among the many...problems left by the departing colonial powers [was] a requirement to solve the logistics of communication in order to govern... and to modernize' (2004: 8). Thus, the principal questions were which languages to develop (e.g. colonial, Indigenous, lingua franca) for which purposes in the context of nation building (Ricento, 2000: 197–200).[2]

In addressing these issues, early LPP scholarship reflected a belief in the efficacy of language planning (Wright, 2004: 9). Einar Haugen, the first to introduce the term language planning in the scholarly literature in 1959, described it as the 'exercise of judgment in the form of choices among available linguistic forms' (1972a: 512). This framework was later famously reformulated by Robert Cooper as a multi-faceted question: 'What *actors* attempt to influence what *behaviors* of which *people* for what *ends* under what *conditions* by what *means* through what *decision-making process* with what *effect*?' (1989: 98). From this perspective, LPP is conceived as rational decision-making: 'The agent commonly evaluates competing language plans within the framework of cost/benefit analysis,' Ricento and Hornberger explain (1996: 406).

In a departure from these earlier assumptions, more recent scholarship interrogates the ideological, social-structural and historical bases of LPP, emphasizing relationships among language, power and inequality (May, 2001; Pennycook, 2001; Tollefson, 2002). Critical approaches view policies as ideological constructs that reflect and (re)produce the distribution of power within the larger society. Tollefson (1991, 2002, 2006) characterizes this as an historical-structural approach. The critical perspective is committed to praxis, recognizing that even as LPP is a mechanism for structuring inequalities, it can open up what Hornberger (2006a) calls 'ideological and implementational spaces' for social-educational change.

In both the rationalistic and critical paradigms, policy has alternatively been viewed as arising *from* planning interventions – as, for example, in Kaplan and Baldauf's notion of policy as a 'body of ideas, laws, ... rules and practices intended to achieve the planning change in the society' (1997: xi) – or giving rise *to* language planning, as in Ricento's definition of planning as the 'development, implementation, and evaluation of specific language policies' (2006: 18; cf. Baldauf, 2006: 148–149). It was Hornberger (1994, 1996a, 2006b) who brought these models of the planning-policy relationship together in an integrative framework that cross-indexed *types* of language planning (status, acquisition and corpus) with language policy and cultivation *goals* (e.g., policy goals of standardization or officialization; cultivation goals of revival, maintenance, spread).[3] 'The truth is,' she points out, 'that the LPP designation is useful ... as a reminder of how inextricably related language planning and policy are' (2006b: 25).

This complexity has been conceptually elaborated in ecological models of LPP. Voegelin *et al.* (1967) and Haugen (1972b) are credited with introducing the ecology metaphor in the field of linguistics. 'The key property of any ecology is structured diversity,' Mühlhäusler observes, and 'ecological language planning advocates the rebuilding of self-regulating diversity' (2000: 306, 310). Recognizing that in any sociocultural environment, 'some languages are more equal than others,' an ecological approach 'draws attention to the role of [LPP] in dynamic relationships among speakers, social contexts, and languages,' Hornberger and Hult write (2008: 282, 292). Phillipson and Skutnabb-Kangas (1996: 436) include the promotion of linguistic human rights, multilingualism and 'equality in communication' in an ecology-of-language paradigm. Linguistic ecology, then, can be thought of as a 'supra-metaphor' for the LPP onion. Later in this chapter I discuss Hornberger's productive use of this conceptual approach in examining multilingual education policy and practice, but first I turn to methodological approaches and advances in researching the LPP onion.

The critical sociocultural-ethnographic turn

Hornberger's integrative framework and the onion and ecology metaphors signal more recent orientations toward LPP, in which planning and policy are conceived not as separable acts, but as mutually constitutive, interdependent and co-occurring sociocultural processes (McCarty, 2004, 2011). Language policies 'are living, dynamic forces that find their viability and articulation in the most local of spaces,' Ramanathan maintains, and must be 'understood in terms of how they get translated into actual practice' (2005a: 89–90). To rephrase Heath *et al*.'s discussion of 'culture as a verb,' policy too is best understood as a verb; it 'never just "is," but rather "does" ' (2008: 7).

One crucial implication of this approach is that LPP research is not restricted to or even focused primarily on official, macro-level policy declarations or texts. This is not to ignore the consequential nature of official policy, but to place those policy processes in context as part of a larger sociocultural system (McCarty, 2011; Sutton & Levinson, 2001). Language policy 'exists even where it has not been made explicit or established by authority,' Spolsky writes, and can be inferred from people's language practices, ideologies and beliefs (2004: 8). Schiffman (1996), Shohamy (2006) and others have distinguished between overt and covert, *de jure* and *de facto* language policies: '[Language policy] can exist at all levels of decision making about languages,' Shohamy stresses, 'as small as individuals and families, making decisions about the languages to be used . . . at home' as well as in 'schools, cities, regions, nations, territories, or in the global context' (2006: 48). King *et al*.'s (2008) work on family language policy, Hornberger and Johnson's (2007) and McCarty's (2011) ethnographies of language policy, Menken and García's (2010) exploration of teachers as policy-makers, Ramanathan's (2010a, 2010b) studies of language policy and health, and Shohamy and Gorter's (2008) exploration of linguistic landscapes exemplify the range of research being conducted within this broadened definition of the field.

The shift in focus to a more dynamic, process-oriented view of policy reflects a concomitant shift in scholarly attention from the universal to the local (Baldauf, 2006; Canagarajah, 2005b). 'There is a move,' Pennycook writes, ' . . . to capture what actually happens in particular places and at particular times' (2010: 1). Noting this shift in the state of the field as early as 1996, Hornberger put it this way:

> [I]n sociolinguistics more generally, and indeed the social sciences as a whole, scholarly attention has steadily shifted toward the individual and the local community as active agents in dialogue and interaction with their social environment, and away from a governmental, institutional, or societal level focus. It is also true that everywhere we look in the world, . . . local initiatives are gaining over national and international ones in terms of producing long-term change. (1996a: 11)

These shifts coincide with corresponding sociocultural 'turns' in language and literacy and policy studies. The New Literacy Studies advanced by Street (1984, 1993, 2001), Gee (2008), Collins (1995; Collins & Blot, 2003),

Lankshear *et al.* (1997) and the New London Group (1996) countered dominant views of literacy as a decontextualized, politically neutral, technical and hence 'standardizable' skill, elucidating the embeddedness of multifarious literacy practices within particular sociocultural settings and power regimes. As Wiley points out, the New Literacy Studies 'demonstrates a strikingly parallel approach to underlying assumptions' in critical approaches to LPP (1996: 116). In like manner, the anthropology of policy illuminates how decontextualized reifications of static text-based policy cloak the power relations through which policies are constructed and perform their social role (Shore & Wright, 1997: 8). Applying this approach to education policy, Levinson *et al.* advocate for a view of 'the entire policy process as a complex set of interdependent sociocultural practices' – 'a practice of power' (2009: 767–768).

These reorientations require 'a shift in our practices of knowledge making,' Canagarajah observes (2005a: xiv). With its overriding concern with cultural interpretation, ethnography is ideally suited to critically examine these complex LPP processes, exposing grounded manifestations of explicit and implicit policy-making at multiple levels and interstices of the metaphorical LPP onion. As Canagarajah writes, '[w]hatever the type or level of policy-making addressed, ethnography can bring out surprising findings about language relationships that elude those acting from outside the community' (2006: 159).

In 2007, Hornberger and Johnson introduced the ethnography of language policy, explaining that it can:

> ... include textual and historical analyses of policy texts but must be based on an ethnographic understanding of some local context. The texts are nothing without the human agents who act as interpretive conduits between the language policy levels (or layers of the LPP onion). (2007: 528)

In a subsequent exposition they add that 'casting an ethnographic eye on language planning at individual, classroom, school, community, regional, national, and global levels can and does serve to uncover the indistinct voices, covert motivations, embedded ideologies, invisible instances, or unintended consequences of LPP as it is created, interpreted, and appropriated in particular contexts' (Hornberger & Johnson, 2011: 24; see also Johnson, 2009).

We can trace the genealogy of the ethnography of language policy to the sociology of language introduced by Fishman (1968); the educational linguistics advanced by Spolsky (1978, Spolsky & Hult, 2008) and developed in Dell Hymes's and Hornberger's educational linguistics program at the University of Pennsylvania (Hornberger, 2001, 2003a); and the union of educational and linguistic anthropology that emerged in the 1960s and 1970s. From educational anthropology came a view of education as a cultural process. From linguistic anthropology came a view of talk as a 'constitutive feature' of human social life (Goodwin & Duranti, 1992), as reflected in the ethnography of communication pioneered by John Gumperz and Dell Hymes (1964, 1972). In the decades following, Hornberger tells us, 'education became a primary arena for sociolinguistic research' (2003a: 245, 246). Out of these interdisciplinary unions came now-classic ethnographic studies of the functions of language in educational settings (Cazden et al., 1972; Green & Wallat, 1981), children's language practices in and out of school (Gilmore & Glatthorn, 1982) and culturally diverse ways of speaking and learning (Heath, 1983; Philips, 1983). As Hornberger describes, in this paradigm (socio)linguistic competence is 'by definition variable within individuals (from event to event), across individuals, and across speech communities' (2003a: 247).

This research catalyzed 'four decades of rich interdisciplinary work, still going strong,' Hornberger writes (2003a: 245).[4] 'Still going strong' is also a perfect characterization of Nancy Hornberger. Her scholarly corpus is incredibly rich – much too extensive to do justice to in this overview. Instead, I want to highlight two principal pillars of that work, framing them in terms of the questions and 'certainties' (Hornberger, 2009) for multilingual education policy and practice they raise.

Can Schools Be Agents of Language and Cultural Maintenance and Revitalization?

A major artery of LPP research addresses the viability of minoritized languages and speech communities in the face of larger homogenizing and stratifying forces. Readers of this volume are familiar with the grim statistics on worldwide language loss: Of some 6800 languages currently spoken on the planet, as many as 90% are predicted to fall silent by century's end (Nettle & Romaine, 2000; UNESCO, 2003). Of these, the majority will be Indigenous languages (McCarty et al., 2008). Fishman has compellingly theorized the macro-level causes of language shift: 'The destruction of languages is concretely mirrored [in the destruction] of the weak by the strong, of the unique and traditional by the uniformizing' (1991: 4). What is less well understood – and what ethnography is so well equipped to ferret out – are the local realities and role of LPP in shift, maintenance and revitalization.

In 1988, Hornberger published the first book-length ethnographic study to address these issues, a case study of bilingual education policy and practice in the largely Indigenous and rural Department of Puno, Peru. With the goal of understanding the relationship between official policy and local language practices, she asks:

(1) Can language maintenance be planned? and,
(2) Can schools be effective agents for language maintenance? (1988: 19)

The answers are as complex as the ethnography itself. At the center of the LPP onion in this case were local language uses and ideologies that positioned Quechua as the extra-school, *ayllu* or home-community language, and Spanish as the language of the school and other outside institutions. Hornberger described how the decreasing isolation and low social status of Quechua speakers mitigated against the micro-level (*ayllu*) language transmission nexus, while problems of implementation and overall government instability undermined macro-level policies for Quechua maintenance. Weighing these interlocking factors, she concluded:

> If a bilingual education program is to make any contribution to language maintenance, it seems most likely that it should be an enrichment... program. Enrichment, or two-way, bilingual education reflects a valuing of Quechua by society not only for Quechua speakers but also for non-Quechua speakers. Thus we return to the importance of the overall societal context in any consideration of language maintenance. (1988: 236)

This masterful study presaged later eco-linguistic research and contains certitudes from which we continue to learn. As Hornberger describes them in her AAAL plenary speech, Certainty No. 1 is that while national, macro-level policies open up 'ideological and implementational spaces for multilingual education,' those spaces are not 'unproblematically accepted or adopted' by local social actors (2009: 199). '[T]op-down policy is not enough,' she insists, citing Certainty No. 2; 'any policy may fail if there is no bottom-up, local support' (2009: 199).

Since the publication of Hornberger's Quechua ethnography, a flourishing ethnographic literature has explored the role of bi/multilingual education policy in maintaining minoritized tongues, including (by publication date): Davis's (1994) ethnography of communication in Luxembourg; Freeman's (1998) study of discourse practices at the Oyster Bilingual School in Washington, DC; Aikman's (1999) study of intercultural education and mother tongue literacy among the Arakmbut in the Peruvian Amazon; Jaffe's (1999) examination of language politics and ideology on Corsica; Heller's (1999) sociolinguistic ethnography of Francophone adolescents in Anglophone Canada; King's (2001) research on Quichua language shift and revitalization in Ecuador;[5] House's (2002) examination of Navajo language shift; McCarty's (2002) 'critical life history' of bilingual-bicultural education in a Navajo community school; Patrick's (2003) ethnography of language use among the Inuit of Arctic Québec; Ramanathan's (2005b) critical ethnography of vernacular-medium education in Gujarat; and Wyman's (in press) study of Yup'ik youth culture and language survivance in the Far North.

Over this same period, numerous edited volumes using ethnographic approaches have further enriched our understanding of the role of educational language policy in promoting or constraining Indigenous language and literacy development: Hornberger (1996b) and McCarty and Zepeda (1995, 1998) provided accounts of bottom-up language and literacy planning in the Americas; Henze and Davis (1999) explored identity and authenticity in LPP in the Pacific Rim; May (1999) surveyed Indigenous community-based education; May and Aikman (2003) presented a comparative investigation into new developments in Indigenous education theory and practice; King and Hornberger (2004) examined Quechua sociolinguistics; McCarty and Wyman (2009) researched Indigenous youth language practices; and Rockwell and Gomes (2009) worked to 'rethink' Indigenous education from a Latin American perspective. Canagarajah (2005b), García *et al.* (2006), Heller and Martin-Jones (2001), Hornberger (2003c), Hult (2010), Lin and Martin (2005), McCarty (2011), Ramanathan and Morgan (2007) and Skutnabb-Kangas *et al.* (2009) offered additional comparative case studies of local enactments of multilingual education policies and practices in settings around the globe. This research has also extended to heritage and community language education, which by definition is 'about developing heritage language learners' biliteracy in both the dominant societal language and the heritage language, whether these be indigenous, immigrant, ethnic, second or foreign languages in any particular context' (Hornberger, 2005: 102).

Nancy Hornberger was right: This rich interdisciplinary work is indeed 'still going strong!' More than 20 years after her initial Quechua study, Hornberger (2008a) continues to challenge our thinking about the role of educational LPP in sustaining linguistic and cultural diversity, asking plainly: 'Can schools save Indigenous languages?' Offering case studies and commentaries from Sámiland, Latin America, Aotearoa/New Zealand, Israel, Africa and Native North America, Hornberger and her coauthors show the potential of multilingual education to open spaces for language revitalization – Certainty No. 10 (Hornberger, 2009: 207) –

even as they acknowledge that 'schools alone are not enough to do the job' (Hornberger, 2008b: 1). Yet, more than 'saving' languages, this work is about 'the necessity for Indigenous peoples to take the lead in these matters,' Hornberger emphasizes (2008b: 10). 'Local knowledges, local identities, local languages, local practices, local literacies ... are among the things local being claimed by Indigenous educators in these settings – Certainty No. 8 (2009: 206–207).[6] Language being 'one of the most visible elements of Indigenous identity,' she adds, the project of language reclamation also 'affords choices for affirming our own' – Certainty No. 9 (2009: 207).

These certitudes exemplify a constant current in Nancy Hornberger's work: the empowerment of local stakeholders, especially education practitioners. The 'teacher exercises language policy power through pedagogical decisions that can ... incorporate minority languages, thus creating a space in which multilingualism is used as a resource,' Hornberger and Johnson point out (2007: 527). I turn now to this second pillar of her work: the questions and certainties entailed by placing the classroom practitioner 'at the heart' of the LPP onion (Ricento & Hornberger, 1996: 417).

Where is the Practitioner in LPP Practice?

> In [my] work, and through various metaphors – from creating successful contexts for biliteracy to bottom-up language planning, from unpeeling and slicing the language policy onion to opening up implementational and ideological spaces for multilingual education, from activating Indigenous voices to saving Indigenous languages – I have sought to foreground ... the fundamental importance of recognizing, incorporating, building on, and extending the language repertoires learners bring to the classroom. Key in all of this ... is the crucial role of educators in their classrooms and the decisions they make about language use, both their own and their students'.

So wrote Nancy Hornberger in the Foreword to Menken and García's recent book on educators as language policy-makers (Hornberger, 2010: xiii). Reflecting the scholarly reorientations discussed earlier, Menken and García position educators 'at the epicenter' of the policy process: 'In this way,' they say, 'we move beyond top-down, bottom-up, or even side-by-side divisions to a conceptualization of language policy as a far more dynamic, interactive, and real-life process' (2010: 4).

An appreciation for the role of education practitioners as animators of language policy came early in Nancy Hornberger's life, when, as a fifth-grader, her teacher 'voluntarily taught Spanish before school hours' (Hornberger, 1988: xv). In college, Hornberger became a practitioner herself, volunteering to teach children of Quechua migrant workers in Arequipa, Peru. 'These experiences provided the starting points,' she says, for a lifetime of language study and work in the Andes (1988: xv).

Her 1988 study brought these starting points to the fore of LPP studies, and it is worth returning to that study to illustrate the ways in which local educators 'may themselves be the ones opening [or closing] spaces for multilingual education' – another instantiation of Certainty No. 2 (Hornberger, 2009: 200). The book is a treasure trove of ethnographic insights; here, I focus on Hornberger's observation of a single lesson to elucidate her larger point. In a second-grade classroom, the teacher asks Quechua-speaking students to draw and label (in Spanish) specific vegetable foods. Despite the fact that these are foods with which the children are familiar, they are stymied by this seemingly simple task. Finally, the teacher resorts to drawing the foods for the students to copy. 'In fact,' Hornberger writes, the 'impression one would have after hours and hours spent observing in these classrooms is that the pupils are incapable of reasoning' (1988: 202). When instruction is provided in Quechua, however, 'this lamentable cycle' is broken (1988: 202). In this case, bilingual scaffolding fosters 'transfer of language and literacy development' across multiple modalities, media and codes, enabling 'learners to access content through the linguistic resources they bring to the classroom while simultaneously acquiring new ones' – Certainty No. 7 (Hornberger, 2009: 205).

In this ethnographic vignette we see exemplified key conceptual tools Hornberger has elaborated for theorizing (and promoting) practitioner agency. First is her well-known continua framework, which, as she describes, shows 'the multiple and complex interrelationships between bilingualism and literacy and the importance of the contexts, media, and content through which biliteracy develops' (2003b: xiv; for a full explanation of the continua of biliteracy, see Hornberger & Skilton-Sylvester, 2000; for studies applying the continua framework, see Hornberger, 2003c). All points in the continua interact and interrelate, and when activated – as with the bilingual scaffolding above – perceived cognitive-linguistic deficiencies are revealed to be not the failing of the learners but of the pedagogical approach.

Second, understanding and proactively engineering these school- and classroom-based processes requires knowledge of the larger sociolinguistic ecology and the inequities among languages and speakers that obtain. 'Ecology of language,' Hornberger maintains, 'recognizes that planning for any one language . . . necessarily entails planning for all languages impinging on that one. The power relations . . . among languages and their speakers cannot be ignored' (2006c: 280). For minoritized languages, the goal is to 'achieve a balance along a full range of continua of biliteracy,' thereby counteracting 'hegemonic social processes and permit[ting] all students' languages to become valuable resources for themselves and their communities' (Hornberger & Hult, 2008: 284). This brings us to Certainty No. 3: 'Ecological language policies take into account the power relations among languages and promote multilingual uses in all societal domains' (Hornberger, 2009: 200).

Finally, this vignette highlights a theme that resounds in all of Nancy Hornberger's work: the activation of the voice(s) of those who fight to counter language-repressive regimes. Voice, she explains, 'is the speaking consciousness . . . , articulated as social practice, in dialogue with others and in situated contexts' (2006c: 284). In multilingual education policy and planning, the activation of practitioners' voices co-activates student voices, tilting 'use of the [minoritized] language away from . . . discrimination and oppression and toward emancipation, self-determination, and empowerment' (Hornberger, 2006c: 289). This directs us back to Certainty No. 8: 'Multilingual education activates voices for reclaiming the local' (2009: 206).

Studies in support of these certainties abound (including those in this book); space prohibits a full discussion here. All of this research illuminates what Hornberger (1996a: 3) has called literacy's 'two-faced potential' – and, by extension, that of LPP – to 'both open and bar doors of opportunity.'

'We Who Imagine Multilingual Schools'

In this chapter I have only touched on the high points of Hornberger's corpus and the LPP literature. I have addressed but eight of her 10 certainties, yet readers will find reflections of all 10 in other chapters. At its core, this body of work surfaces the possibilities for what Hornberger's mentor, Richard Ruiz (1984), calls a language-as-a-resource approach. Despite the injustices of language-restrictionist policies, Hornberger's work points us toward the indefatigable promise of human agency in cracking open spaces of hope and possibility. 'I am more convinced than ever that we who imagine multilingual schools have the long-term advantage,' she reflects, concluding a discussion of recent English-only policies in García *et al.*'s (2006) *Imagining Multilingual Schools*. 'Threat and fear and restriction can never prevail in the grand scheme of things,' Hornberger insists, 'but a profuse and rich diversity of ways of speaking, meaning, thinking, valuing and being will' (2006a: 234).

For we who, like Nancy Hornberger, 'imagine multilingual schools,' this is the foremost certainty of all.

Notes

1. Parts of this overview were adapted from the introductory chapter in McCarty (2011).
2. See Fishman *et al.* (1968) for an early exposition of these goals in LPP research and practice.
3. See also the parallel 'framework for language planning goals by levels and awareness' presented by Baldauf (2006: 150–151).
4. See Hornberger and Johnson (2011) for a review of this research.
5. King's (2001) study, in particular, complements Hornberger's early ethnography. King examined language use, attitudes and instruction in two Quichua communities in Ecuador, one in which a shift to Spanish was far advanced, and another that was rapidly moving from Quichua monolingualism to Spanish monolingualism. Despite the fact that Ecuador has an official policy of intercultural education, for members of both communities 'Quichua remains on the periphery of their daily lives' (King, 2001: 185). The school affords 'an important foothold' for Quichua maintenance, but is insufficient to overcome the extreme economic and social pressures favoring Spanish. King shows ethnographically how those pressures are reflected in conflicting ideologies that, on the one hand, link Quichua to ethnic identity, and, on the other, position Spanish as the language of the *buena gente* or 'decent people' (2001: 39; see also King, 1999, 2000).
6. Romaine makes a similar point, saying that putting the onus 'on restoration of intergenerational transmission as the social criterion' of successful language revitalization runs 'the risk of dismissing the value of the journey, which is at least as, if not more important . . . as long as each step is regarded as valuable to the community concerned' (2006: 465).

References

Aikman, S. (1999) *Intercultural Education and Literacy: An Ethnographic Study of Indigenous Knowledge and Learning in the Peruvian Amazon.* Amsterdam/Philadelphia: John Benjamins.
Baldauf, R.B., Jr. (2006) Rearticulating the case for micro language planning in a language ecology context. *Current Issues in Language Planning* 7 (2, 3), 147–170.
Canagarajah, S. (2005a) Introduction. In A.S. Canagarajah (ed.) *Reclaiming the Local in Language Policy and Practice* (pp. xiii–xxx). Mahwah, NJ: Lawrence Erlbaum.
Canagarajah, A.S. (ed.) (2005b) *Reclaiming the Local in Language Policy and Practice.* Mahwah, NJ: Lawrence Erlbaum
Canagarajah, S. (2006) Ethnographic methods in language policy. In T. Ricento (ed.) *An Introduction to Language Policy: Theory and Method* (pp. 153–169). Malden, MA: Blackwell.

Cazden, C.B., John, V.P. and Hymes, D. (eds) (1972) *Functions of Language in the Classroom*. New York: Teachers College Press.

Collins, J. (1995) Literacy and literacies. *Annual Review of Anthropology* 24, 75–93.

Collins, J. and Blot, R. (2003) *Literacy and Literacies: Texts, Power, and Identity*. Cambridge, UK: Cambridge University Press.

Cooper, R.L. (1989) *Language Planning and Social Change*. Cambridge, UK: Cambridge University Press.

Davis, K.A. (1994) *Language Planning in Multilingual Contexts: Policies, Communities, and Schools in Luxembourg*. Amsterdam/Philadelphia: John Benjamins.

Fishman, J.A., Ferguson, C.A. and Das Gupta, J. (eds) (1968) *Language Problems of Developing Nations*. New York: John Wiley and Sons.

Fishman, J.A. (ed.) (1968) *Readings in the Sociology of Language*. The Hague: Mouton.

Fishman, J.A. (1991) *Reversing Language Shift: Theoretical and Empirical Foundations of Assistance to Threatened Languages*. Clevedon: Multilingual Matters.

Freeman, R. (1998) *Bilingual Education and Social Change*. Clevedon: Multilingual Matters.

García, O., Skutnabb-Kangas, T. and Torres-Guzmán, M. (eds) (2006) *Imagining Multilingual Schools: Languages in Education and Glocalization*. Clevedon: Multilingual Matters.

Gee, J.P. (2008) *Social Linguistics and Literacies: Ideology in Discourses*. New York: Routledge.

Gilmore, P. and Glatthorn, A.A. (eds) (1982) *Children In and Out of School: Ethnography and Education*. Washington, DC: Harcourt Brace Jovanovich and Center for Applied Linguistics.

Goodwin, C. and Duranti, A. (eds) (1992) *Rethinking Context: Language as an Interactive Phenomenon*. Cambridge, UK: Cambridge University Press.

Green, J. and Wallat, C. (eds) (1981) *Ethnography and Language in Educational Settings*. Norwood, NJ: Ablex.

Gumperz, J.J. and Hymes, D. (eds) (1964) The ethnography of communication. *American Anthropologist* 66 (6), 137–153.

Gumperz, J.J. and Hymes, D. (eds) (1972) *Directions in Sociolinguistics: The Ethnography of Communication*. New York: Basil Blackwell.

Haugen, E. (1972a) Linguistics and language planning. In E.S. Firchow, K. Grimstad, N. Hasselmo and W.A. O'Neil (eds) *Studies by Einar Haugen Presented on the Occasion of his 65th Birthday – April 19, 1971* (pp. 510–530). The Hague: Mouton.

Haugen, E. (1972b) *The Ecology of Language: Essays by Einar Haugen*. Stanford, CA: Stanford University Press.

Heath, S.B. (1983) *Ways with Words: Language, Life, and Work in Communities and Classrooms*. Cambridge, UK: Cambridge University Press.

Heath, S.B., Street, B.V. and Mills, M. (2008) *On Ethnography: Approaches to Language and Literacy Research*. New York: Teachers College Press and National Conference on Research in Language and Literacy (NCRLL).

Heller, M. (1999) *Linguistic Minorities and Modernity: A Sociolinguistic Ethnography*. London: Longman.

Heller, M. and Martin-Jones, M. (eds) (2001) *Voices of Modernity: A Sociolinguistic Ethnography*. London: Longman.

Henze, R. and Davis, K.A. (guest eds) (1999) Authenticity and identity: Lessons from Indigenous language education. Special issue, *Anthropology and Education Quarterly* 30 (1), 3–21.

Hornberger, N.H. (1988) *Bilingual Education and Language Maintenance: A Southern Peruvian Quechua Case.* Dordrecht, Holland: Foris.

Hornberger, N.H. (1994) Literacy and language planning. *Language and Education* 8 (1, 2), 75–87.

Hornberger, N.H. (1996a) Indigenous literacies in the Americas. In N.H. Hornberger (ed.) *Indigenous Literacies in the Americas: Language Planning from the Bottom Up* (pp. 3–11). Berlin: Mouton de Gruyter.

Hornberger, N.H. (ed.) (1996b) *Indigenous Literacies in the Americas: Language Planning from the Bottom Up.* Berlin: Mouton de Gruyter.

Hornberger, N.H. (2001) Educational linguistics as a field: A view from Penn's program on the occasion of its 25th anniversary. *Working Papers in Educational Linguistics* 17 (1–2), 1–26.

Hornberger, N.H. (2003a) Linguistic anthropology of education (LAE) in context. In S. Wortham and B. Rymes (eds) *Linguistic Anthropology of Education* (pp. 245–270). Westport, CT: Praeger.

Hornberger, N.H. (2003b) Introduction. In N.H. Hornberger (ed.) *Continua of Biliteracy: An Ecological Framework for Educational Policy, Research, and Practice in Multilingual Settings* (pp. xii–xxiii). Clevedon: Multilingual Matters.

Hornberger, N.H. (ed.) (2003c) *Continua of Biliteracy: An Ecological Framework for Educational Policy, Research, and Practice in Multilingual Settings.* Clevedon: Multilingual Matters.

Hornberger, N.H. (2005) Heritage/community language education: U.S. and Australian perspectives. *International Journal of Bilingual Education and Bilingualism* 8 (2, 3), 101–108.

Hornberger, N.H. (2006a) *Nichols* to *NCLB:* Local and global perspectives on US language education policy. In O. García, T. Skutnabb-Kangas and M.E. Torres-Guzmán (eds) *Imagining Multilingual Schools: Languages in Education and Glocalization* (pp. 223–237). Clevedon: Multilingual Matters.

Hornberger, N.H. (2006b) Frameworks and models in language policy and planning. In T. Ricento (ed.) *An Introduction to Language Policy: Theory and Method* (pp. 24–31). Malden, MA: Blackwell.

Hornberger, N.H. (2006c) Voice and biliteracy in Indigenous language revitalization: Contentious educational practices in Quechua, Guarani, and Māori contexts. *Journal of Language, Identity, and Education* 5 (4), 277–292.

Hornberger, N.H. (ed.) (2008a) *Can Schools Save Indigenous Languages? Policy and Practice on Four Continents.* New York: Palgrave Macmillan.

Hornberger, N.H. (2008b) Introduction: Can schools save Indigenous languages? Policy and practice on four continents. In N.H. Hornberger (ed.) *Can Schools Save Indigenous Languages? Policy and Practice on Four Continents* (pp. 1–12). New York: Palgrave Macmillan.

Hornberger, N.H. (2009) Multilingual education policy and practice: Ten certainties (grounded in Indigenous experience). *Language Teaching* 42 (2), 197–211.

Hornberger, N.H. (2010) Foreword. In K. Menken and O. García (eds) *Negotiating Language Policies in Schools: Educators as Policymakers* (pp. xi–xiii). New York: Routledge.

Hornberger, N.H. and Hult, F.M. (2008). Ecological language policy. In B. Spolsky and F.M. Hult (eds) *The Handbook of Educational Linguistics* (pp. 280–296). Malden, MA: Blackwell.

Hornberger, N.H. and Johnson, D.C. (2007) Slicing the onion ethnographically: Layers and spaces in multilingual language education policy and practice. *TESOL Quarterly* 41 (3), 509–532.

Hornberger, N.H. and Johnson, D.C. (2011) Ethnography of language policy. In T.L. McCarty (ed.) *Ethnography and Language Policy* (pp. 273–289). New York: Routledge.

Hornberger, N.H. and Skilton-Sylvester, E. (2000) Revisiting the continua of biliteracy: International and critical perspectives. *Language and Education* 14 (2), 96–122.

House, D. (2002) *Language Shift Among the Navajos: Identity Politics and Cultural Continuity*. Tucson: University of Arizona Press.

Hult, F.M. (guest ed.) (2010) Scales of multilingualism: Toward multilayered analysis of linguistic diversity. Special issue, *International Journal of the Sociology of Language* 202.

Jaffe, A. (1999) *Ideologies in Action: Language Politics on Corsica*. Berlin: Mouton de Gruyter.

Johnson, D.C. (2009) Ethnography of language policy. *Language Policy* 8 (2), 139–159.

Kaplan, R.B. and Baldauf, R.B., Jr. (1997) *Language Planning: From Practice to Theory*. Clevedon: Multilingual Matters.

King, K.A. (1999) Language revitalization processes and prospects: Quichua in the Ecuadorian Andes. *Language and Education* 13 (1), 17–37.

King, K.A. (2000) Language ideologies and heritage language education. *International Journal of Bilingual Education and Bilingualism* 3 (3), 167–184.

King, K.A. (2001) *Language Revitalization Processes and Prospects: Quichua in the Ecuadorian Andes*. Clevedon: Multilingual Matters.

King, K.A. and Hornberger, N.H. (guest eds) (2004) Quechua sociolinguistics. Special issue, *International Journal of the Sociology of Language* 167.

King, K.A., Fogle, L. and Logan-Terry, A. (2008) Family language policy. *Language and Linguistics Compass* 2, 1–16.

Lankshear, C., Gee, J.P., Knobel, M. and Searle, C. (1997) *Changing Literacies*. Buckingham, UK: Open University Press.

Levinson, B.A.U., Sutton, M. and Winstead, T. (2009) Education policy as a practice of power: Theoretical tools, ethnographic methods, democratic options. *Educational Policy* 23 (6), 767–795.

Lin, A.M.Y. and Martin, P.W. (eds) (2005) *Decolonisation, Globalization: Language-in-Education Policy and Practice*. Clevedon: Multilingual Matters.

May, S. (ed.) (1999) *Indigenous Community-based Education*. Clevedon: Multilingual Matters.

May, S. (2001) *Language and Minority Rights: Ethnicity, Nationalism and the Politics of Language*. Harlow, Essex, England: Longman/Pearson Education.

May, S. and Aikman, S. (guest eds) (2003) Indigenous education: New possibilities, ongoing constraints. Special issue, *Comparative Education* 39 (2).

McCarty, T.L. (2002) *A Place to be Navajo – Rough Rock and the Struggle for Self-Determination in Indigenous Schooling*. Mahwah, NJ: Lawrence Erlbaum.

McCarty, T.L. (2004) Dangerous difference: A critical-historical analysis of language education policies in the United States. In J.W. Tollefson and A.B.M. Tsui (eds) *Medium of Instruction Policies: Which Agenda? Whose Agenda?* (pp. 71–93). Mahwah, NJ: Lawrence Erlbaum.

McCarty, T.L. (ed.) (2011) *Ethnography and Language Policy.* New York: Routledge/ Taylor and Francis.

McCarty, T.L. and Wyman, L.T. (guest eds) (2009) Indigenous youth and bilingualism. Special issue, *Journal of Language, Identity, and Education* 8 (5).

McCarty, T.L. and Zepeda, O. (guest eds) (1995) Indigenous language education and literacy. Special issue, *Bilingual Research Journal* 19 (1), 1–4.

McCarty, T.L. and Zepeda, O. (guest eds) (1998) Indigenous language use and change in the Americas. Special issue, *International Journal of the Sociology of Language* 132.

McCarty, T.L., Skutnabb-Kangas, T. and Magga, O. (2008). Education for speakers of endangered languages. In B. Spolsky and F.M. Hult (eds) *The Handbook of Educational Linguistics* (pp. 297–312). Malden, MA: Blackwell.

Menken, K. and García, O. (eds) (2010) *Negotiating Language Policies in Schools: Educators as Policymakers.* New York: Routledge.

Mühlhäusler, P. (2000) Language planning and language ecology. *Current Issues in Language Planning* 1 (3), 306–367.

Nettle, D. and Romaine, S. (2000) *Vanishing Voices: The Extinction of the World's Languages.* Oxford, UK: Oxford University Press.

New London Group (1996) A pedagogy of multiliteracies: Designing social futures. *Harvard Educational Review* 66 (1), 60–92.

Patrick, D. (2003) *Language, Politics, and Social Interaction in an Inuit Community.* Berlin: Mouton de Gruyter.

Pennycook, A. (2001) *Critical Applied Linguistics: A Critical Introduction.* Mahwah, NJ: Lawrence Erlbaum.

Pennycook, A. (2010) *Language as a Local Practice.* New York: Routledge.

Philips, S.U. (1983) *The Invisible Culture: Communication in Classroom and Community on the Warm Springs Indian Reservation.* New York: Longman.

Phillipson, R. and Skutnabb-Kangas, T. (1996). English only worldwide or language ecology? *TESOL Quarterly* 30 (3), 429–452.

Ramanathan, V. (2005a) Rethinking language planning and policy from the ground up: Refashioning institutional realities and human lives. *Current Issues in Language Planning* 6 (2), 89–101.

Ramanathan, V. (2005b) *The English-Vernacular Divide: Postcolonial Language Politics in Practice.* Clevedon: Multilingual Matters.

Ramanathan, V. (ed.) (2010a) Language policies and health. Special issue, *Language Policy* 9 (1).

Ramanathan, V. (2010b) *Bodies and Language: Health, Ailments, Disabilities.* Bristol: Multilingual Matters.

Ramanathan, V. and Morgan, B. (guest eds) (2007) Language policies and TESOL: Perspectives from practice. Special issue, *TESOL Quarterly* 41 (3).

Ricento, T. (2000) Historical and theoretical perspectives in language policy and planning. *Journal of Sociolinguistics* 3 (2), 196–213.

Ricento, T. (2006) Theoretical perspectives in language policy: An overview. In T. Ricento (ed.) *An Introduction to Language Policy: Theory and Method* (pp. 3–23). Malden, MA: Blackwell.

Ricento, T. and Hornberger, N.H. (1996) Unpeeling the onion: Language planning and policy and the ELT professional. *TESOL Quarterly* 30 (3), 401–427.
Rockwell, E. and Gomes, A.M.R. (guest eds) (2009) Rethinking Indigenous education from a Latin American perspective. Special issue, *Anthropology and Education Quarterly* 40 (2).
Romaine, S. (2006) Planning for the survival of linguistic diversity. *Language Policy,* 5 (4), 441–473.
Ruiz, R. (1984) Orientations in language planning. *NABE Journal* 8 (2), 15–34.
Schiffman, H. (1996) *Linguistic Culture and Language Policy.* London: Routledge.
Shohamy, E. (2006) *Language Policy: Hidden Agendas and New Approaches.* London: Routledge.
Shohamy, E. and Gorter, D. (eds) (2008) *Linguistic Landscape: Expanding the Scenery.* New York: Routledge.
Shore, C. and Wright, S. (eds) (1997) *Anthropology of Policy: Critical Perspectives on Governance and Power.* New York: Routledge.
Skutnabb-Kangas, T., Phillipson, R., Mohanty, A.K. and Panda, M. (eds) (2009) *Social Justice through Multilingual Education.* Bristol: Multilingual Matters.
Spolsky, B. (1978) *Educational Linguistics: An Introduction.* Rowley, MA: Newbury House.
Spolsky, B. (2004) *Language Policy.* Cambridge, UK: Cambridge University Press.
Spolsky, B. and Hult, F.M. (eds) (2008) *The Handbook of Educational Linguistics.* Malden, MA: Blackwell.
Street, B.V. (1984) *Literacy in Theory and Practice.* New York: Cambridge University Press.
Street, B.V. (ed.) (1993) *Cross-Cultural Approaches to Literacy.* Cambridge, UK: Cambridge University Press.
Street, B.V. (ed.) (2001) *Literacy and Development: Ethnographic Perspectives.* London: Routledge.
Sutton, M. and Levinson, B.A.U. (eds) (2001) *Policy as Practice: Toward a Comparative Sociocultural Analysis of Educational Policy.* Westport, CT: Ablex.
Tollefson, J.W. (ed.) (1991) *Planning Language, Planning Inequality: Language Policy in the Community.* London: Longman.
Tollefson, J.W. (ed.) (2002) *Language Policies in Education: Critical Issues.* Mahwah, NJ: Lawrence Erlbaum.
Tollefson, J.W. (2006) Critical theory in language policy. In T. Ricento (ed.) *An Introduction to Language Policy: Theory and Method* (pp. 42–59). Malden, MA: Blackwell.
UNESCO (2003) *Language Vitality and Endangerment.* Paris: UNESCO.
Voegelin, C.F., Voegelin, F.M. and Schutz, N.W. Jr. (1967) The language situation in Arizona as part of the Southwest cultural area. In D. Hymes and W. E. Bittle (eds) *Studies in Southwestern Ethnolinguistics: Meaning and History in the Languages of the American Southwest* (pp. 11–32). The Hague: Mouton.
Wiley, T.G. (1996) Language planning and policy. In S.L. McKay and N.H. Hornberger (eds) *Sociolinguistics and Language Teaching* (pp. 103–147). Cambridge, UK: Cambridge University Press.
Wright, S. (2004) *Language Policy and Language Planning: From Nationalism to Globalization.* New York: Palgrave Macmillan.
Wyman, L. (forthcoming) *Youth Culture and Linguistic Survivance.* Bristol: Multilingual Matters.

Chapter 7

Implementational and Ideological Spaces in Bilingual Education Policy, Practice, and Research

DAVID CASSELS JOHNSON

Introduction

Nancy Hornberger's record of publications spans more than two decades and her pioneering research on the interaction between language policy, Indigenous/minority languages and bilingual education has been an inspiration for students, scholars, educators and activists all over the world. In this chapter, I examine the spaces Hornberger has opened and cultivated for bilingual education policy, practice and research. I highlight important themes and findings in her work with particular attention to the notion of ideological and implementational spaces, two concepts that have been important in my own work on language policy and bilingual education. Focusing on implementational and ideological spaces in bilingual education language policy reveals connections between macro-level language policies and micro-level language education policy and practice and illuminates the agency across the multiple layers of policy creation, interpretation and appropriation.

Hornbergian Spaces for Bilingual Education Policy, Practice and Research: A Review

A caveat up front: Like many of the other authors in this book, I was a student of Nancy Hornberger's. I attended the Educational Linguistics program from 2001 to 2007 at the University of Pennsylvania and she was the chair of my dissertation committee. Thus, I am not an impartial judge of her work; I claim no objectivity. T.S. Eliot said that 'immature poets imitate but mature poets steal' and, indeed, many of Hornberger's ideas are so embedded in my own work, so ingrained in my own thinking, that it has taken a review of her publications, from 1987 to 2009, to re-illuminate just how much my own work is inspired by hers. Here, I focus the review on (1) how this work, in and of itself, creates implementational and ideological spaces for bilingual education research and practice, and (2) the application of these concepts in my own work on bilingual educa-tion and language policy in the School District of Philadelphia (Johnson, 2007).

The micro-macro connection: Language policy and bilingual education

Hornberger examines how macro-level language policies open and close spaces for the implementation of bilingual education and how, in turn, local efforts to institute bilingual educational practices develop spaces for the promotion of Indigenous and minority languages. In the past two decades, much of the research in the field of language policy has critically focused on the *power* of language policies to marginalize minority languages and subjugate minority language users (*e.g.*, Pennycook, 2002, 2006; Shohamy, 2006; Tollefson, 1991, 2002); yet, Hornberger has argued (and shown) that national language policies that value multilingualism as a resource can create political openings for bilingual education which promote Indigenous and minority languages (Hornberger, 2006a, 2009; Hornberger & Johnson, 2007).

Still, such language policies alone might not be enough to ensure the survival of Indigenous languages, especially if there is no bottom-up sup-port: '[L]anguage policies with a language-as-resource orientation can and do have an impact on...revitalization of endangered Indigenous lan-guages. Of course, this is not to say that protecting Indigenous languages is simply a matter of declaring a language policy to that effect. There is ample evidence to the contrary' (Hornberger, 1998: 444). Indeed, as she has demonstrated in her ongoing work in South America, multilingual national language policies do not necessarily translate into multilingual classroom practice for multiple reasons including the gap between policy creation and implementation, the ephemeral and ever-changing nature of policy and the language attitudes of the communities themselves (Hornberger, 1987a, 1988).

While they may not always be enough, multilingual language poli-cies have opened spaces for bilingual education throughout the world (Hornberger, 2000, 2001, 2009). In turn, bilingual education, and espe-cially maintenance or developmental bilingual education (Hornberger,

1991), has become a powerful ally to the maintenance and/or revitalization of Indigenous and minority languages (Hornberger, 1997, 2006, 2008;
Hornberger & Johnson, 2007). Hornberger has long recognized the power
of educators to create classroom spaces that draw on the multilingual
resources of students and shows, for example, how teachers in the School
District of Philadelphia promote the biliterate development of Cambodian
children (in Khmer) and Puerto Rican children (in Spanish) (Hornberger,
1990; Hornberger & Micheau, 1993). The rich history of bilingual education in Philadelphia has been possible because of the Bilingual Education
Act (BEA), which has provided funding for the implementation of bilingual programs throughout the years. However, even without this macro-
level policy support, as is the case with the Henry C. Lea School, which
is not a bilingual school and does not receive BEA support, Hornberger
shows how teachers can create space for biliterate development. Thus,
even within *non*-bilingual schools, teachers can take advantage of their
students' L1s as resources and 'there is no one "program"... that will
necessarily provide the best learning context for all biliterate learners... [T]he specific characteristics of the optimal contexts for their learning can be defined only in each specific circumstance or case' (Hornberger,
1998: 449).

   This earlier ethnographic work on the powerful role that educators
play in language policy helped inspire, in part, the now seminal article
in a *TESOL Quarterly* special issue on language policy co-authored with
Ricento (Ricento & Hornberger, 1996) in which they argue that, because
multiple actors have influence across multiple language policy and planning (LPP) layers, language policy research needs to account for activity
across the multiple layers of what they metaphorically referred to as the
language policy onion. A decade later, Hornberger and I (Hornberger
& Johnson, 2007) resurrected this metaphor, again in a *TESOL Quarterly* special issue on language policy, to examine the powerful role that
educators play in interpreting and appropriating language policy. We
compare findings from ethnographies of language policy in two very
different contexts – the School District of Philadelphia in Pennsylvania,
US and the Master's degree program in the Program for Professional
Development in Bilingual Intercultural Education for the Andean Region
(PROEIB Maestría) – and argue that while macro-level policy can set
boundaries on what is considered educationally normal or feasible,
'local educators are not helplessly caught in the ebb and flow of shifting ideologies in language policies – they help develop, maintain, and
change that flow' (Hornberger & Johnson, 2007: 527; see also Johnson,
2007: 39).

Implementational and ideological spaces

While it is clear that she has long been interested in the 'space' that language policies both create and close for bilingual education (*e.g.* see the use of 'political openings' in Hornberger, 1998), Hornberger introduced the terms *implementational* and *ideological space* in a 2002 article published in the first issue of *Language Policy*, in which she positions these concepts within the ecology of language metaphor: '[M]ultililingual language policies are essentially about opening up ideological and implementational space in the environment for as many languages as possible, and in particular endangered languages, to evolve and flourish rather than dwindle and disappear' (Hornberger, 2002: 30).

In a series of pieces following the 2002 article, she further clarifies and enriches these concepts (Hornberger, 2005a, 2005b; Hornberger & Johnson, 2007), which are integrally related to one another but distinct nonetheless. Multilingual language policies that promote multilingualism as a resource, like Bolivia's National Education Reform of 1994, open *ideological space* for multilingualism and bilingual education but this space is, in a sense, only a potential space, because language educators and language users must take advantage of this space by implementing multilingual educational practices. In other words, these opened ideological spaces 'carve out' *implementational spaces* at classroom and community levels which language educators and users, in turn, must 'fill up' with multilingual educational practices. Such ideological spaces need the support of local educators and language users but they can also be strengthened by other language policies – for example, the Lau v. Nichols court decision opened ideological space for bilingual education in the United States but it took the Lau Remedies and the Bilingual Education Act of 1968 to create the *implementational space* for bilingual education (Hornberger, 2005a).

Other language policies, like the US No Child Left Behind Act (NCLB) of 2002, *close* ideological space for multilingualism but, just as educators must fill up the implementational spaces created by multilingual language policies, educators can also take advantage of local implementational spaces for incorporating minority languages as resources even though the ideological space created by the macro-level language policy is restrictively monolingual. In turn, these local implementational spaces carved out for multilingual educational practices can 'serve as wedges to pry open ideological ones' (Hornberger, 2005b: 606).

The notion of 'spaces' in language educational policy and practice was not invented by Hornberger and she, herself, traces it to Chick (2001), who suggests that recent South African language policies opened space for counter discourses that reject traditional monolingual discourses in South African schools. Along with Chick, Hornberger cites others who have looked at the spaces created by multilingual policies and/or classroom practices for the incorporation of students' linguistic and cultural resources (Alexander, 2003; Gutiérrez *et al.*, 1999; Ismail & Cazden, 2005).

Elsewhere (Johnson, 2010a), I compare the Hornbergian concepts of ideological and implementational space in language policy to Ball (1993/2006), who has proposed that spaces for educator agency open up in the representation, re-representation, interpretation and re-interpretation of educational policy. A multiplicity of policy interpretations within the policy process and the attempts 'to represent and re-represent policy...spread confusion and allow for play in and the playing-off of meanings. Gaps and spaces for action and response are opened-up or re-opened as a result' (Ball, 2006: 45). Similarly, Bowe and Ball (1992: 14) use the term 'spaces for manoeuvre' to describe how, throughout the policy cycle, educators take advantage of potentially ambiguous policy intentions created by omissions and contradictions in policy language. For Bowe and Ball, then, the prying open of spaces lays in the hands of educators and other policy implementers who take advantage of the confusion created by ambiguous policy language and the multi-layered nature of policy creation, interpretation and implementation to suit their own aims.

Implementational and Ideological Spaces for Bilingual Education: Five Findings (Grounded in Ethnographic Experience)

In her 2008 plenary talk at the American Association of Applied Linguistics Conference in Washington, D.C., and subsequent article in *Language Teaching* (Hornberger, 2009), Hornberger provides ten certainties about multilingual education policy and practice. This section borrows that formatting technique and proffers a list of assertions about implementational and ideological spaces for bilingual education based on data collected in an ethnography of language policy in the School District of Philadelphia (SDP). These results emerged from a 3-year (2002–2006) multi-sited ethnography of language policy that examined language policy creation, interpretation and appropriation for bilingual learners in the SDP (Johnson, 2007, 2009, 2010a, 2010b). Ethnographic data collection emerged out of a series of action-oriented research projects with bilingual teachers and administrators on bilingual teacher professional development, standardized test data analysis, articulation of bilingual programs K-12 and the development of a language policy for and by language educators in the SDP. These projects engendered participant-observation and fieldnote collection and for the sake of data triangulation, formal and informal interviews were conducted with teachers, administrators, and Pennsylvania and federal policy administrators. Of particular interest here are the ideological and implementational spaces left for developmental bilingual education by the US federal education policy, NCLB and the language policy within it, Title III, which took the place of the Bilingual Education Act starting in 2001.

1. Title III of NCLB limited but did not completely close ideological and implementational space for developmental bilingual education

While I agree with Hornberger (2005a) that NCLB has decreased the ideological space for developmental bilingual education in the US, educators in the SDP were able to utilize implementational space within the policy anyway. Language policies are not necessarily monolithic, ideologically consistent and static documents that show up on some educators' doorsteps uncontested. The confluence of many different voices, influenced by different ideological orientations, creates policies with discrepancies and space for improvisation. NCLB was no different – the revisions and congressional debate surrounding those revisions reveal that earlier House drafts of Title III were even more restrictively English-focused, while Senate versions were less so, than what was eventually adopted. Instead of a manifestation of singular intentions, an analysis of the congressional record reveals the multiplicity of intentions and ideologies about language (education) that engendered NCLB policy text and the subsequent variation in interpretation by the policy creators (Johnson, 2009, 2010b). Notably, both anti- and pro-bilingual education advocates were ardent supporters of NCLB in general, and Title III in particular. What emerges is a text that satisfies as many lawmakers as possible, and no one fully, and is therefore, *by nature*, somewhat vague – a result of the political wrangling through which policy language must pass.

Further, not only did NCLB's creators disagree about its intentions, but federal administrators responsible for its implementation echo the emphasized 'flexibility' in NCLB text (105 instances of the word 'flexibility' appear), and argue that school districts have complete freedom to implement the language education programs of their choosing. For example, Brinda Sea,[1] the director of the State Consolidated Grant

Division[2] at Office of English Language Acquisition, avers that the federal department of education does not promote or prefer any particular method and are, in fact, prohibited from doing so (interview, 24 May 2006).

It is not surprising, then, when different readers proffer different interpretations and then appropriate the policy in different ways. This is exactly what happened in the SDP – some educators were drawn in by NCLB's intense focus on English and assumed it was an English-focused policy that demanded transitional or English-only language education; others interpreted the policy as open enough to allow developmental bilingual education and, in turn, used NCLB money to fund developmental bilingual programs. Thus, while NCLB limited ideological space for developmental bilingual education, educators had the power to ignore these ideological leanings and pry open implementational spaces anyway. Others were swayed by the monolingual discourse of NCLB and appropriated the policy in kind.

2. Educators open and close implementational space for developmental bilingual education through selective appropriation of policy text and discourse

While restrictive language policies can close ideological spaces for bilingual education, local educators can take advantage of the implementational spaces for bilingual education, even within policies like NCLB, by attending to the language in the policy that allows for developmental bilingual education. Consider the following texts from two administrators in the SDP – Emily Dixon-Marquez and Lucía Sanchez – both of whom were responsible for ESL/bilingual education at different times. Here, they are reflecting on the interaction between Title III and bilingual education:

Dixon-Marquez: [In Title III] there's an emphasis on English language acquisition – but it doesn't mean that's all they're going to fund – we haven't changed our programs dramatically – we're pretty much going to do what we've been doing (Interview, 11 April 2003)

And later, from a policy meeting with bilingual teachers:

Dixon-Marquez: For the first time in the history of this state, we have [Title III] money for ELL's and the definition of an ESL program is broad enough to include bilingual (Teacher Meeting, 20 March 2004)

On the other hand, Sanchez had a very different interpretation of Title III:

Sanchez: Title III was created to improve English language acquisition programs by increasing the services or creating situations where the students would be getting supplemental services to move them into English language acquisition situations. (Interview, 13 June 2005)

In the SDP, different interpretations have led to different appropriations of the same policy. Dixon-Marquez was an active advocate for developmental bilingual education and interpreted Title III as flexible enough to allow for such programs while Sanchez felt that 'bilingual education' was best used to transition English Language Learners (ELLs) into all-English instructional settings and, in turn, interpreted Title III as restrictively focused on English and thus sought to implement transitional, and not developmental, bilingual programs. Both administrators used Title III money to different ends.

3. Educators can create their own local ideological and implementational spaces for multilingualism

During this study, a group of administrators and teachers developed their own language policy for the SDP (see Johnson, 2010a). The genesis and subsequent drafting was dominated by a discourse community that championed bilingualism for all learners and developmental bilingual education. Two administrators – Emily Dixon-Marquez and Maggie Chang – and the outside consultant – Eve Island – played a critical role in this process and helped create the following guiding mission statement for the development of the policy:

> The School District of Philadelphia acknowledges that we live in an increasingly multicultural/multilingual global society. The diverse cultures of students are a well-spring of resources... [T[he District firmly believes that administrators, teachers, students, parents, and community partners, working together in an environment of mutual respect, can bring about positive changes necessary to ensure our youth equality of education.

Besides the clear language as resource orientation (Ruiz, 1984) the mission statement provides policy text support for promoting an environment in which community and school district members from all levels of institutional authority have input. This mission statement was the ideological foundation for the initial stages of development and the language is representative of the reigning ideas – fostered by Dixon-Marquez, Chang, and Island – about language diversity and bilingual education: that Philadelphia schools are advantaged by their linguistic and cultural diversity; that a pedagogy that takes advantage of this diversity is best served by incorporating members of the community; and that the ultimate goal is educational equality for all students.

The ideological space created and sustained through the development of the SDP language policy was resistant to Title III's English-only discourse for three possible reasons. First, many of the policy developers in the SDP were not focused on the English-only discourse of Title III and instead were devoted to the task at hand – developing bilingual programs. Second, the administrators who were very aware of Title III's language were not swayed by its English-oriented discourse. They did not feel 'under the gun', as Dixon-Marquez put it (Johnson, 2010a: 72), to sculpt their programs to the monolingual flavor of Title III. Finally, Island, Chang and Dixon-Marquez all promoted a more egalitarian discourse community of policy makers that incorporated the views and beliefs of educators from various levels of institutional authority. Together, and from the ground up so to speak, they engendered the SDP Language Policy which (in early drafts at least) promoted developmental bilingual education over transitional and English-focused programs (Johnson, 2010a; Johnson & Freeman, 2010).

4. Educators selectively appropriate research on bilingual education to pry open implementational spaces in NCLB

The varied interpretations of educational linguistic research played a crucial role in both the interpretation and appropriation of language policy in the SDP. Island, herself a well-published researcher, appropriated research (including her own) and voices from an outside community of bilingual education advocates and applied linguistic scholars (like Richard Ruiz) to contextualize and support educator efforts to develop developmental bilingual policy and pedagogy. Positioning the research(ers) as allies, and the SDP practitioners as experts, empowered teachers to become active agents in policy making. Concomitantly, she challenged traditional divisions between policy 'creators' and 'implementers' and exemplified how policies that reduce inequality and promote the maintenance of minority languages can be developed more democratically (Johnson, 2010b; Johnson & Freeman, 2010).

Those educators who were cognizant of the research supporting developmental bilingual education engendered and supported a discourse community of administrators, teachers and researchers that supported one and two-way developmental programs. For example, Dixon-Marquez, the Title VII and Title III grant writer, viewed the requirement that programs must be based on scientifically based research as beneficial because the research she cited – especially the Collier and Thomas (1997, 2002) studies – supported the programs she wanted to promote in the SDP. Within this ideological space, developmental bilingual programs were positioned as superior to transitional programs and the Collier and Thomas (1997, 2002) studies were appropriated as allies.

However, a change in administration led to a change in how the 'research' was appropriated and while Island and Dixon-Marquez referenced outside research and researchers in an attempt to enhance teacher agency, Lucía Sanchez positioned the research as setting rigid standards (i.e. transition into English) to which SDP language policy, and the teachers, must adapt. Sanchez's interpretation of Title III was filtered through her definition of 'bilingual education' as necessarily transitional. Further, the expertise of the teachers was diminished in favor of outside experts – 'scientists' and 'linguists' as she called them (see Johnson, 2010b: 86) – whose research was misinterpreted and then used to place restrictions on SDP language policy in favor of transitional bilingual education.

5. The focus on accountability has limited the implementational space for developmental bilingual education (which potentially has a negative impact on the ideological space)

While NCLB in general, and the language policy within it, Title III, does not condone or restrict any particular language education program, the focus on standardized tests in *English* has made it difficult for many schools and school districts to maintain the integrity of their bilingual education programs (Menken, 2008; Menken & Shohamy, 2008). Shohamy (2006) has argued that such language testing amounts to *de facto* language policy because, if educators are forced to teach to an English-language test, they will be forced to teach in English. This was true of the bilingual education program at Orlando Cepeda Middle School whose teachers felt more and more pressure to teach to the increasingly English-focused tests, a pressure that was engendered by NCLB but mediated by new leadership in the district (namely, Sanchez). One of the teachers, Mary Streams, reported that:

> [T]hey give us these tests and they say that 'these are the most important things in the world to us right now' and 'how are you gonna have kids ready for tests in English if you're not preparing for them in

English – so, two years ago we made the shift ourselves to teach more in English. (interview, 3 March 2005)

Even though they were opposed to making the switch, Streams and the other Cepeda teachers felt so much pressure to teach to the English-language tests, they modified their developmental program. While they had been accustomed to administrators, like Dixon-Marquez, supporting their efforts to keep their developmental program, Sanchez not only supported the increasing instruction in English, she turned it into official policy by re-writing the language policy of the district to focus on transitional bilingual education.

This new policy offended the Cepeda teachers and when Sanchez enacted another top-down policy decision that denied Spanish-language standardized content assessments to the Cepeda students, the teachers began resisting. First, the Cepeda teachers began an email writing campaign to SDP leaders including the CEO of the SDP. Then, the teachers encouraged parental complaints about the testing decision and once the parents began calling the school to complain, a meeting was planned between Cepeda teachers, Sanchez, the principal of Cepeda, a teachers' union representative and a school counselor. In preparation for the meeting, about a dozen bilingual students planned a protest for the arriving entourage and made signs declaring things like, 'If you want to test my intelligence, test me in my own language!' The students received permission from a supportive principal and, along with some parents, set up a picket line, through which Sanchez had to drive. The protest and meeting were marginally successful in that Spanish-dominant students were allowed to attend a special session for taking a Spanish-language content assessment. Streams reported that about a half of her students attended.

Conclusion

While NCLB has limited the ideological space for developmental bilingual education, many educators in the School District of Philadelphia ignored this ideological shift and, instead, pried open implementational space in the policy for developmental bilingual education, which relied on the development of a local ideological space that promoted developmental bilingual education. However, this space would soon change when Sanchez took over as ESL/Bilingual coordinator. She interpreted Title III as restrictively English focused, an interpretation that collided with her own interpretation of 'bilingual education' as an educational program that is necessarily transitional. While the ideological leanings of

NCLB shaped the educational landscape in the SDP, the policy shifts relied on local administrators and educators whose interpretation of bilingual education policy, practice and research impacted their interpretation and appropriation of NCLB in general, and Title III in particular.

While critical approaches to LPP and bilingual education policy, which focus on the power of language policies to marginalize minority language use and users, have become increasingly prevalent (and rightfully so), examining the implementational and ideological spaces in language policies reveals agency across the multiple layers of language policy creation, interpretation and appropriation. The supporters and creators of a policy – who may have varying goals or intentions – are able to open and close ideological and implementational spaces for bilingual education; however, the interpreters and appropriators (administrators and teachers) have agency to pry open implementational spaces, and create their own ideological space. Certainly, language policies can instantiate already existing, and generate new, hegemonic discourses that normalize particular ways of educating, but researchers and educators need to recognize that, they too, inform the discourses surrounding these policies. Focusing exclusively on the subjugating power of policy helps perpetuate the idea that language policy is a necessarily monolithic mechanism for educational hegemony and helps reify critical conceptualizations as disempowering realities. We need to balance our critical analyses of policy power while simultaneously finding, examining and exploiting spaces for educator agency because if the arc of our research bends toward continued analyses of single-noted hegemony, the arc of language policy may bend in the same direction.

Notes

1. While the institutional names are real, all quoted research participants are given pseudonyms.
2. This department is responsible 'for the administration of new formula grants and for providing technical assistance to State and Local educational agencies.'

References

Alexander, N. (2003) *Language Education Policy: National and Sub-national Identities in South Africa.* Stasbourg: Council of Europe.
Ball, S.J. (2006) *Education Policy and Social Class: The Selected Works of Stephen J. Ball.* London and New York: Taylor & Francis.
Bowe, R. and Ball, S.J. (1992) *Reforming Education and Changing Schools: Case Studies in Policy Sociology.* London and New York: Routledge.

Chick, K. (2001) Constructing a multicultural national identity: South African classrooms as sites of struggle between competing discourses. *Working Papers in Educational Linguistics* 17, 27–45.

Collier, V.P. and Thomas, W.P. (1997). *School Effectiveness for Language Minority Children*. Washington D.C.: National Clearinghouse for Bilingual Education.

Collier, V.P. and Thomas, W.P. (2002). *A National Study of School Effectiveness for Language Minority Students' Long-Term Academic Achievement*. Berkeley, CA: CREDE, University of California.

Gutiérrez, K.D., Baquedano-López, P. and Tejeda, C. (1999) Rethinking diversity: Hybridity and hybrid language practices in the third space. *Mind, Culture, and Activity: An International Journal* 6, 286–303.

Hornberger, N.H. (1987a) Bilingual education success but policy failure. *Language in Society* 16 (2), 205–226.

Hornberger, N.H. (1987b) Bilingual education and Quechua language maintenance in highland Puno, Peru. *NABE Journal* 11 (2), 117–140.

Hornberger, N.H. (1989) Continua of biliteracy. *Review of Educational Research* 59 (3), 271–296.

Hornberger, N.H. (1990) Creating successful learning contexts for biliteracy. *Teachers College Record* 92 (2), 212–229.

Hornberger, N.H. (1991) Extending enrichment bilingual education: Revisiting typologies and redirecting policy. In O. García (ed.) *Bilingual Education: Focusschrift in Honor of Joshua A. Fishman on the Occasion of his 65th Birthday, Volume 1* (pp. 215–234). Philadelphia: John Benjamins.

Hornberger, N.H. (1997) Literacy, language maintenance, and linguistic human rights: Three telling cases. *International Journal of the Sociology of Language* 127, 87–103.

Hornberger, N.H. (1998) Language policy, language education, language rights: Indigenous, immigrant, and international perspectives. *Language in Society* 27, 439–458.

Hornberger, N.H. (2000) Bilingual education policy and practice in the Andes: Ideological paradox and intercultural possibility. *Anthropology and Education Quarterly* 31 (2), 173–201.

Hornberger, N.H. (2001) Ideological paradox and intercultural possibility: Andean language-in-education policy and practice and its relevance for South Africa. *South African Journal of Applied Language Studies* 19 (3&4), 215–230.

Hornberger, N.H. (2002) Multilingual language policies and the continua of biliteracy: An ecological approach. *Language Policy* 1 (1), 27–51.

Hornberger, N.H. (2005a) Nichols to NCLB: Local and global perspectives on U.S. language education policy. *Working Papers in Educational Linguistics* 20 (2), 1–17.

Hornberger, N.H. (2005b) Opening and filling up implementational and ideological spaces in Heritage language education. *Modern Language Journal* 89, 605–609.

Hornberger, N.H. (2006) Voice and biliteracy in indigenous language revitalization: Contentious educational practices in Quechua, Guarani, and Māori contexts. *Journal of Language, Identity, and Education* 5 (4), 277–292.

Hornberger, N.H. (ed.) (2008). *Can Schools Save Indigenous Languages? Policy and Practice on Four Continents*. New York: Palgrave Macmillan.

Hornberger, N.H. (2009) Multilingual education policy and practice: Ten certainties (grounded in Indigenous experience). *Language Teaching* 42 (2), 197–211.

Hornberger, N.H. and Johnson, D.C. (2007) Slicing the onion ethnographically: Layers and spaces in multilingual language education policy and practice. *TESOL Quarterly* 41 (3), 509–532.

Hornberger, N.H. and Micheau, C. (1993) Getting far enough to like it: Biliteracy in the middle school. *Peabody Journal of Education* 69 (1), 30–53.

Ismail, S.M. and Cazden, C.B. (2005) Struggles for indigenous education and self-determination: Culture, context, and collaboration. *Anthropology and Education Quarterly* 36, 88–92.

Johnson, D.C. (2007) *Language Policy within and without the School District of Philadelphia.* PhD thesis, University of Pennsylvania.

Johnson, D.C. (2009) Ethnography of language policy. *Language Policy* 8, 139–159.

Johnson, D.C. (2010a) Implementational and ideological spaces in bilingual education language policy. *International Journal of Bilingual Education and Bilingualism* 13 (1), 61–79.

Johnson, D.C. (2010b) The relationship between applied linguistic research and bilingual language policy. *Applied Linguistics* 31 (1), 72–93.

Johnson, D.C. and Freeman, R. (2010) Appropriating language policy on the local level: Working the spaces for bilingual education. In K. Menken and O. García (eds) *Negotiating Language Policies in Schools: Educators as Policymakers* (pp. 13–31). London: Routledge.

Menken, K. (2008) *English Learners Left Behind: Standardized Testing as Language Policy.* Clevedon: Multilingual Matters.

Menken, K. and Shohamy, E. (eds) (2008) *No Child Left Behind* and U.S. language education policy. Special issue, *Language Policy* 7 (3).

Pennycook, A. (2002) Language policy and docile bodies: Hong Kong and Governmentality. In J. Tollefson (ed.) *Language Policy in Education: Critical Issues* (pp. 91–110). Mahwah, NJ: Lawrence Erlbaum.

Pennycook, A. (2006) Postmodernism in language policy. In T. Ricento (ed.) *An Introduction to Language Policy: Theory and Method* (pp. 60–76). Malden, MA: Blackwell.

Ricento, T. and Hornberger, N.H. (1996) Unpeeling the onion: Language planning and policy and the ELT professional. *TESOL Quarterly* 30 (3), 401–427.

Ruiz, R. (1984). Orientations in language planning. *NABE Journal* 8 (2), 15–34.

Shohamy, E. (2006) *Language Policy: Hidden Agendas and New Approaches.* London and New York: Routledge.

Tollefson, J.W. (1991) *Planning Language, Planning Inequality: Language Policy in the Community.* London: Longman.

Tollefson, J.W. (ed) (2002) *Language Policies in Education: Critical Issues.* Mahwah, NJ: Lawrence Erlbaum.

Chapter 8
Quechua Language and Education Policy in the Peruvian Highlands

SERAFÍN M. CORONEL-MOLINA

Peru is a multilingual, pluricultural and multiethnic country. Despite this fact, Peruvian mainstream society has long ignored the existence of its Indigenous population. This stance is linked to not only the widespread negative attitudes towards Indigenous languages in the country, but also the more general difficulties of implementing language planning for Indigenous languages. Peru has adopted a range of sweeping official policies that recognize Peru's cultural and linguistic diversity, particularly in the 20th century. Nevertheless, it seems that no matter what efforts groups and language planning organizations make on behalf of Quechua, the main Indigenous language of the country, they have failed to change the discriminatory attitudes towards the Quechua language, and by extension towards the people who speak that language.

As Nancy Hornberger has emphasized across much of her work and writings, including her extensive research in Peru, full understanding of any language policy requires analysis of both top-down and bottom-up perspectives. Fifteen years ago, Hornberger signaled – in the introduction of her 1996 book, *Indigenous Literacies in the Americas: Language Planning for the Bottom Up* – the importance of 'showing the richness and potential of on-the-ground, grassroots initiatives for language and literacy planning. Such an emphasis is a reflection of both the reality of our times and of trends in scholarship' (1996: 11). Hornberger then pointed to the ongoing shift in sociolinguistics as well as in social science as a whole towards 'the individual and the local community as active agents in dialogue and interaction with their social environment, and away from a governmental, institutional, or societal level focus' (1996: 11). As language policy scholarship has shifted in the last 20 years to a greater emphasis on individual language practices and community efforts, and as Hornberger's own work in Peru has illustrated (1988), the limited power of these government and 'top-down' efforts to shape public attitudes and popular practices has become increasingly clear.

This chapter outlines some of governmental-level policies (from Presidents Leguía through García) in Peru, but with an emphasis on the gaps between the organizational, institutional, governmental (top-down) levels, and the popular, grass-roots (bottom-up) level efforts, as well as between explicit and implicit language policies. As this limited overview will suggest, despite nearly a century of Indigenous language activism and policy, the attitudes and actions of the average Spanish-speaking citizen (and even many Quechua-speaking citizens who have been convinced of the lack of value of their language), and the implicit policies, represented through daily language practices, have changed relatively little. For Quechua to have a chance of survival, these attitudes and practices are those most in need of changing in all sectors of society, not only among mainstream members, but among Quechua speakers themselves (Coronel-Molina, 1999: 177).

Official Government Policy and *Indigenismo*

Augusto B. Leguía was perhaps the first president to officially recognize the multicultural nature of Peruvian society. Leguía served as president from 1919 to 1931, and during his terms of office, he proclaimed a policy of 'official *indigenismo*.' The intent was to give stronger social and political force to the *Indigenismo* movement, which had begun at the end of the 19th century with a literary and cultural base. To this end, Leguía created the Office for Indigenous Affairs in 1920, and established *El Día del Indio* 'Day of the Indian' as a national holiday. Together, these actions 'signaled the government's intention of institutionally assimilating the Indian into the mainstream life of the nation. So did the official recognition of Indian communities in the new Constitution of 1920, the first such recognition in the history of the republic' (Klarén, 2000: 247). Equal if not more important was Leguía's creation of the *Tawantinsuyo* Committee for Pro-Indigenous Rights, a 'radical indigenista national project' (de la Cadena, 2000: 89), that brought together both Indigenists and self-identified Indigenous leaders from around the country in an effort to demand Indigenous literacy and citizenship rights (García, 2005: 69).

Despite his apparent support for Indigenous rights, Leguía's desire to modernize the country possibly negatively impacted rural Andean ways of life, including aiding the already slowly growing shift from Quechua to Spanish. Leguía was determined to update and modernize not only Lima, but the national communication and transportation systems across the country as well (Klarén, 2000). In connecting all parts of the country with better roadways, Leguía ultimately made migration and communication among different parts of the country much easier, bringing the Quechua-speaking areas into greater contact with Spanish and necessitating that many Quechua communities adopt Spanish for economic survival (Cerrón-Palomino, 1997: 62). Leguía's modernization efforts thus contributed to greater contact between Quechua- and Spanish-speaking populations, with the concomitant rise in Quechua–Spanish bilingualism among Quechua speakers and the eventual shift completely from Quechua to Spanish in many cases (Cerrón-Palomino, 1997).

Manuel González Prada, and later Víctor Raúl Haya de la Torre and José Carlos Mariátegui were three other well-known Peruvian intellectual figures who supported and contributed to the Indigenist movement from its beginnings in the 1880s through the 1930s. In varied ways, these figures expressed their concern for the 'oppressed Indian masses,' a common catch-phrase of this period. And each sought ethnic, cultural and linguistic vindication and revitalization for Indigenous groups (Klarén, 2000: 246). Mariátegui was probably the first intellectual to distinguish three literary genres dealing with the so-called 'Indian question': *indianista* (indianist), *indigenista* (indigenist) and *indígena* (indigenous). Of these three, the most popular was the *indígena*, which was the only one truly capable portraying the 'true essence' of Indigenous life, since it was the only one which was produced by the Indigenous peoples themselves about their own life experiences. However, Mariátegui recognized that 'until indigenous people reclaimed their rights and emerged from their places of marginalization, they should be protected and represented by *indigenistas*' (García, 2005: 65). The *indianista* genre was little more than a romanticized representation of life as an indigene.

After World War I, young *indigenistas* were less interested in simply studying Indians, and more interested in 'militant and revolutionary objectives. Some saw the Indian as the agent of a socialist-agrarian revolution, while others emphasized a new revolutionary nationalism based upon what they saw as a glorious Indian past ignored' (Klarén, 2000: 246). This was true in Lima as well as in Cuzco and the rest of the highlands.

Later, in the 1940s and 1950s, Luis Valcárcel lent himself to a manifestation of *Indigenismo* that de la Cadena calls 'purist indigenism a la Valcárcel.' This movement sought to reduce assimilationist projects in Peru and advocated for bilingual Quechua and Spanish literacy campaigns. José María Arguedas, together with Valcárcel, was particularly active in these campaigns (de la Cadena, 2000: 324–325). They also were active in the promotion of the first Quechua–Spanish bilingual education programs in the country (García, 2005: 72). However, a fatal flaw of this movement was that its leaders were elite, non-Indigenous intellectuals. Thus, the native populations never felt a true connection to the effort, and it failed to give rise to later 'ethnic pride' Indigenous movements (de la Cadena, 2000: 325).

Unfortunately, in subsequent decades, the force of the Indigenist movements faded and was replaced once again by 'the old Hispanist position inherited from the colony,' which reconceptualized the 'Indian question' in terms of incorporating (read 'culturally assimilating') them into mainstream society. Correspondingly, 'the extension of the domestic market, in response to the pressure of capitalist development, and the education of the native mass were put forth as an alternative solution to the national problem' (Cerrón-Palomino, 1989: 25; see also Mannheim, 1991: 63).

Within this development-oriented context, in the mid-1940s, experimental bilingual education programs were instituted as one means of educating the masses. These first attempts at bilingual education were not geared towards maintenance of ancestral languages, but rather were transitional in nature, with the expressed goal of educating the 'Indians' in their native tongues while they were in the process of learning Spanish. Once Indigenous students became fluent enough in Spanish, bilingual education ceased and they were taught exclusively in Spanish.

Although there was no concern at this time for officializing any Indigenous languages, there was a limited amount of attention given to developing standardized alphabets for them. To that end, a standardized alphabet was proposed by a Ministerial Resolution of 29 October 1946, but this alphabet was never enforced (Cerrón-Palomino, 1989: 25). This was one small move in the direction of codification of Quechua. A more successful effort was made later, during the military regime of General Juan Velasco Alvarado in the first half of the 1970s, resulting not only in a more uniform spelling system but also in didactic materials and textbooks (Cerrón-Palomino, 1989: 29). In reality, status planning (e.g., the establishment of Quechua as a *lingua franca*) goes back to Incan times followed by the Councils of Lima in colonial times. Corpus planning, the development of the writing system through codification and elaboration of dictionaries, grammars and catechisms, etc. was also initiated in colonial times by chroniclers, interpreters and religious agents, among them Jesuits and Franciscans (see e.g. Adelaar & Muysken, 2004; Cerrón-Palomino, 1989; Coronel-Molina, 2007, in press; Durston, 2007; Heath & Laprade, 1992; Hornberger & King, 2006; Mannheim, 1991).

President Velasco Alvarado came to power in 1968 after a military *coup d'etat*. Although a dictator, Velasco Alvarado enacted sweeping reforms, many of which were interpreted as pro-Indigenous. He included Tupac Amaru II (a glorified Incan leader) alongside the familiar *criollo* heroes of Peruvian independence in an attempt to unify the nation in a 'much more inclusive and popular fashion' (Klarén, 2000: 121–122). Furthermore, he instituted a nationalist policy to end feudalism in the Andean region, including agrarian reform and sociocultural and linguistic vindication of the Andean peoples, thus fulfilling the hopes and ambitions of previous generations of Indigenists.

Velasco Alvarado also enacted major education changes, passing the General Education Law (Government Decree 19326 of 3/21/1972), which instituted maintenance bilingual education (Hornberger, 1988). He also enacted Government Decree 21156 in May 1975, which promoted Quechua to the status of official national language, together with Spanish, quite a victory for Quechua status *and* acquisition planning at that time: 'The law stated that after April 1976, the teaching of Quechua would be obligatory at all educational levels. Further, all legal proceedings involving monolingual Quechua speakers would have to be conducted in Quechua' (García, 2005: 75). In this way, the law effectively extended Quechua to new domains: education of all citizens, not just the Indigenous, and law, 'two areas where language had been previously used as a mechanism of domination over Indigenous speakers' (García, 2005: 76).

The Velasco Alvarado government decided to codify six Peruvian dialects (Anchash-Huailas, Ayacucho-Chanca, Cajamarca-Cañaris, Cuzco-Collao, Junín-Huanca & San Martín-Chachapoyas). The experts chosen to carry out this work started with the development of a unified alphabet that was capable of representing all the sounds of the various dialects, including those found in some but not in others. After this, a reference grammar and dictionary for each of the six varieties was developed and published (Cerrón-Palomino, 1997: 61).

Unfortunately, 'the measure to promote Quechua failed before more than a few steps toward its implementation were taken' (Cerrón-Palomino, 1989: 25). In fact, Godenzzi questions whether Velasco Alvarado actually had the welfare of the Indigenous people at heart, or whether 'these measures were nothing more than ideological resources, without any greater technical foundation than service to political interests' (1992: 62–63). By the end of 1975, Velasco's reforms were causing growing discontent among the elite classes, including within the government itself. Velasco suffered a *coup d'etat* of his own, and General Francisco Morales Bermúdez instituted the next dictatorship, in which the neo-indigenist stance of Velasco was abandoned and a call was made to transfer power to civilians. The result of this was a new constitution in 1979 which retracted the previous law and reduced Quechua and Aymara to 'official use zones' and made Spanish the only official national language.

Despite the overthrow of Velasco's projected reforms, Velasco's populist move in officializing the ancestral language served as a powerful agent to revive the linguistic awareness of Indigenous groups, so that in the future they would not neglect to incorporate, within their demands, the call for a recognition of Quechua as a national and official language together with Spanish and other Indigenous languages of the country (Cerrón-Palomino, 1997: 61).

Thus, though Velasco's attempts perhaps failed at the official and political level, they did raise the awareness of both *criollos* and Indigenous peoples, and in this sense was ultimately a positive influence for the neo-indigenist movement. And although Velasco's overthrow effectively meant the end of the reforms that he had proposed and begun instituting, at least at the governmental level, the ideas had been planted. With the government's effective withdrawal from such stands and proposals as official Quechua and bilingual education programs, the way was opened for other organizations to come in and take up where the government had left off.

Institutions such as the technical cooperation program GTZ (German Technical Cooperation Society) and numerous non-governmental organizations (NGOs) took up the banner of bilingual education in collaboration with official entities associated with the educational branch of the government. These collaborations tended to be regional and experimental, such as the Project of Experimental Bilingual Education (PEBE) based in Puno, and financed by GTZ. This project offered a maintenance model for bilingual education, in which children were taught both in their mother tongues and in Spanish throughout their elementary school years, in an attempt to help them maintain the former and become proficient in the latter. These experimental programs were the subject of Hornberger's dissertation work (1988).

PEBE contributed significantly to Peruvian language planning. Its contribution to status planning was made by valorizing the native language for use in formal education, a new domain for Quechua. Corpus planning received its contribution through the elaboration of textbooks and pedagogical materials in Quechua. Finally, PEBE contributed to acquisition planning by revitalizing language use through the educational system and encouraging native speakers to maintain their language use rather than shifting to Spanish.

Once the term for the experimental project ended, the government was supposed to take over the program and extend it throughout the southern region. Unfortunately, however, successive governments apparently never had any real intention of taking on the challenges of such a bilingual education program and so it has yet to be implemented on a wider scale (Cerrón-Palomino, 1997: 62). García suggests that this failure on the part of the government to take up bilingual education may have been deliberate:

> Gradually, the educational system was seen as a vital terrain that the state had to control and protect from the forces of subversion. In the 1980s, this concern was only exacerbated by the political fact that the leadership of Sendero Luminoso and many of its supporters had emerged from the universities and public schools of Peru. Education, once a place where Indigenous people could be brought into the nation, was becoming a minefield between the forces of order and those of insurrection. (García, 2005: 76)

With the rise of the *guerrilla* group *Sendero Luminoso* and a tense political climate, the government seemed to come to view maintenance bilingual education as one more possible site of contestation, potentially further dividing the citizenry. During this period, Indigenous mobilization at the national level was not a desirable activity, given the popularly held, although mistaken, view that *Sendero Luminoso* was at heart an Indigenous insurgency movement (García, 2005: 76). In part for this reason, Indigenous linguistic rights were not given high priority.

Even so, some progress was made in the area of language policy and planning. Of particular significance to both corpus and status planning was the officialization of both a Quechua and an Aymara alphabet in 1985, under the first administration of President Alan García (1996–1990). It was a boon for corpus planning because of the standardization of the writing system, and for status planning because the alphabets were officialized in the legal code. Furthermore, in 1987, President García reopened the National Office of Bilingual Education, after nearly 10 years of inactivity. A number of conferences and debates were held around the country on the standardization of Indigenous languages, cultural identity and educational reform (García, 2005). Despite all these improvements in favor of Indigenous languages in general, Alan Garcia's first administration (1996–1990) was marked by corruption, profound economic crisis and abuse of power and human rights violations.

It was under Alberto Fujimori's first term (1990–1995) that *Sendero Luminoso* was finally disbanded and its leader, Abimael Guzmán, was captured in 1992. Fujimori took drastic measures politically and economically to begin rebuilding the country with improved 'roads, schools, medical and agricultural facilities, electricity and running water, and [support for] organizations emphasizing community development' (García, 2005: 48). It was within this context that Indigenous rights activists again slowly began advocating for Indigenous linguistic rights. However, Fujimori's second term (1995–2000) was also marked by repeated allegations of corruption, abuse of power and major human rights violations at all levels.

Under the administration of Alejandro Toledo (2001–2006), there seemed to be hope for continued advancement with regard to linguistic rights. New laws were passed not only to offer education in the students' native languages, but also for teachers to speak the language of the region in which they are teaching. In addition, training in bilingual intercultural education (BIE) was made available to the teachers, which sought to enable them to fulfill the letter of the law (*Ley General de Educación, Decreto Ley*, 2003: 19–20). Furthermore, a new law was passed which aimed to further the recognition, promotion, revalorization and revitalization of Indigenous languages at the national level and in public and administrative spheres. This law was designed to make explicit the legal linguistic rights of non-Spanish-speaking Peruvian citizens (*Ley Nacional de Lenguas*, 2005).

Since 2006, Alan García Pérez has lead as president for the second time. His term has been marked not only by economic growth (and lower rates of poverty), but also by conflicts with Indigenous groups, in particular in the Amazon with respect to oil and logging rights. The current language and educational policy of Alan García Pérez is detrimental to Indigenous groups. There is a lack of support to bilingual intercultural education and the linguistics rights of Indigenous people (Invent–Diálogos de educación, 2010). Despite this lack of support, after three years of intense legislative battle the plenary session of the Peruvian Congress approved on 23 June 2010 the *Ley para la Preservación y Uso de las Lenguas Originarias del Perú* ('Law for the Preservation and Use of the Original Languages of Peru') proposed by Congresswoman Maria Sumire de Conde through the Congressional Commission of Indigenous People. This law intends to benefit millions of Peruvians who speak Quechua, Aymara and Amazonian languages as their mother tongue, and to encourage their use in public spheres rather than in only domestic domains (Miryam Yataco, personal communication, 24 June 2010). This unique and important initiative seeks to benefit and strengthen language maintenance and revitalization of Indigenous languages, and bilingual/multilingual education in Peru in the years to come.

Language Attitudes and Challenges to Bilingual Education

Over the last several decades BIE has gained greater acceptance among Indigenous organizations and indigenist advocates. They see BIE as 'an integral part of the struggle for both cultural and political rights. In fact, bilingual intercultural education has become a phrase pointing to broader concerns over democracy, self-determination, citizenship, and social justice' (García, 2005: 82). Even so, many highland communities still reject the idea of BIE (or bilingual education of any sort), thinking that the activists and educators seeking to implement these programs are simply 'outsiders trying to impose disadvantageous educational changes.' Speakers of Quechua and other Indigenous languages argue that to become fully accepted members of the nation, they need to be proficient in Spanish, and learning in Quechua will take this opportunity away from them (García, 2005: 92).

Interestingly, these are the same reactions that Hornberger found 25 years ago when she did research on the PEBE program in Puno. As Zúñiga *et al.* report, based on their own study of southern Peruvian departments:

> The majority of parents, and even more so the teachers, admit bluntly that Quechua and Aymara speaking children learn better if they are taught in their Indigenous languages and Spanish; in other words, if the pedagogy that is planned and developed is bilingual. The demand for bilingual education is, then, in the majority in all the departments. (Zúñiga *et al.*, 2000: 67)

Regardless of the point of view expressed by the activists, educators and Quechua parents, these observations highlight the importance of language policy for a given group's sense of belonging. Nevertheless, despite the new regulations and a greater attempt to enforce them, at least at present there still does not appear to be much progress being made in terms of educational equity in the Andean regions. Although teachers might understand the native languages of their students to some degree, they still suffer significant shortages, among them supplies, materials and the appropriate intercultural pedagogical training (see López, 2002; Zúñiga *et al.*, 2003).

Although a range of progressive and Indigenous-oriented new laws have been passed, it takes time and resources to implement such new policies, and even more time to change long-standing attitudes. Currently, public education is available and required for all school-age children in Peru. However, until recently, this education was widely available only in

Spanish, with few allowances made for monolingual students whose language was *not* Spanish (Godenzzi, 1997: 240). The few bilingual education situations in previous decades were scattered and experimental. Such a situation immediately put non-Spanish-speaking students at a clear disadvantage, and at the same time, communicated to them the lack of value of the language they speak (and it could well be this aspect that caused the reaction, mentioned above, of many of the parents who were against bilingual education in any form).

The renewed efforts to design and implement bilingual intercultural educational curricula contribute to the potential revalorization of Quechua, which further both status and acquisition planning goals. Other recent initiatives include the top-down planning implied in the constitutional and juridical measures also previously mentioned; greater inclusion of Indigenous languages in mass media, particularly radio and in some areas newspapers; and increasing exposure on the Internet and other Information and Communication Technologies (ICTs) (see Coronel-Molina, 2005; Hornberger & Coronel-Molina, 2004). In addition, Heath and Laprade consider that the activities of the *Instituto de Estudios Peruanos* (IEP, or Institute of Peruvian Studies) are contributing to a 'greater visibility and legitimacy' of Quechua, together with 'the preparation of bilingual teaching materials and publications of folk literature' (1982: 134).

These two authors, writing 20 years ago, took an optimistic view of the situation of Quechua, going so far as to assert that 'Quechua is gaining in ideological acceptance and in some practical uses as a language capable of performing many of the same functions as Spanish' (Heath & Laprade, 1982: 135). With the experience of the last two decades, but also looking ahead, I have mixed feeling about this assessment: even at the height of the neo-indigenist movement, it would be difficult to claim that any large number of the mainstream population had suffered an ideological change to accept Quechua in public spaces. At most, it could be said that they were more willing to accept that Quechua speakers not give up their own language in favor of Spanish, but certainly monolingual Spanish speakers were (are) not rushing the gates to make Quechua a part of their lives.

Still, the *de facto* policies of the citizens themselves are much more powerful than any governmental decree because they are based on unconscious, unrecognized attitudes and ideologies which often lead to linguistic discrimination. Godenzzi highlights how such linguistic discrimination tends to have far-reaching societal effects: 'The southern Andean region constitutes an area of strict social hierarchy, with the cultural and linguistic diversity of the Quechua population often serving as a pretext for social discrimination and exclusion from national political life'

(1997: 240). This is not surprising, since 'bilingualism does not support Quechua or Aymara; on the contrary, it erodes them: this is a natural consequence of the struggle between unequally equipped languages and societies' (Cerrón-Palomino, 1989: 27). However, despite the complex situation of the Peruvian social and linguistic landscape, it is essential for Indigenous people to learn Spanish and possible another language (but without abandoning their native languages) in order to face the challenges of this century. If bilingualism erodes Indigenous languages, perhaps it is necessary to expand the functional domains of these languages by multiplying efforts at all levels in order to maintain and invigorate them, and use them in public domains and in cosmopolitan areas (for more on this point, see Coronel-Molina, 1999, 2005; Hornberger & Coronel-Molina, 2004; Hornberger & King, 2001; King, 2001).

Conclusion

Over the last century, then, we see a low value placed by the dominant class on the Quechua language in Andean societies. Through both covert and overt language policies carried out at all levels of society, this devaluation has been communicated to the speakers of that language, effectively convincing them that in order to survive, especially in the cities where there is the greatest chance to earn more than a subsistence living, it is best to speak Spanish and perhaps to forget that they ever spoke Quechua (Albó, 1999: 42; Cerrón-Palomino, 1989: 24, 25, 27; López, 1990: 105; Marr, 1998). Such economic and social forces are contributing to the slow death of Quechua (Cerrón-Palomino, 1989; Hornberger & Coronel-Molina, 2004; von Gleich, 1994), and the current trend to try to revitalize it faces a difficult challenge.

Contradictorily, there have been specific, concrete language planning efforts for Quechua, particularly in the 20th century. Corpus planning has probably received the most attention, with focus on standardizing the written language both orthographically and lexically. Cerrón-Palomino points out that such work is critical for the maintenance of Quechua, since an oral language will always be at a disadvantage when faced with a written language (1989: 28). However, considerable work has also been done in the areas of status planning and acquisition planning in Peru. All of this research shows the importance placed on language planning not only by international researchers but by language planners, linguists and language speakers native to the countries themselves.

This points to the tension that has always existed between rhetoric, or overt policy, and practice, or covert policy, at both the organizational/

institutional/governmental (top down) level, and the popular, grass-roots (bottom-up) level. That is, the research and developments outlined above shows just how much work is going into language planning by governments, non-governmental organizations, linguists and language planners, and in some cases, by Quechua-speaking communities themselves, contributing to overt, explicitly stated policy. However, the attitudes and actions of the average Spanish-speaking citizen, and even many Quechua-speaking citizens who have been successfully convinced of the lack of value of their language, represent implicit, covert policy, or the norms of daily practice. For Quechua to have a fighting chance of survival, the covert level is the one most in need of changing in all sectors of society, not only among mainstream members, but among Quechua speakers themselves who (may) have been negatively influenced in their own opinions of the value of their language, or in the value of other varieties of Quechua. Of course, it can only help for top-down and bottom-up groups to learn to work together as well.

References

Adelaar, W.F.H. and Muysken, P.C. (2004) *The Languages of the Andes*. Cambridge, UK: Cambridge University Press.

Albó, X. (1999) *Iguales Aunque Diferentes. Hacia unas Políticas Interculturales y Lingüísticas para Bolivia*. La Paz: Ministerio de Educación / UNICEF / CIPCA.

Cerrón-Palomino, R. (1989) Language policy in Peru: A historical overview. *International Journal of the Sociology of Language 77*, 11–33.

Cerrón-Palomino, R. (1997) Pasado y presente del quechua. *Yachay Wasi 4*, 49–64.

Coronel-Molina, S.M. (1999) Functional domains of the Quechua language in Peru: Issues of status planning. *International Journal of Bilingual Education and Bilingualism 2* (3), 166–180.

Coronel-Molina, S.M. (2005) Lenguas originarias cruzando el puente de la brecha digital: nuevas formas de revitalización del quechua y el aimara. In S.M. Coronel-Molina and L.L. Grabner-Coronel (eds) *Lenguas e Identidades en los Andes: Perspectivas Ideológicas y Culturales* (pp. 31–82). Quito, Ecuador: Abya Yala.

Coronel-Molina, S.M. (2007) Language policy and planning, and language ideologies in Peru: The case of Cuzco's High Academy of the Quechua Language (Qheswa simi hamut' ana kuraq suntur). Unpublished Ph.D. thesis, University of Pennsylvania.

Coronel-Molina, S.M. (in press) Sociohistorical perspective of Quechua language policy and planning in Peru. In J. Fishman and O. García (eds) *Handbook of Language and Ethnic Identity* (vol. 2). Oxford: Oxford University Press.

de la Cadena, M. (2000) *Indigenous Mestizos: The Politics of Race and Culture in Cuzco, Peru, 1919–1991*. Durham, NC: Duke University Press.

Durston, A. (2007) *Pastoral Quechua: The History of Christian Translation in Colonial Peru, 1550–1650*. South Bend, IN: University of Notre Dame Press.

García, M.E. (2005) *Making Indigenous Citizens: Identity, Development, and Multicultural Activism in Peru.* Palo Alto, CA: Stanford University Press.

Godenzzi, J.C. (1992) El recurso lingüístico del poder: coartadas ideológicas del quechua y el castellano. In J.C. Godenzzi (ed.) *El Quechua en Debate: Ideología, Normalización y Enseñanza* (pp. 51–77). Cuzco, Peru: Centro de Estudios Regionales Andinos 'Bartolomé de Las Casas.'

Godenzzi, J.C. (1997) Literacy and modernization among the Quechua speaking population of Peru. In N.H. Hornberger (ed.) *Indigenous Literacies in the Americas: Language Planning from the Bottom Up* (pp. 237–249). Berlin: Mouton de Gruyter.

Heath, S.B. and Laprade, R. (1982) Castilian colonization and Indigenous languages: The case of Quechua and Aymara. In R.L. Cooper (ed.) *Language Spread: Studies in Diffusion and Social Change* (pp. 118–147). Bloomington: Indiana University Press.

Hornberger, N.H. (1988) *Bilingual Education and Language Maintenance: A Southern Peruvian Quechua Case.* Berlin: Mouton de Gruyter.

Hornberger, N.H. (ed.) (1996) *Indigenous Literacies in the Americas: Language Planning from the Bottom Up.* Berlin: Mouton de Gruyter, Contributions to the Sociology of Language.

Hornberger, N.H. and Coronel-Molina, S.M. (guest eds) (2004) Quechua in the Andes: Language shift, maintenance and revitalization. Special issue, *International Journal of Sociology of Language* 167, 9–67.

Hornberger, N.H. and King, K.A. (2001) Reversing Quechua language shift in South America. In J. Fishman (ed.) *Can Threatened Languages Be Saved?* (pp. 166–194). Clevedon: Multilingual Matters.

Hornberger, N.H. and King, K.A. (2006) Quechua as lingua franca. *Annual Review of Applied Linguistics* 26, 177–194.

Invent–Diálogos de educación (2010) Perú: ¿Adiós a los maestros bilingües? – Online document: http://www.dialogos-en-educacion.org/actualidades/peru-adios-los-maestros-bilinguees. Accessed 20 October 2010.

King, K.A. (2001) *Language Revitalization Processes and Prospects: Quichua in the Ecuadorian Andes.* Clevedon: Multilingual Matters.

Klarén, P.F. (2000) *Peru: Society and Nationhood in the Andes.* New York/Oxford: Oxford University Press.

Ley General de Educación (2003, July 29) *Diario Oficial El Peruano.* Ley No. 28044, 248, 944–956.

Ley Nacional de Lenguas (2005) Ley Nacional de Lenguas – Online document: http://www.pucp.edu.pe/eventos/intercultural/pdfs/inter15.PDF. Accessed 20 October 2010.

López, L.E. (1990) El bilingüismo de los unos y los otros: diglosia y conflicto lingüístico en el Perú. In E. Ballón-Aguirre and R. Cerrón-Palomino (eds) *Diglosia Linguo-Literaria y Educación en el Perú* (pp. 91–128). Lima, Peru: CONCYTEC (Consejo Nacional de Ciencia y Tecnología) / GTZ (Deutsche Gesellschaft für Technische Zusammenarbeit).

López, L.E. (2002) La educación intercultural bilingüe ¿respuesta a la multietnicidad, pluriculturalidad y multilingüismo latinoamericanos? In M. Yamada and C.I. Degregori (eds) *Estados Nacionales, Etnicidad y Democracia en América Latina* (pp. 7–30). State Nation and Ethnic Relation IV. JCAS Symposium Series 15. Osaka: Japan Center for Area Studies, National Museum of Ethnology.

Mannheim, B. (1991) *The Language of the Inka Since the European Invasion.* Austin: University of Texas Press.

Marr, T. (1998). The language left at Ticlio: Social and cultural perspectives on Quechua loss in Lima, Peru. Unpublished Ph.D. thesis, University of Liverpool.

von Gleich, U. (1994) Language spread policy: The case of Quechua in the Andean republics of Bolivia, Ecuador, and Peru. *International Journal of the Sociology of Language* 107, 77–103.

Zúñiga, M., Cano, L. and Gálvez, M. (2003) *Construcción de Políticas Regionales: Lenguas, Culturas y Educación.* Ayacucho, Peru: Instituto de Estudios Regionales José María Arguedas.

Zúñiga, M., Sánchez, L. and Zacharías, D. (2000) *Demanda y Necesidad de Educación Bilingüe. Lenguas Indígenas y Castellano en el Sur Andino.* Lima: Ministry of Education of Peru/GTZ/KfW.

Chapter 9

An Ecological Perspective for Planning Chinese Language in the United States

SHUHAN C. WANG

Chinese languages in the United States have transformed, in stages, from immigrant languages spoken by laborers to high-status foreign languages with global currency (e.g. Lo Bianco, 2007). In the 21st century, the demand for Chinese as a Foreign/World Language[1] has been steadily increasing. According to a national survey of K-12 foreign-language programs conducted by the Center for Applied Linguistics, from 1997 to 2008, elementary schools offering Chinese-language instruction increased from 0.3% to 3%, and secondary schools from 1% to 4% (Rhodes & Pufahl, 2010). Similarly, post-secondary student enrollment grew from 2.4% to 3.3% from 1998 to 2006 (Furman et al., 2007). As heralded by a *New York Times* article, 'Foreign Languages Fade in Class – Except Chinese' (Dillon, 2010), demand for Chinese-language programs shows no sign of slowing, even amidst global economic contraction and local school district stress.

The high demand for Chinese-language instruction and the growing number of classes and teachers calls for an in-depth analysis of the Chinese case so that we can learn from past experiences and chart new directions for stakeholders – policy-makers, language planners and researchers, educators, parents, community members and students. Since September 11, 2001, the study and teaching of critical languages, including Chinese, Arabic, Hindi, Persian and Urdu, has been actively promoted in the US. The lessons learned from the Chinese case can shed light for other Less Commonly Taught Languages (LCTLs) currently under development.

This chapter takes an ecological perspective to analyze language planning, policy and practice in the case of the Chinese languages in the US, and addresses the following questions: (1) What has been the status and development of the Chinese languages over time in the US, and how have these developments affected language learning programs or language education? (2) What were the conditions and factors that contributed to the languages' transformation? (3) What are the implications for future Chinese-language education in the US? And, (4) what are the implications for other LCTLs?

Conceptual Framework

The evolution of the Chinese languages in the US calls our attention to the role of language policy and planning (LPP) in language education. The concern of LPP is often for large-scale and national efforts, usually undertaken by governments (Kaplan & Baldauf, 2008). Within the LPP discipline, there are three major strands: status planning relating to language function; corpus planning relating to language form; and acquisition planning relating to language learners and users (Cooper, 1989; Hornberger & Hult, 2008; Kaplan & Baldauf, 1997, 2008). Prior to the 1990s, there were no organized federal or state government LPP efforts to promote the study of Chinese in the US, although grassroots movements of Chinese minority groups have been evident since the early 20th century, as discussed below. However, the Chinese languages present a rich 'de facto' LPP case, providing illustrative examples of status, corpus and acquisition planning, particularly in the context of language education in the US.

LPP as a field increasingly recognizes that the study of a given language in a society or polity must be viewed from an ecological perspective that accounts for the complex relationships among languages, players, policies and contexts (e.g. Hornberger & Hult, 2008; Kaplan & Baldauf, 2008; Mühlhäusler, 2000; Wang, 2007, 2008). Building on Haugen's (1972) and other researchers' work, Hornberger synthesizes the ecology of language in the following way:

> I am primarily interested in three themes of the ecology metaphor which are salient to me in writings on the ecology of language; all of them are present in Haugen's original formulation. These are: that languages, like living species, evolve, grow, change, live, and die in relation to other languages and also in relation to their environment; for ease of reference, I will call these the *language evolution* and *language environment* themes. A third theme is the notion that some languages, like some species and environments, may be endangered and that the ecology movement is about not only studying and

describing those potential losses, but also counteracting them; this I will call the *language endangerment* theme. (Hornberger, 2003: 320–321)

Hornberger is concerned – here and throughout much of her scholarship – with how minority or Indigenous languages face assimilation or loss within the dominant society; thus the endangerment theme is prominent. In my work analyzing Chinese as a heritage language used and maintained by Chinese immigrants in the US, the theme of endangerment captures the push and pull of forces between language shift and language preservation (Wang, 2004). However, in the context of Chinese as a foreign/world language, the central theme is the effect of efforts to spread a foreign language in a new environment. Therefore, in discussing language education planning and policy, I replace the language endangerment theme with *language effect* as it applies to contexts of both language maintenance and foreign/world language spread. The ecology of language also lends itself as an approach to investigate, critically think about and analyze 'contextual interconnections in language contact situations and their wider implications for sociopolitical actions' (Hornberger & Hult, 2008: 282). Building upon this body of work, I developed an integrated matrix as an analytical tool that applies an ecological perspective to the investigation of various strands of LPP (Table 9.1).

'Planning and Policy' in the title of the matrix refers to governmental statements, legislative efforts, funding support and actions. 'Practice' refers to the actions, behaviors and programs that players at all levels of education have engaged in to promote or prohibit language learning and teaching. On the top level of this matrix is the ecological perspective with its three themes of environment, evolution and effect. 'Environment' reflects both macro- and micro-level factors. Macro-level environment factors may include economic, political and national security concerns between home and host countries; public attitudes toward the language and people who use it; and legislative efforts and funding support for that language. Micro-level environment factors may include who the speakers of this language are, how they arrived in the host country, under what conditions, in what number and where they settled. Their religious beliefs and cultural practices, social integration and educational levels come into question, and so does their perceived allegiance to the English language and US society (Hornberger & Wang, 2008). The prestige (status) and perceived usefulness of their language is another driving factor in learning or teaching the language.

Evolution of a language refers to how this language, over time, in the macro- and micro-environments described above, has been maintained as

Table 9.1 An ecological language education matrix for planning, policy and practice

	Ecological Perspective				
	Environment & Evolution				Effects
	Language Planning and Policy in Action: Approaches to Overt or Covert Goals				
Status Planning		*Corpus Planning*			*Acquisition Planning*
	Time period?	*Time period?*	*Time period?*	*Time period?*	Function of Language Education
Type of Language Education		Top-down Support: Formal Education System?			
Foreign language?					
Bilingual/English Language Learners?					
Heritage/Religious/Culture Schools?		Bottom-up Effort: Home/Community?			
Home Language?					

Source: Adapted from Baldauf (2005); Cooper (1989); Wang (2007)

a home/heritage language, assimilated to another or the dominant language, or introduced into the formal education system as a foreign/world language. It is important to examine the development of a corpus of the language and variants being promoted or used in a host environment. In measuring the effect of LPP, questions such as the status or prestige of the language and the incentives and opportunities to study that language must be addressed. Efforts and outcomes in terms of language maintenance, shift, death or spread, or number and sustainability of language programs and student learning achievements should be documented and analyzed.

On the next level are language planning and policy in action, which lay out approaches to influencing 'ways of speaking or literacy practices within a society' (Baldauf, 2004: 1). Here I analyze the effect of LPP in terms of status planning, that is, the status of Chinese in various historical periods in terms of language education types: home, heritage, bilingual or foreign/world language education. I examine the corpus planning of Chinese through: (1) the intra-Chinese diversity issue, outlining what dialects of Chinese are being used by whom; and (2) how the issues of language reform within Chinese have affected Chinese-language programs. Finally, my discussion of acquisition planning focuses on the factors that contribute to the maintenance, shift or spread of Chinese language in the US.

In this matrix, I differentiate bottom-up effort from top-down support: the efforts made by individuals and ethnic groups in the unofficial and private space of the society; and the policy, funding and programs made by the formal education system in the official and public space. Home language maintenance or heritage language schools, whether for cultural, linguistic or religious purposes, fall into the grassroots domain, whereas bilingual education or foreign/world language education, being part of the formal education system, fall into the top-down support domain.

These two types of efforts dovetail in the environmental and evolution themes, so they serve as organizing principles of the following discussion. At the close of the chapter, I use data from the Chinese case to 'fill in the blanks' in this matrix to illustrate an ecological approach to LPP.

Bottom-up Efforts: Chinese as a Home and Heritage Language

On the macro-level, US policy and public attitudes toward immigrant languages used in the private sphere of ethnic communities have largely been 'tolerance oriented,' neither prohibiting nor encouraging the maintenance of heritage language and culture (Macías & Wiley, 1998: x). Under this laissez-faire policy, many immigrant groups have established heritage schools that Fishman describes as *reversing language shift*, striving to preserve heritage languages and cultures in the dominant society, as seen in German, Greek, Hebrew, Korean or Yiddish schools in the US (Alliance for the Advancement of Heritage Languages, 2010; Fishman, 1991). Chinese heritage language schools have similar aims and origins.

On the micro-level, Chinese heritage language schools are products of cultural practice. There is a long-standing Chinese tradition of setting up private, one-room schools in towns or villages, prior to the availability of public education. Chinese families in the diaspora often organized their own schools, usually in the basement of a church or a few rented classrooms from a nearby university or school, to teach children their ancestral language and culture on the weekends (Wang, S.C., 2004; Wang, X., 1996).

Paralleling the immigration patterns of the Chinese, there are three major groups of Chinese community schools in the US, each of which is independent, with little interaction between groups. The first group consists of Chinese schools in and around Chinatowns in large cities such as San Francisco, Chicago and New York. Many of these were formed in the 19th century to teach the children of the few Chinese merchants who were allowed to bring their families to the US. Because most of this group came from Guangdong (or Canton), their schools taught in Cantonese (Chan & Tsang, 1983; Wong, 1945). Later, when public schools began to accept Chinese students, these community schools changed into either after-school programs or weekend schools.

Since the Immigration Act of 1968 and throughout the 1970s, there was a steady influx of graduate students and business people coming from Taiwan or Hong Kong, comprising what is known as the second wave of Chinese immigrants (Takaki, 1989). They established Chinese schools that taught Mandarin, often with a few additional classes in Cantonese. From 1987 to the early 2000s, because of the political drive toward independence in Taiwan, a small branch of these Chinese schools began to teach Taiwanese, a dialect related to Min, also known as Fukienese.

During the decade from 1974 to 1984, as a result of the Vietnam War and subsequent US policy in the area (Wong, 1988), an influx of ethnic Chinese from Cambodia, Vietnam and Laos arrived, settled into Chinatowns, and transformed them into Asiantowns (Wang, 2004). Some of the Chinese schools began to offer instruction in Mandarin, Vietnamese, Hmong or Cambodian as a home language and English as a Second Language (Hardman, 1994; Skilton-Sylvester, 1997). Because these Chinese schools serve a large number of immigrant children, many were incorporated into local educational systems and have become bilingual or immersion schools or service centers for new arrivals. Alice Fong Yu Chinese-English Immersion School in San Francisco exemplifies this trend.

After the Tian'anmen Square protests and violence in 1989, a third wave of Chinese immigrants, mostly professionals, students and their families, from the People's Republic of China (P.R.C) began to arrive to the US (Zweig & Chen, 1995). Mandarin is both the subject of study and the medium of instruction in the Chinese heritage schools they established. Because the immigration settlement pattern of this group is similar to that of immigrants from Taiwan and Hong Kong, so are the accomplishments, challenges and issues faced by their Chinese schools (Wang, S.C., 2004; Wang, X., 1996).

In 1993, under the auspices of the National Foreign Language Center (NFLC), the Chinese heritage schools established by the immigrants from China (the third wave) formed a national organization called the *Chinese School Association in the United States* (CSAUS). In 2008, it is reported that there were 100,000 students and 7000 teachers in 410 heritage schools (Han, 2010). In 1994, also with the support of NFLC, the Taiwan/Hong Kong heritage schools (the second wave) formed the *National Council of Associations of Chinese Language Schools* (NCACLS). In 2009, because immigration from Taiwan has decreased, there are now 70,599 students and 5354 teachers in 401 schools, a 30% decline from 1995 (Yen, 2010).

Since the 1990s, many Chinese schools have experienced a new phenomenon – the presence of non-Chinese families who adopted children from China. According to Families with Children from China (FCC), the number of such adoptions grew from a few dozen in 1985 to 23,903 in 2004 nationwide (FCC, 2004: para. 5). This special population adds another dimension to the already complex issue of heritage language and culture transmission (Hornberger & Wang, 2008).

Top-down Support

Chinese language in bilingual education

Under the policies of Bilingual Education Act (1968) and the No Child Left Behind (NCLB, Public Law 107–110, 2001), the status of Chinese language is subject to an assimilationist ideology that has continued to drive different forms of Americanization through education (Hornberger & Johnson, 2007; Johnson, 2010; Lo Bianco, 2001). Although the landmark case of Lau v. Nichols (1974) affirmed the rights of Chinese-speaking children to meaningful education (Ruiz, 1984), Chinese and other immigrant languages often face hostility, and are often associated with fears of immigration and questioned allegiance to the US (Hornberger & Wang, 2008; Wong, 1988). The development of heritage languages and their effectiveness in helping immigrant students learn English and other subjects have been glaringly absent from discourse on implementing policies for English Language Learners (ELLs) (Evans & Hornberger, 2005; Hornberger & Johnson, 2007; Johnson, 2010).

Chinese as an emerging foreign/world language: 1960–2000

In formal foreign-language education, Chinese is a newcomer compared with commonly taught European languages such as French, German or Spanish. The National Defense Education Act Title VI of 1958, now Title VI of the Higher Education Act, introduced Chinese as one of the non-Western European languages offered in a limited number of graduate programs in select universities, but has had little impact in promoting Chinese in K-12 schools (Moore *et al.*, 1992: 1–2). Historically, two major private initiatives were instrumental in introducing Chinese to US schools: the Carnegie Foundation in the early 1960s and throughout the 1980s, and the Geraldine Dodge Foundation from the 1980s through the early 2000s. Unfortunately, neither of these major initiatives established significant numbers of sustainable Chinese-language programs in the US, although they began to build the foundation of an infrastructure for the Chinese-language field (Moore *et al.*, 1992; Wang, 2007, 2008).

Federal funding for Chinese in the K-12 level has been limited to the Foreign Language Assistance Program (FLAP), first enacted in 1988, which awards funds to state and local educational agencies for three years to develop model programs that establish, improve or expand foreign-language study in elementary and secondary schools. In the 1992 reauthorization of the Elementary and Secondary Education Act (ESEA), Chinese was identified as one of the 'critical languages' that should receive funding priority, but the funding was too little and too competitive to have a significant impact. Taken together, before 2004, Chinese foreign-language enrollment in secondary schools (Grades 7–12) was only 24,000 (Draper & Hicks, 2000), and 34,153 in post-secondary institutions (Welles, 2003). In contrast, the number of students enrolled in heritage language programs in 2003 was 150,000, almost three times more than those in the formal education system (McGinnis, 2005). During this period, the status of Chinese was still primarily that of a home and heritage language.

Chinese as an important foreign/world/global language: 2004 to present

The year 2004 was a defining one for the evolution of Chinese-language education in the US, with two pivotal events heralding the transformation of Chinese from an emerging to a fashionable foreign or 'global' language. The first of these was the National Language Conference held by the Departments of Defense, State and Education, in partnership with the Intelligence Community and the Center for the Advanced Study of Language of the University of Maryland. The White Paper published after the conference became a roadmap for a series of federal initiatives for critical languages that will be outlined later (National Language Conference, 2005). The second event was the College Board's decision to offer the Chinese Advancement Placement (AP) examination after survey results showed that 2400 schools expressed interest in the prospect of a Chinese AP (Asia Society, 2005); the exam allows high-school students to earn college-level credits for studying Chinese.

The National Security Language Initiative (NSLI) was enacted in 2006, supported by the federal agencies mentioned above. Although not intended as a comprehensive foreign language educational policy, NSLI addressed the national need for language competence and linked national security with education (Language Flagship, 2010; NSLI, 2008).

Among federal initiatives, STARTALK is probably the most far-reaching, as it offers intensive summer learning opportunities for students and teachers in K-16 (kindergarten through post-secondary) in Arabic, Chinese, Hindi, Persian, Turkish, Swahili and Urdu (also Dari and Russian teacher programs in 2010). Managed by the National Foreign Language Center at the University of Maryland (NFLC, 2010), from 2007 to 2009, STARTALK Chinese programs have served 5762 students and 1908 teachers nationally. With an average funding of $15 million per year, this initiative will continue until 2013 (STARTALK, 2010), and is expected to have long-lasting impact on the nation's foreign-language education. What sets STARTALK apart is its focus on programs for teacher development (Wang, 2009) and infrastructure building on the national level, a point that will be elaborated later.

The Chinese-language field now receives additional top-down support that has not been seen in previous periods. For example, numerous municipal and state governments have developed 'Foreign Language Roadmaps' (e.g. Texas, Ohio, Oregon, & Utah) or 'Chinese Language Initiatives' (e.g. Minnesota and New York), recognizing the study of Chinese language and culture as strategic for economic competitiveness and for developing the global competence of their future workers (Asia Society

& China Institute, 2009; Asia Society & College Board, 2008; Minnesota Department of Education, 2007). International and national players are instrumental, including the Office of Chinese Language Council International (commonly known as Hanban) of the People's Republic of China, the College Board, Asia Society and various professional organizations (Wang, 2008). Twenty-first century media and digital tools have been adapted into numerous resources and programs for learners of Chinese, mostly Mandarin, broadening access and opportunities to learn anytime and anyplace.

Implications of the Chinese Case for Language Policy and Planning

Status planning

The status of Chinese languages has undergone different stages of transformation. In the 19th and early 20th centuries, Chinese (as a collective term for all dialects) was identified as a language of 'coolies' or laborers, which stirred up strong nativist sentiments and made it impossible for Chinese to be assimilated, even in the eyes of the law (e.g., the Nationality Act, 1870; the Page Law, 1875; the Chinese Exclusion Act, 1882; and the Immigration Act, 1924; also see Hing, 1993; Takaki, 1989). Since the 1950s and up to the present time, under the policies of bilingual education and education for ELLs, Chinese as a home language continues to be at the *unum* (assimilationist) rather than the *pluribus* (pluralist) end of the US national motto, *E pluribus Unum* ('out of many, one') (Lo Bianco, 2001).

Since the mid-1980s, concurrently with the rise of Taiwan, Hong Kong and Singapore (all Chinese-speaking regions), Chinese has slowly gained ground in the world language field. The themes of societal economic competitiveness and language competency as a new set of skills for individuals in the global age have gained prominence (CED, 2006), coinciding with the rise of China as a world superpower. After 2004, the identity and marketability (Grin, 2006; Zhou, 2006) of Chinese languages have taken off in the US and the world (Lo Bianco, 2007).

While the prestige, usefulness and desirability of Chinese have rapidly changed, the fact remains that Chinese still makes up only about 3% or 4% of language program offerings or student enrollment in K-12 and post-secondary sectors, dwarfed by the numbers of Spanish or French programs and learners (Furman *et al.*, 2007; Rhodes & Pufahl, 2010). However, the US and Chinese governments' heavy investment in promoting the study of Mandarin creates the anxiety that Chinese absorbs most of the resources and space in a school's world language curriculum. It is not likely that Chinese will soon be a 'killer language' like English (Kaplan & Baldauf, 2008: 45); nevertheless, if Chinese continues to grow, language planners and policy makers may need to consider how to manage an anti-Chinese backlash in world language education in US schools.

Corpus planning

Parallel to the issue of keeping linguistic diversity in the macro-foreign-language environment, intra-Chinese-language diversity poses its own challenges. As mentioned previously, a variety of Chinese dialects (Cantonese, Taiwanese & Mandarin) have been taught in US education systems. As Mandarin is heavily promoted, the very notion of 'heritage language' has become more fluid and evolving. In a Chinese-language classroom, teachers must keep in mind that not all Chinese heritage language learners are Mandarin speakers, and dialect speakers may face extra burdens or identity conflicts when learning Mandarin (Hornberger & Wang, 2008). Tending the 'biodiversity' of Chinese is important for many heritage language students.

Because the P.R.C. was essentially behind the iron curtain between the 1950s and 1980s, there was little debate in the formal education system about the Chinese corpus, but since the 1980s the Chinese-language field has seen rigorous debates about what should be considered 'Standard' pronunciation, lexicon and writing scripts (DeFrancis, 1984; Everson & Xiao, 2009; Kubler, 2006). It is widely known that the linguistic divergence of Chinese has become more prevalent since 1949, when the Nationalist (Guomingdang) and the Communist (Gongchandang) split resulted in the formation of Taiwan (Nationalist) and the People's Republic of China (Communist). While the varieties of Mandarin used in P.R.C. and Taiwan remain intact and are mutually intelligible, there are differences that trigger more psychological, emotional and identity issues than linguistic issues (Everson & Xiao, 2009; Kubler, 2006). During the late 1980s and throughout the 1990s, in almost every Chinese-language meeting or conference, rigorous and emotional debates raged over which version of Mandarin to teach, the P.R.C. or the traditional varieties commonly used in Taiwan.

Since the beginning of the 21st century, as China has been recognized as a world power, such debates have become fewer and less vehement. Generally, the consensus of the field has been to use Hanyu Pinyin for teaching pronunciation, and to introduce students to only one form of writing, either simplified or traditional, and familiarize them later with the other form (Asia Society, 2006). For heritage schools, such issues of corpus are less important because the schools usually adopt the system that most parents use.

Acquisition planning

Acquisition planning must negotiate a complicated and interwoven system of national language needs and the supply and demand of students, teachers and programs. Infrastructure, which consists of policy, funding, program types, curriculum, materials, assessment of student learning outcomes, program evaluation and community/parental support, etc., must also be considered. The Chinese case illustrates how these components and mechanisms of needs, supply and demand interact.

First of all, the field is built on a foundation established from the bottom up by the highly educated immigrant parents from Taiwan, Hong Kong and P.R.C. Although Chinese heritage language school systems continue to struggle with 'revers[ing] language shift' (Fishman, 1991), these systems have built an infrastructure for a language learning system that includes curriculum, materials, and assessment, albeit much of it 'homemade.' They have produced a large number of Chinese learners who possess proficiency and literacy that is beyond what two-year high school or tertiary language programs can produce. They are the largest source of Chinese-language teachers, many of whom can be trained and certified to teach in public schools. They are a community of practice that can provide linguistic and cultural resources for formal Chinese-language programs. These heritage language schools provide rich nutrients that nurture the Chinese languages' growth (Wang, S.C., 2004; Wang, X., 1996).

Second, the gradual buildup of the language learning system since the 1960s has provided the necessary conditions and support for the boom after 2004. During these four decades, two professional organizations (CLASS and CLTA) and programs supported by the formal education system, heritage systems, the government and private providers have been built and connected. Materials, assessment and curricula have begun to develop, albeit on a small scale. A research tradition about Chinese-language acquisition, teaching methodology, and teacher development, and a network of experts and researchers, is established.

Finally, the Chinese field benefits from having top-down support from the US and Chinese governments; bottom-up efforts from heritage language school systems; active promotion from non-government organizations and professional organizations; and an infrastructure of language learning and teaching. From an ecological perspective, all these elements are essential.

Table 9.2 The Chinese case as shown in an ecological language planning, policy and practice matrix

	Ecological Perspective				
	Environment & Evolution				Effects
	Language Planning and Policy in Action: Approaches to Overt or Covert Goals				
Status Planning	*Corpus Planning*				*Acquisition Planning*
	19th Century to 1949	1950–1969	1970–2004	2004–Present	
Type of Language Education					Function of Language Education
Formal Education System (with Top-down Support)					
Foreign / World Language		Mandarin in select IHE & K-12 schools	Mandarin (Cantonese & Taiwanese in select schools)	Mandarin (Cantonese & Taiwanese in select schools)	Language spread
Bilingual Ed / English Language Learners		Bilingual Education Act (1968) No Child Left Behind (2001)			Assimilation / Language shift
Home / Community (Bottom-up Effort)					
Heritage Language (in community schools)	Cantonese	Cantonese	Mandarin, Cantonese, Taiwanese	Mandarin, Cantonese, Taiwanese	Maintenance / Reversing language shift
Home Language	Cantonese, Taishanese, Chaozhou, Hakka, gradually Mandarin & other dialects such as Shanghainese & Taiwanese	Mandarin, Taiwanese, Cantonese, & other Chinese dialects	Mandarin, Cantonese, Taiwanese	Mandarin, Taiwanese, Cantonese, Taishanese, Chaozhou, Hakka, & other Chinese dialects	Maintenance

Conclusion

So far, I have used the matrix as a guide to analyze the Chinese case in the US. My discussion is summarized in the matrix with data reflecting the Chinese case (Table 9.2).

Based on the Chinese case, what are the future directions and recommendations for the Chinese field and other LCTLs?

Recommendations for the Chinese field

Recommendation 1: Expand and Solidify Language Learning Systems to Support the Rapid Growth of the Chinese Language Field. Instead of rushing to establish more Chinese-language programs, strengthen comprehensive language learning systems that address the supply and demand of students, teachers, curricula, materials, assessment, traditional classroom and digital delivery models, and provide the necessary funding, research and technical assistance for schools and communities. As mentioned earlier, this is what STARTALK has been doing since its inception in 2007, which benefits language-specific and the general world language fields.

Recommendation 2: Develop Students' Biliteracy in Chinese and the Native Language. It is not enough to expose students with a flavor of Chinese language and culture. Educators, researchers and stakeholders in K-12, higher education, and heritage language communities need to analyze the conditions in which they teach and carefully study their students' needs, abilities, motivations, identities and evidence of learning outcomes. Hornberger's continua of biliteracy framework (Hornberger, 2003; Skilton-Sylvester, 1997) provides excellent theoretical and practical considerations for developing students' biliteracy in target and native languages.

Recommendation 3: Connect Theory with Practice in Chinese LPP Activities and Extend the Lessons Learned to World Language Education in General. There needs to be much coordination of policy, funding and practice in all levels and sectors to ensure the healthy growth of the Chinese field and its relationships with other languages. Additionally, policy makers need to include world language study as a core subject for student learning account-ability, while considering how to develop coherent US language education policies for ELLs, Bilingual Education, Foreign Language Education and Heritage Language Education. Hornberger and Hult (2008: 295) suggest two major questions to consider:

- How are relationships among different languages reflected in policy documents?
- How do language policies at multiple levels of social organization interact?

Without a broad-based and in-depth discussion of these questions and a thorough review of language policies and their implications, the US will continue to have fragmented and often contradictory poli-cies and approaches to language education. Borrow-ing Hornberger's terms, in the near future there is very limited ideological or implementational space (Hornberger, 2009) moving toward upholding a mul-tilingual education policy in the US.

Recommendations for less commonly taught languages

I hope the *Ecological Language Education Matrix for Planning, Policy and Practice* overviewed here has both theoretical and practical applications that will help other LCTLs to examine their language-specific fields. Each language has its own ecological system; the key is to pay attention to the dynamic interactions among languages (and variants), policy, practice and players within the system and strategize about how to leverage resources and remove barriers.

In closing, I quote a statement from Hornberger that eloquently sums up what language education in a global age should strive for:

Multilingual education is, at its best, (1) multilingual in that it uses and values more than one language in teaching and learning, (2) intercultural in that it recognizes and values understanding and dia-logue across different lived experiences and cultural worldviews, and (3) education that draws out, taking as its starting point the knowl-edge students bring to the classroom and moving toward their partic-ipation as full and indispensable actors in society – locally, nationally, and globally. (Hornberger, 2009: 198)

Indeed, in any ecology, all things are living; so is a language that is dear to the hearts of its speakers.

Note

1. In this article, I use foreign language and world language interchangeably. In K-12 education, foreign language is also labeled as world language because that language is not 'foreign' to a heritage language student. In the post-secondary level, however, foreign language is still the preferred label.

References

Alliance for the Advancement of Heritage Languages (2010) Heritage languages in America – Online document: http://www.cal.org/heritage/.

Asia Society (2005) *Expanding Chinese Language Capacity in the United States: What Would it Take to Have 5 Percent of High School Students Learning Chinese by 2015?* New York: Asia Society.

Asia Society (2006) *An Introductory Guide: Creating a Chinese Language Program in Your School.* New York: Asia Society.

Asia Society and China Institute (2009) *Developing Global Competence for a Changing World: Learning Chinese in New York schools. Report of the New York Task Force on Chinese Language and Culture Initiatives.* New York: Asia Society.

Asia Society and College Board (2008) *Chinese in 2008: An Expanding Field.* New York: Asia Society.

Baldauf Jr., R.B. (2004) Language planning and policy: Recent trends, future directions. Paper presented at the conference of the American Association of Applied Linguistics, Portland, Oregon.

Baldauf Jr., R.B. (2005) Language planning and policy research: An overview. In E. Hinkel (ed.) *Handbook of Research in Second Language Teaching and Learning* (pp. 957–970). Mahwah, NJ: Lawrence Erlbaum.

Chan, K.S. and Tsang, S.L. (1983) Overview of the educational progress of Chinese Americans. In D.T. Nakanishi and M. Hirano-Nakanishi (eds) *The Education of Asian and Pacific Americans: Historical Perspectives and Prescriptions for the Future* (pp. 39–48). Phoenix, AZ: Oryx Press.

Committee for Economic Development (CED) (2006) *Education for Global Leadership: The Importance of International Studies and Foreign Language Education for U.S. Economic and National Security.* Washington, DC: Committee for Economic Development.

Cooper, R.L. (1989) *Language Planning and Social Change.* Cambridge: Cambridge University Press.

DeFrancis, J. (1984) *The Chinese Language: Fact and Fantasy.* Honolulu, HI: University of Hawaii Press.

Dillon, S. (2010) Foreign languages fade in class – Except Chinese. *New York Times*, 21 January , A18.

Draper, J.B. and Hicks, J.H. (2000) *Foreign Language Enrollments in Public Secondary Schools.* Alexandria, VA: American Council on the Teaching of Foreign Languages.

Evans, B. and Hornberger, N.H. (2005) No child left behind: Repealing and unpeeling federal language education policy in the United States. *Language Policy* 4 (1), 87–106.

Everson, M.E. and Xiao, Y. (eds) (2008) *Teaching Chinese as a Foreign Language: Theories and Applications*. Boston: Cheng & Tsui.

Families with Children from China (FCC) Homepage – Online document: http://www.fwcc.org.

Fishman, J.A. (1991) *Reversing Language Shift: Theoretical and Empirical Foundations of Assistance to Threatened Languages*. Clevedon: Multilingual Matters.

Furman, N., Goldberg, D. and Lusin, N. (2007) *Enrollment in Languages Other than English in the United States Institutions of Higher Education, Fall 2006*. New York: Modern Language Association.

Grin, F. (2006) Economic considerations in language policy. In T. Ricento (ed.) *An Introduction to Language Policy* (pp. 77–94). Oxford: Blackwell.

Han, Q. (2010) *Valuable Resources for Chinese Language Education from Heritage Schools*. Presentation at the National Chinese Language Conference, Washington, DC, 22–24 April.

Hardman, J.C. (1994) Language and literacy development in a Cambodian community in Philadelphia. Unpublished PhD thesis, University of Pennsylvania.

Haugen, E. (1972) The ecology of language. In A.S. Dil (ed.) *The Ecology of Language* (pp. 325–339). Stanford, CA: Stanford University Press.

Hing, B.O. (1993) *Making and Remaking Asian America through Immigration Policy 1850–1990*. Stanford, CA: Stanford University Press.

Hornberger, N.H. (2003) Multilingual language policies and the continua of biliteracy: An ecological approach. In N.H. Hornberger (ed.) *Continua of Biliteracy: An Ecological Framework for Educational Policy, Research, and Practice in Multilingual Settings* (pp. 315–339). Clevedon: Multilingual Matters.

Hornberger, N.H. (2009) Multilingual education policy and practice: Ten certainties (grounded in Indigenous experience). *Language Teaching* 42 (2), 197–211.

Hornberger, N.H. and Hult, F.M. (2008) Ecological language education policy. In B. Spolsky and F.M. Hult (eds) *Handbook of Educational Linguistics* (pp. 280–296). Malden, MA: Blackwell.

Hornberger, N.H. and Johnson, D.C. (2007) Slicing the onion ethnographically: Layers and spaces in multilingual language education policy and practice. *TESOL Quarterly* 41 (3), 509–532.

Hornberger, N.H. and Wang, S.C. (2008) Who are our heritage language learners? Identity and biliteracy in heritage language education in the United States. In D. Brinton, O. Kagan and S. Bauckus (eds) *Heritage Language Education: A New Field Emerging* (pp. 3–35). New York: Routledge.

Johnson, D.C. (2010). Implementational and ideological spaces in bilingual education language policy. *International Journal of Bilingual Education and Bilingualism* 13 (1), 61–79.

Kaplan, R.B. and Baldauf Jr., R.B. (1997) *Language Planning: From Practice to Theory*. Clevedon: Multilingual Matters.

Kaplan, R.B and Baldauf Jr., R.B. (2008) An ecology perspective on language planning. In A. Creese, P. Martin and N.H. Hornberger (eds) *Encyclopedia of Language and Education*, vol. 9: *Ecology of Language* (pp. 41–52). New York: Springer.

Kubler, C.C. (ed.) (2006) *NFLC Guide for Basic Chinese Language Programs*. Washington, D.C.: National Foreign Language Center.

Language Flagship (2010) Homepage – Online document: http://www. thelanguageflagship.org/.

Lo Bianco, J. (2001) *What is the Problem? A Study of Official English.* Paper presented at the conference of American Association for Applied Linguistics, 24–27 February, St. Louis, MO.

Lo Bianco, J. (ed.) (2007) The emergence of Chinese. *Language Policy* 6 (1), 3–26.

Macías, R.F. and Wiley, T.G. (1998) Introduction. In H. Kloss (ed.) *The American Bilingual Tradition* (pp. xxv–xxix). Washington, DC and McHenry, IL: Center for Applied Linguistics and Delta Systems [Reprint of Kloss, H. (1977) *The American Bilingual Tradition.* Rowley MA: Newbury House.].

McGinnis, S. (2005) *Statistics on Chinese Language Enrollment* – Online document: http://clta-us.org/flyers/enrollment_stats.htm.

Minnesota Department of Education (2007) *Chinese Language Programs Curriculum Development Project* – Online document: http://education.state.mn.us/MDE/ groups/Communications/documents/Report/030708.pdf.

Moore, S.J., Walton, A.R. and Lambert, R.D. (1992) *Introducing Chinese into High Schools: The Dodge Initiative* (National Foreign Language Center Monograph Series). Washington, DC: Johns Hopkins University.

Mühlhäusler, P. (2000) Language planning and language ecology. *Current Issues in Language Planning* 1 (3), 306–367.

National Foreign Language Center at the University of Maryland (NFLC) (2010) Homepage – Online document: http://www.nflc.org.

National Language Conference (2005) *A Call to Action for National Foreign Language Capabilities White Paper.* Proceedings of the National Language Conference sponsored by the Department of Defense and the Center for the Advanced Study of Language, 22–24 June 2004, University of Maryland, College Park, MD.

National Security Language Initiatives (NSLI) (2008) Homepage – Online document: http://www2.ed.gov/about/inits/ed/competitiveness/nsli/index. html.

Rhodes, N.C. and Pufahl, I. (2010) *Foreign Language Teaching in U.S. Schools: Results of a National Survey.* Washington, DC: Center for Applied Linguistics.

Ruiz, R. (1984) Orientations in language planning. *NABE Journal* 8, 15–34.

Skilton-Sylvester, E. (1997) Inside, outside, and in-between: Identities, literacies, and educational policies in the lives of Cambodian women and girls. Unpublished PhD thesis, University of Pennsylvania.

STARTALK (2010) Homepage – Online document: http://startalk.umd.edu.

Takaki, R. (1989) *Strangers from a Different Shore.* Boston, MA: Little, Brown.

Wang, S.C. (2004) Biliteracy resource eco-system of intergenerational transmission of heritage language and culture: An ethnographic study of a Chinese community in the United States. Unpublished PhD thesis, University of Pennsylvania.

Wang, S.C. (2007). Building societal capital: Chinese in the United States. *Language Policy* 6 (1), 27–52.

Wang, S.C. (2008) The ecology of the Chinese language in the United States. In N.H. Hornberger, A. Creese and P. Martin (eds) *Encyclopedia of Language and Education*, vol. 9: *Ecology of Language* (pp. 169–181). New York: Springer.

Wang, S.C. (2009) Preparing and supporting teachers of less commonly taught languages. *Modern Language Journal* 93 (2), 282–287.

Wang, X. (ed.) (1996) *A View from Within: A Case Study of Chinese Heritage Community Language Schools in the United States.* Washington, DC: Johns Hopkins University.

Welles, E.B. (2003) Foreign language enrollments in United States institutions of higher education, Fall 2002. *ADFL Bulletin* 35 (2–3), 7–26.

Wong, J.S. (1945) *The Fifth Chinese Daughter.* New York: Harper and Brothers.

Wong, S.C. (1988) The language situation of Chinese Americans. In S.L. McKay and S.C. Wong (eds) *Language Diversity: Problem or Resource? A Social and Educational Perspective on Language Minorities in the United States* (pp. 193–228). New York: Newbury House.

Yen, J.L. (2010) *Connect and Inspire through Cultural Heritage.* Presentation at the National Chinese Language Conference, 22–24 April, Washington, DC.

Zhou, M. (2006) Theorizing language contact, spread, and variation in status planning: A case study of modern standard Chinese. *Journal of Asian Pacific Communication* 16 (2), 159–174.

Zweig, D. and Chen, C. (1995) *China's Brain Drain to the United States: Views of Overseas Chinese Students and Scholars in the 1990s.* Berkeley, CA: University of California, Institute of East Asian Studies.

Afterword: Cooking with Nancy

RICHARD RUIZ

Nancy Hornberger has been peeling and unpeeling and slicing and unslic-ing the language planning onion for quite a long time.[1] This book can be seen as an onion cookbook by her students and colleagues – borrowing and extending her recipes to create their own. So, now that Nancy can order from the senior menu at her local restaurant, we might ask how close these recipes are to Nancy's original dishes.

First, however, I should start with some history. Nancy's passion for language and education are of long-standing. Although we in higher edu-cation may like to take credit for igniting and directing her passion, she acknowledges the early experiences she had in school, and specifically those with her first-grade teacher, Miss Lohnberg, as the starting point in her continuing journey to understand language and its role in society (Hornberger, 2010).

Even before graduating from Radcliffe College (Harvard University) in the History and Literature program in 1972, Nancy taught for a short while in a public school in Arequipa, Peru. In that role she also produced teaching materials and taught children of Quechua-speaking parents. Shortly after graduation, she worked as a consultant, teacher and cur-riculum developer in bilingual education for the Quechua Community Ministry and the *Instituto de Pastoral Andino* in Cusco. By the time she arrived at the University of Wisconsin in Madison for her doctoral pro-gram in 1980, she had already clearly exceeded the experience of her student peers, as well as that of many of her professors.

She has always been an able and bold presenter of her work. Cahnmann's ethnopoetic approach to ethnography and language (this book) reminds me of one of the first conferences I attended with Nancy as my student – the Southern Anthropological Society Conference in April, 1981 in Fort Worth, Texas. Cahnman writes of the expressive possibili-ties of ethnography, and speculates that Nancy's work could have been informed by her vocal performances with the University of Pennsylvania choir. I have similar memories of Nancy in Fort Worth; since we were in

Texas, someone on the conference organizing committee decided to get
one of the locals to teach all of these stodgy academics the two-step. As
is my wont in these situations, I stayed in the far reaches of the room,
diverting my eyes when anyone even appeared to be looking for a part-
ner. Nancy was one of the first on the dance floor, willing to learn from
this new cultural experience as perhaps any ethnographer should. I can
see that she would have encouraged her students to be as bold, whether
in writing or reciting poetry, dancing on unfamiliar ground, or presenting
papers in front of unknown academics.

Nancy Hornberger's dissertation at the University of Wisconsin (1985)
won the outstanding dissertations competition held annually by the
National Association for Bilingual Education; it is 651 pages long (not
including 22 pages of front matter, but including the longest acknowledgement section I have ever seen) – easily the thickest book in my collection.
No one should be surprised by that. It is a testament to her dedication,
persistence and thoroughness. In her dissertation, she demonstrates that
from the beginning of her life as an academic, her primary interest was
to give voice to those who were on the margins of society; her extensive
field notes are a clear demonstration of that interest. The meticulous attention to her field notes, the basic tool of the ethnographer, is what strikes
her former student Angela Creese (this book) as one of the hallmarks of
Hornberger's work: 'Fieldnotes document details of practice. They are
productions and recordings of the researchers' noticings with the intent
of describing the research participant's actions emically.' Even Nancy's
reports on the progress of her dissertation research (1983) while she was a
Fulbright Scholar were extensive and detailed:

> As time went on, I got to know more families, and adult members of
> the community would come and visit me, usually in the early morn-
> ing or late afternoon, and I would visit their homes. I also participated
> in and observed several important *fiestas* of the community (school
> anniversary, district *fiesta*, *Todos Santos*) when more members of the
> community were present. My observations ranged from continuous
> participation in the daily life of the community (e.g., giving rides to
> the community members, sharing kerosene, rat poison, or meals, play-
> ing at *recreo* with the schoolchildren, discussing child-rearing with
> mothers, etc.) to formal five-minute tabulations of Quechua-Spanish
> language use in the classroom.

Martin-Jones (this book), in describing the impact of Hornberger's work
on her own development, highlighted what would later be called 'language planning from the bottom up': 'Here was a researcher who, like

me, was committed to approaching the study of language policy and bilingual education from the vantage point of the classroom, of teachers and learners and of local communities and who was convinced, as I was, that ethnography was best suited to this purpose, because of its emphasis on interpretive processes and on the situated nature of such processes.' Martin-Jones' overview is a reminder of how far-reaching Nancy's contribution has been to the field of sociolinguistics. It is also a reminder to me of how much one's students can surpass their professors.

Similarly, Creese's discussion of Nancy's work (this book) demonstrates the considerable reach of her contributions: 'Hornberger seeks to extend and build, critique and develop and in making hitherto unnoticed links across arguments and theories, allows us develop new perspectives and think anew.' It was my impression from early on that this was one of Nancy's defining traits: the pursuit of the novel in the familiar. While anthropologists are supposed to 'make the strange familiar and the familiar strange,' Hornberger exceeds that by problematizing what seems commonplace and self-evident. I give one early example. In her dissertation proposal (1982), she states that a focus on Quechua language *maintenance* through bilingual education in Peru 'will contribute to knowledge of social change.' In this declaration she rightly anticipates a seeming-contradiction that frankly eluded her professors and about which she was not asked during her examination: she writes that

> it is, perhaps, paradoxical to suggest that the maintenance of anything could be a part of change. After all, does not change by its very nature suggest the removal of what is there and its replacement by something else? Nevertheless, I suggest here that the maintenance of (or shift from) the Quechua language is directly related to change in Andean society. The explanation for this paradox is straightforward: if the overall tendency in Andean society has been for the last several hundred years towards the suppression and eradication of the Quechua language, then a reversal of such a tendency would indeed signify a change.

Her habit of asking these sorts of questions has enriched the descriptions of everyday life she includes in her ethnographic accounts.

But Nancy's commitment does not stop at asking the questions. As Varghese (this book) illustrates, '[h]er work has shown how educators can enact positive changes in restrictive language policy environments and how the local practices of these educators need to be examined and described to show the openings that are created.' Similarly, Johnson (this book) discusses how Hornberger recognizes that education is about power relations, but even those who may seem to be subordinate in these relations wield their own power, the power to 'create classroom spaces that draw on the multilingual resources of students' and communities, whether in Peru or Philadelphia. He cites an early Hornberger work highlighting the importance of grass-roots support for language maintenance: '[L]anguage policies with a language-as-resource orientation can and do have an impact on . . . revitalization of endangered Indigenous languages. Of course, this is not to say that protecting Indigenous languages is simply a matter of declaring a language policy to that effect. There is ample evidence to the contrary' (Hornberger, 1998: 444).

In these ways, the Hornberger body of work is timely – and as important as ever – for addressing the present wrongs. I write from Arizona, where recently the anti-immigrant spirit is stronger than ever. The State Senate has passed a law (Senate Bill 1070, now in judicial review) requiring the police to verify the status of those who might look 'illegal'; we have a Superintendent of Schools who has promoted legislation outlawing ethnic studies in public schools (also see Skilton-Sylvester, this book), and who threatens teachers with accents with termination. (See, for the Arizona political context, Wright [2005], as well statements by the National Council of Teachers of English [2010] and the University of Arizona Linguistics Faculty [2010] on the accents of teachers.) In such an oppressive atmosphere, we need to find teachers willing to risk their jobs to benefit children. In fact, I am convinced that the only way to be a responsible teacher of English language learners (maybe any teacher at all) in Arizona is to be subversive of the constraints placed on good practice; it is our job to find, develop and support these teachers. We can and do use the cases Nancy presents in her work as guides for this sort of subversive teacher preparation.

In conclusion, let me return to the beginning. Nancy Hornberger came to the University of Wisconsin-Madison to study international and comparative education in the Department of Educational Policy Studies (EPS). She no doubt had in mind working alongside established scholars in this field such as Andreas Kazamias, Robert Koehl, Bob Tabachnick and Tom Skidmore. But her interest was language policy in education; it will always be a mystery to me, as it might be to Nancy, why the senior members of the Department did not share that interest in language. I count it as one of the great coincidences in my academic life that I was, therefore, left as the one person in EPS who could talk with her about how language fit in educational policy. Soon, those of us who recognized that fit joined in what I called the Language and Education Planning group (LEP – an obvious ironic commentary on one of the negative labels of the day). The LEPs, among them Dianne Bowcock, Maria Dalupan, Nancy Hornberger, Julia Richards and Joan Strouse, created some great opportunities for discussion and reflection on language and education. As I note in a recent paper (Ruiz, 2010), discussions with these students called my attention to a hole in my original orientations model for language planning. I had posited a dichotomy between 'language-as-problem' and 'language-as-resource'; the cases that the LEPs brought to our discussions forced me to think about a third prong, 'language-as-right.'[2] Of course, Nancy Hornberger's focus on Indigenous language maintenance and the rights of language minority communities shone a great light into the hole of the model. It is the sort of light she continues to shine into the core of the language planning onion.

Notes

1. Cf. Ricento and Hornberger (1996), where they introduce the idea that language policy and planning (LPP) is like an onion that needs to be 'unpeeled' to understand better the processes of language change in minority communities. (See also Martin-Jones in this volume for an insightful review of this construct.) This theme has persisted: Hornberger and Johnson (2007) suggest 'slicing the onion' as well to reveal spaces for language revitalization. Finally, see also the very responsible suggestion by Menken and García (2010) that the onion be 'stirred' from time to time, as well. When I introduced her as a keynote speaker at the Georgetown University Round Table in 2006, I kidded her about her word choice; I had always peeled onions (as well as potatoes, bananas and oranges), so I wondered whether un-peeling was the opposite, i.e. putting them back together. She took it well. (To be fair, she has used 'slicing' in relation to the language planning onion, but not un-slicing, an invention of mine designed to carry the kidding a little further.)
2. The original orientations paper was presented in Cancun in 1981, although I had presented a preliminary model in lectures at the University of Wisconsin starting in 1980. A series of strange incidents delayed the publication of the paper until 1984, by which time I could present the fuller version of the model. See Ruiz (1981, 1984).

References

Hornberger, N.H. (1982) Research prospectus: Bilingual education and Quechua language maintenance in southern highland Peru. Unpublished manuscript, University of Wisconsin-Madison.

Hornberger, N.H. (1983) Three-month report to the Commission for Educational Exchange Between the United States and Peru. Unpublished manuscript.

Hornberger, N.H. (1985) Bilingual education and Quechua language maintenance in Highland Puno, Peru. Unpublished Ph.D. dissertation, University of Wisconsin-Madison.

Hornberger, N.H. (1998) Language policy, language education, language rights: Indigenous, immigrant, and international perspectives. *Language in Society* 27, 439–458.

Hornberger, N.H. (2010) Foreword. In K. Menken and O. García (eds) *Negotiating Language Policies in Schools: Educators as Policymakers* (pp. xi–xiii). New York and London: Routledge.

Hornberger, N.H. and Johnson, D. (2007) Slicing the onion ethnographically: Layers and spaces in multilingual language education policy and practice. *TESOL Quarterly* 41 (3), 509–533.

Menken, K. and García, O. (eds) (2010) *Negotiating Language Policies in Schools: Educators as Policymakers*. New York and London: Routledge.

National Council of Teachers of English (2010) NCTE speaks out on Arizona Department of Education ruling on teacher speech: Evaluate teachers on their competence, not on their accents – Online document: http://www.ncte.org/library/NCTEFiles/Involved/Action/NCTEpositiononAZELLrules.pdf.

Ricento, T. and Hornberger, N.H. (1996) Unpeeling the onion: Language policy and planning and the ELT professional. *TESOL Quarterly* 30 (3), 401–427.

Ruiz, R. (1981, December). Orientations in language planning: An essay on the politics of language. Paper presented at the International Conference on Language Problems and Public Policy, Cancun, Mexico.

Ruiz, R. (1984) Orientations in language planning. *NABE Journal* 8 (2), 15–34.

Ruiz, R. (2010) Reorienting language-as-resource. In J. Petrovic (ed.) *International Perspectives on Bilingual Education: Policy, Practice, and Controversy* (pp. 155–172). Charlotte, NC: Information Age Publishing.

University of Arizona Linguistics Faculty (2010) English teachers' fluency initiative in Arizona – Online document: http://www.u.arizona.edu/~hammond/ling_statement_final.pdf on 28 July 2010.

Wright, W. (2005) English language learners left behind in Arizona: The nullification of accommodations in the intersection of federal and state language and assessment policies. *Bilingual Research Journal* 29 (1), 1–30.

Index

- implications for policy, 163–166
- policy and practice matrix, 166t
- status planning, 163–164
citizenship education and content matters,
  68–78
classroom multilingualism research, 6–8
community contexts and rural school, 3
content
- changing in refugee camps and US, 87–91
- ESL literacy classes, 87–91
- matters in biliterate citizenship education,
  68–78
- not diluted but rather scaffolded, 21
context
- changing in refugee camps and US, 87–91
- ESL literacy classes, 87–91
- Hornberger's emphasis, 69
- refugee women's shifting practices, 87–91
Continua of Biliteracy, 10, 59–66
- dimensions, 96f
- new literacy studies and continua of
  biliteracy, 65–66
Conversation Analysis, 31
Coronel-Molina, Serafín, ix–x, xxiv, 140–153
Creese, Angela, x, xxiii, 41–56
critical sociocultural-ethnographic turn,
  111–114
critical theory, 6, 110
cultural citizenship and content, 75–76

data collection managing and analyzing, 51
de la Torre, Victor Raúl Haya, 142
Dixon-Marquez, Emily, 132
Dodge Poetry Festival, 100–101
dynamic, process-oriented view, 112

ecology of language, 119, 129, 155
educational linguistics, xviii–xxii
- global and local connections in, xviii–xxv
- transdisciplinary field, xviii
El Día del Indio (Day of the Indian), 141
English as Second Language (ESL), 19,
  85–92, 132, 136
English in Bollywood, 37–38
English literacy
- classes in refugee camp, 88
- description of learning, 89
epistemological debates in ethnography, 47
equity and justice, 64
ESL. *See* English as Second Language (ESL)
ethnography
- epistemological debates, 47
- language policy, 113
- long-standing research tradition, 5

ethnopoetics, 99

female refugees, 81
fieldnotes
- Blommaert description of, 45
- making local practices globally relevant,
  49–52
- presenting emic perspective, 44–49
- researching multilingual education, 49–52
- team ethnography, 49–52
Foreign Language Assistance Program
  (FLAP), 161
Fulbright Scholar, 174

Gandhi, Mohandas Karamchand, 28
García, Ofelia, 119
Georgia, 101–102
global and local connections in educational
  linguistics, xviii–xxv
- book overview, xxii–xxv
- central themes, xix–xxi
- contributions and contributors, xxi–xxii
global local dilemma, 18–20
Goldkist Poultry, Athens, Georgia, 101–102
Gordon, Daryl, x–xi, xxiv, 81–94
government policy and *Indigenismo*,
  141–147
Grover, Mike, xi, xv–xviii

Hanyu Pinyin, 164
Harvard University, 173
Hindi, 28
- code switching and identity in
  Bollywood, 38–41
- Romanization, 39
- written, 39
Hornberger, Nancy H., xv–xvii, 140. *See also*
  specific topics or areas
- bilingual education and bilingualism, 3–58
- biliteracy continua, 59–108
- contributions to educational linguistics,
  xviii–xxii
- inspiring others, xviii
- policy and planning for linguistic
  diversity in education, 109–172
Hornbergian spaces, 126–127
Hult, Francis M., xi, xviii–xxv

identity in Bollywood, 27–39
ideological acceptance of Quechua, 149
ideological approach and literacy, 63
ideological models, 65
ideological perspectives
- biliteracy content and context, 82–84

For Product Safety Concerns and Information please contact our EU Authorised Representative:

Easy Access System Europe

Mustamäe tee 50

10621 Tallinn

Estonia

gpsr.requests@easproject.com

www.ingramcontent.com/pod-product-compliance
Lightning Source LLC
Chambersburg PA
CBHW050440280326
41932CB00013BA/2188